INCIDENTAL RACIALIZATION

.

Yung-Yi Diana Pan

INCIDENTAL RACIALIZATION

Performative Assimilation in Law School

TEMPLE UNIVERSITY PRESS
Philadelphia • *Rome* • *Tokyo*

TEMPLE UNIVERSITY PRESS
Philadelphia, Pennsylvania 19122
www.temple.edu/tempress

Published 2017

Library of Congress Cataloging-in-Publication Data

Names: Pan, Yung-Yi Diana, 1980– author.
Title: Incidental racialization : performative assimilation in law school / Yung-Yi Diana
 Pan.
Description: Philadelphia : Temple University Press, 2017. | Based on author's thesis
 (doctoral - University of California, Irvine, 2012) issued under title: Learning to become
 a lawyer . . . of color : Asian American and Latino law students negotiate ambitions,
 expectations and obligations. | Includes bibliographical references and index.
Identifiers: LCCN 2016042661 (print) | LCCN 2016059729 (ebook) | ISBN 9781439913840
 (hardback) | ISBN 9781439913857 (paper) | ISBN 9781439913864 (E-Book)
Subjects: LCSH: Law students—United States—Social conditions. | Law—Study and
 teaching—Social aspects—United States. | Hispanic American law students. | Asian
 American law students. | BISAC: SOCIAL SCIENCE / Discrimination & Race Relations.
 | LAW / Legal Education.
Classification: LCC KF287 .P36 2017 (print) | LCC KF287 (ebook) | DDC 340.071/173—dc23
LC record available at https://lccn.loc.gov/2016042661

9 8 7 6 5 4 3 2 1

CONTENTS

ACKNOWLEDGMENTS

It takes a village to write a book, and I owe tremendous gratitude to mine. First, I thank my respondents, who took the time out of their busy schedules to speak with me and trusted me with their stories. Their commitment to this project sustained my drive and motivation.

This project began as my dissertation, and I thank my brilliant committee, Carroll Seron, Linda Vo, Ann Southworth, and especially cochairs Calvin Morrill and Rubén G. Rumbaut, who pushed me toward more complex analyses and challenged me to think about this book's unique significance. Their invaluable intellectual guidance saw me through this project, and they continue to support me in my career. I also thank my undergraduate and graduate mentors, Patti Sakurai, Erlinda Gonzales-Berry, Amy Sueyoshi, and Madeline Hsu, among others who inspired me to pursue academia.

I gained so much more than a Ph.D. at the University of California, Irvine, and I am fortunate to have made lifelong friends. I especially thank David S. Meyer for being an informal advisor (and professional cheerleader) since my first day of graduate school. Meals shared with Bobby Chen, Elizabeth Chiarello, Scott Byrd, Lorien Jasny, and Chris Marcum invariably led to conversations that bolstered the initial conceptualization of this book. Over the years, Daisy Reyes and Megan Thiele have spent hours reading and commenting on numerous chapter drafts. I am so fortunate to share this intellectual community with friends close enough to be family.

Incidental Racialization started to take its current form when I began working as assistant professor of sociology at Brooklyn College of the City University of New York. I am indebted to an encouraging group of colleagues, staff, and students who allowed my writing to flourish. I am most appreciative of my department chair, Carolina Bank Muñoz, who read and commented on chapter and proposal drafts. Tamara R. Mose also provided valuable advice on the book publication process. And for punctuated moments of respite from research, writing, and teaching, I thank Emily T. Molina; I could not imagine a better officemate. The curiosity of sociology students encouraged and inspired me throughout the writing process. I am so thankful to be a part of the Sociology Department at Brooklyn College.

Over the course of my work on the book, I have had the good fortune of expanding my intellectual community, many of whom have also taken time to selflessly read, comment, and provide valuable insight on chapter drafts. I thank Margaret Chin, Gilda Ochoa, Glenda Flores, and Neda Maghbouleh for their important feedback. I further thank Wendy Leo Moore, Eduardo Bonilla-Silva, David Brunsma, and Fiona Kay, who have been more than supportive of my professional endeavor.

Numerous funding sources and awards helped make this project a reality. These include the City University of New York Gittell Junior Faculty Award; the City University of New York Faculty Fellowship Publication Program; the University of California, Irvine, Dissertation Year Fellowship; the Society for the Study of Social Problems Race/Ethnic Minority Graduate Scholarship; and numerous summer research grants from the UC Irvine Department of Sociology.

I am grateful for my editor at Temple University Press, Aaron Javsicas, for his unwavering support of and belief in this book. Nikki Miller has also been tremendously helpful. I thank the anonymous reviewers for their constructive criticism, comments, and suggestions that further sharpened this book's contribution. Of course, any errors are my own.

My family—in the United States and in Taiwan—deserve tremendous praise and thanks. The resolve of my grandparents, Li Wen-Hsiu and Chuang Mao-Lin, as exiled immigrants in Taiwan kept me grounded while writing this book. I am humbled by the experiences of my parents, Yi-Han Chuang and Jen Pan, as working-class immigrants in the United States, and I am always reminded that I am fortunate to have had the opportunity to attend college and graduate school. My siblings, Josh Pan and Chrissy Pan, also inspired me in their own ways. My sincerest gratitude goes to Jeff Rosenberg, whose unconditional love and support over the past nineteen years saw me through the inception and completion of this book. He is the only person to have read the entire book manuscript in its multiple iterations over the years; I am so lucky to have his companionship. Finally, I thank my children for sharing me with this project. Siri was ten months old when I began collecting data for my dissertation in 2009, and Emi was four months old when I finished the final edits on the manuscript in 2016. I thank them for the snuggles, hugs, tantrums, field trips, dirty diapers, and all the joys of parenthood that provide more dimension to my life. I dedicate this book to them.

INTRODUCTION

Law School, Panethnicity, and
Confessions of an Imposter

As much as the dominant white group might say that [race] doesn't matter to them, they notice it too, but they don't say anything. But when you're in their presence, they know "there's a Latina here." They identify you that way. . . . [T]hey are categorizing you in that way. And it's from experience. . . . As much as you want to think that the problem isn't there in terms of discrimination or social isolation, it is there. I feel like you always have a choice to be like, "I don't care. It doesn't matter. I'm going to be who I am," which is really great. But at the same time, you really can't ignore the fact that you're still—you're not white. (Noemi Castillo)[1]

In some ways, it's almost like a double whammy. Like, I'm Asian American, so they expect me to be a model minority and to be polite and acquiescent and quiet. And be a hard worker who doesn't stir up trouble. I stir up trouble, and it freaks them out because it doesn't fit [with] what they think an Asian American is. But I'm not quite a black person, or Filipina, or I'm not Latina. And that incongruence freaks people out. (Bryn Singh)

The legal profession is racially diversifying, but law students like Noemi and Bryn describe still feeling as if they do not belong. Both women talk about the assumptions that others make about them: Noemi speaks of white peers categorizing her as Latina and of not being able to hide or ignore her ethnicity, even when she does not want to think about it. Bryn grapples with her peers' racialized and gendered stereotypes of Asian Americans as polite, acquiescent, and quiet hard workers—characteristics that do not describe Bryn. This book examines processes of racialization during law school specifically, but it provides broader insights regarding racial inequalities in society in general. I initially chose to focus on law schools given the growing number and prominence of both Asian American and Latino lawyers. But other factors make law schools compelling research sites, illustrative of dynamics in American society at large. Paradoxically, it is precisely because law schools constitute a particularly rarified realm to which only a few have access that I suggest they can offer unique insights into *how* racialized privilege—and its counterpart, inequality—are produced and maintained.

First, American lawyers need to be proficient, if not fluent, in the English language. Unlike medicine or science, technology, engineering, and mathematics fields, law is immersed in understanding, interpreting, and recreating language. Individuals who are interested in pursuing law must have adequate command of American English. This requires, at the very least, going to college and earning decent grades. The Department of Education reports that 46 percent of Americans held college degrees in 2015. While this is a 13 percent increase since 1995, it is prudent to note that the majority of Americans—54 percent—are not college graduates. Law students fit squarely into the minority of Americans who are college educated. Moreover, once they earn their law degrees, they will be among the 9 percent of Americans who hold a master's degree or higher (National Center for Education Statistics 2016) and part of the less than 0.5 percent of Americans who are attorneys.[2] This fact alone places law students into a socially and economically privileged status.

Further, requirements for practicing law vary by country and jurisdiction. In select countries, including most of the United States, the practice of law requires an advanced degree, such as a juris doctor (JD). The students interviewed and observed for this book were all JD candidates. Equivalent to an MD (doctor of medicine) or a Ph.D. (doctor of philosophy), a JD is the terminal degree required for law practice. As noted previously, earning a JD thus places law students in an elite category that does not reflect the educational attainment of most Americans.

Second, law is a prestigious profession in common law countries, such as the United States, precisely because its practice signifies advanced education and training. *Common law* refers to a legal system built on interpreting precedent so that principles applied to similar facts produce comparable outcomes. In this sense, common law systems practice a form of pseudoscientific inquiry ostensibly characterized by systematic, rather than arbitrary, findings. Attorneys require specialized training not only to become familiar with the content and application of the law but even to understand legal language itself. Popular jokes about cheating or lying attorneys notwithstanding, the law is a respected and stable profession. To possess the title of lawyer connotes intellectual prowess and ability.

Third, the United States remains the economic center of the world, and lawyers are often intricately involved in international endeavors. Major corporations, banks, and government entities retain in-house legal counsel. Unlike the medical profession, which is also seen as prestigious, law is paramount on the international stage and affects the economic direction of this country. It is, therefore, a powerful profession.

And finally, the time necessary to acquire a JD is relatively short compared to training for an MD or a (humanities or social science) Ph.D., for example. In just three years, a law student transforms into a corporate attorney, a judicial clerk, or a business counsel, to name just a few possibilities. This relatively brief but extraordinarily intense training provides researchers with a unique opportunity to investigate how professional socialization happens in a short period, at a particular institution—an institution that, as law students themselves put it, first "scares you to death, then works you to death, then bores you to death."[3]

Law schools are thus intricately tied to the social world yet are uniquely exclusive and house exclusionary spaces within themselves. Thus, they serve as vivid microcosms of how systemic inequalities are sustained and (re)produced. When Asian American and Latino law students enter these spaces, they receive an education in long-established culturally dominant norms and practices *and* in where they as nonwhites fit in relation to those norms and practices. How these students learn to become lawyers is an exercise in learning to be upwardly mobile, racialized Americans. It is essentially a lesson about assimilation into mainstream America—both its promise and its limits.

Asian American and Latino law students entering an elite profession evoke three separate yet interrelated types of assimilation: assimilation into mainstream America; assimilation into the legal profession; and assimilation into panethnicity. Let us begin with how law school both teaches and effects assimilation into mainstream America. The ability to become a professional signifies acceptance by mainstream society. And such acceptance, without (much) protest, generally represents a step toward full membership into the mainstream. The increase in Asian American and Latino law students and lawyers can read as a testament to this successful endeavor—the acceptance of Asian Americans and Latinos within American society.

Law students learn how to become lawyers, a process that requires assimilation into the legal profession. This entails learning to decipher cases, formulate arguments, and speak legalese. But it also involves subtler, less

obvious lessons—for example, assertiveness is an invaluable trait for success in law school and, indeed, the legal profession. Asian American and
Latino law students assimilate to such cultural norms but simultaneously
recognize that they do not represent the modal law student. Most of their
peers are white and hail from families with strong roots in the United States.
As mostly second-generation immigrants, Asian American and Latino law
students represent a different profile. They are nonwhite, and they are continually made aware of their otherness. This happens directly, through their
interactions with peers and professors who often make assumptions about
Asian American and Latino law students' immigrant status, cultural knowledge, and admission into law school (merit versus affirmative action). But
it also happens even through the omission of race in the color-blind classroom—a strategy that preserves whiteness's position of unspoken privilege,
thus actually heightening race's significance. Through these processes, Asian
American and Latino law students assimilate to law school both by learning
about the law and by learning their position as nonwhite persons within the
racialized spaces of law school and the legal profession.

This is not to say that race and ethnicity are completely absent from or
invisible in the law school environment or experience per se; rather, they
are acknowledged and framed in particular ways. Panethnicity thrives in
law school in the form of panethnic student organizations, which provide
academic, professional, and social support to their members. Such organizations rely on broad classifications that group a number of specific, often
highly diverse, ethnic identities—hence, associations for Asian American
students instead of Chinese American or Korean American students and
for Latino students instead of Mexican American or Cuban American students. Law students study with panethnic organization members, eat meals
with them, and attend networking events with them. Importantly, most
of the Asian American and Latino law students in this book were not involved in panethnic associations before law school but chose to align with
specific ethnic identities. But law school changed that, as the respondents
not only joined panethnic student organizations but also came to align
themselves increasingly with panethnic causes and identities. In this way,
Asian American and Latino law students thus also learn to assimilate pan-
ethnically.

Social experiences in broader society, law school, and among copanethnics shape how Asian American and Latino law students understand their
law school socialization. Their otherness—in this case, race—begins to significantly matter as they learn how to become lawyers. Panethnicity is both
asserted by individuals and ascribed by their law school surroundings (Cornell and Hartmann 1998). The product is that these nonwhite, panethnic,
mostly second-generation immigrants experience incidental racialization
while undergoing professional socialization.

Supreme Court Justice, Attorney General, and Legal Advisor: Asian Americans and Latinos in the Spotlight

In August 2009, Sonia Sotomayor, a Puerto Rican woman, was confirmed to the U.S. Supreme Court. Sotomayor's confirmation elicited excitement and pride within the Latino community, as she is the first Latina to sit on the high bench. Civil rights and immigration attorney Antonia Hernandez remarked that Sotomayor's "entry into the most private of clubs in this country" (Hughes 2009) provides hope for young Latinos throughout the United States. In 2005, President George W. Bush appointed Alberto Gonzales, who is ethnically Mexican, to the position of attorney general. Gonzales held this position until 2007, during which time he gained much attention (and generated controversy) for drafting memos regarding Al-Qaeda and Taliban detainees. Vietnamese American Viet Dinh served as assistant attorney general from 2001 to 2003 and was the chief architect of the Patriot Act. Ethnically Korean, Harold Koh was legal advisor to the Department of State from 2009 to 2013, nominated by President Barack Obama. He had previously served as the dean of Yale Law School, from 2004 to 2009.

Sotomayor, Gonzales, Dinh, and Koh are similar in many ways: they all have made headlines in major news outlets, they all have law degrees from elite law schools (Harvard and Yale), and their prominent positions and visibility in the mainstream are often pointed to as providing young Asian Americans and Latinos with positive role models. Twenty years ago, one would be hard-pressed to find Asian Americans and Latinos in such high-profile positions, but today, select members from these two racialized, panethnic groups have indeed acquired visibility and continue to make strides in a profession that, at one time, did not welcome them.[4]

But does visibility in the mainstream translate to successful U.S. integration? On the surface, it may appear so. Trumpeting successes like these, some scholars suggest that Asian Americans and Latinos are making it through upward mobility (Alba and Nee 2003; Bean and Stevens 2003; Brown and Bean 2006). But such analyses fail to offer insight into the complexity of assimilation experiences and how Asian Americans and Latinos interrogate their (pan)ethnicity[5] while learning to become professionals.

Extensive research on race spotlights how phenotype affects everyday experiences. Professionals of color—black, Asian American, Latino—are harassed, discriminated against, or assumed to be foreigners in daily interactions with strangers.[6] Panethnicity or race marks individuals in conspicuous ways, without regard to educational attainment, profession, or wealth. This, then, leads to the question: How does panethnicity matter for neophyte professionals? In this case, for law students?

To answer this question, I first examine research that speaks directly to the experiences of Asian American and Latino professionals, as racialized individuals and as immigrants. Though there is some literature on this subject, none of it is within the broader profession's literature.[7] Of the available works on Asian American and Latino professionals, few directly examine the intersecting processes of racialization and professional socialization. This lacuna fuels my desire to interrogate mainstream integration and racialization. But before we explore the issues, we need some context on how, in general, professional socialization happens.

When Professional Socialization Happens to Good People

Since the mid-1960s, social scientists have taken an interest in the socialization of future doctors, lawyers, surgeons, and social workers, among other professionals.[8] Prior research demonstrates that while these aspiring professionals begin their professional education with individual sets of ideals, each profession has its own dominant culture to which the new initiates must learn to adapt. New medical and law students, for example, begin their schooling imagining the types of doctors or lawyers they expect to become. The rigorous socialization they experience, however, creates anxiety as they learn the new culture and vocabularies of their chosen profession. Most research on this socialization examines how students in general adapt to the dominant standards of their respective disciplines. What is commonly missing from such research is how those who are *not* part of the modal population experience their socialization. In other words, how does this adaptation process affect racial and ethnic minorities as they prepare to join a predominantly white profession, in this case, law school?

What is so special about law schools and lawyers? Why focus on this particular elite profession and not medicine or finance? An additional consideration alongside those I described earlier is the numbers of enrollees. While there has been an increase in Asian American and Latino professionals generally, the surge of Asian American and Latino lawyers and law students has been particularly staggering. Data from the American Bar Association reveal that nonwhite law student enrollment in general has increased approximately 107 percent over the past two decades—from 15,720 in 1989–1990 to 32,505 in 2009–2010 (American Bar Association 2011). In a study of Chicago-area law firms, the number of practicing minority lawyers increased from 2.2 percent in 1975 to approximately 7.3 percent in 1995 (Heinz et al. 2005). With regard to Asian American and Latino law students in particular, the American Bar Association (2011) reports 200.8 and 100.6 percent upticks, respectively, over the course of two decades (see Figure I.1). The legal profession has clearly opened its doors to Asian Americans and Latinos, as demonstrated by these numbers. But beyond this increased numerical presence, we know little about the experiences of these students inside the walls of law schools.

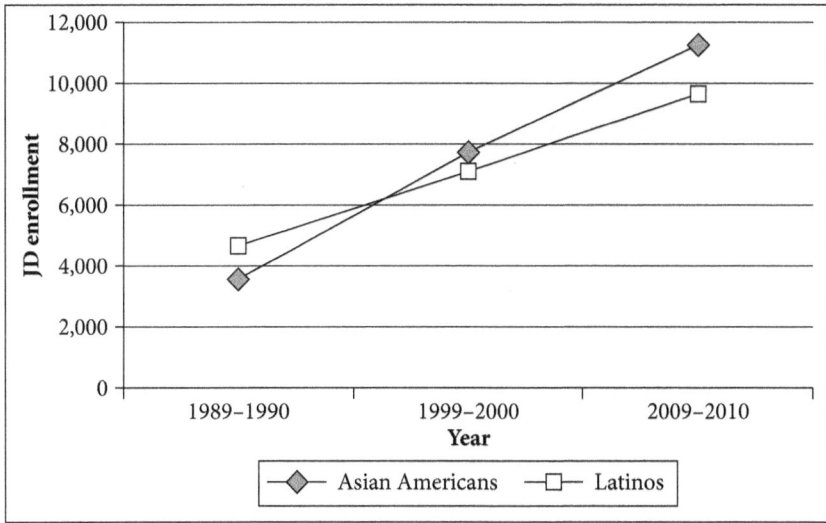

Figure I.1 Increase in law school enrollment from 1989 to 2010
Source: Data derived from American Bar Association 2011

Law School Socialization and Culture

Scott Turow's memoir *One L* (1977) invites readers into the life of a first-year Harvard law student. The reader shares Turow's agonies over the prospect of being called on in class, learning the ropes of the law, and adjusting his life to fit the personal and academic demands of being a law student. The demands and competition of law school render it unique. Unlike other disciplines, while learning the law, one also learns to live by it. As explained by Turow, "Law school begins to become more than just learning a language. You also have to start learning rules, and you'll find pretty quickly that there's quite a premium placed on mastering the rules and knowing how to apply them. . . . The law in almost all its phases is a reflection of competing value systems" (1977, 83). For many law students, learning such rules also compels them to take on the associated values, thus forever changing their moral outlook. The intense and stressful process of learning to love the law and learning to think like a lawyer is a common story told by law students, making legal education seem a race-, gender-, and class-neutral experience. Yet a growing number of social scientists and legal scholars have explored how law schools alienate women, students of color, and students from lower socioeconomic backgrounds (Epstein 1992; Granfield 1992; Mertz 2007; and Moore 2008). This characteristic of the law suggests that law students' race, gender, and socioeconomic backgrounds affect how they think about the law and their future careers as lawyers.

It is relatively easy to identify gender segmentation in classrooms. Compared to their male counterparts, female law students appear more passive and are less likely to contribute to classroom discussions (Banks 1988; Epstein 1993; Guinier, Fine, and Balin 1997; Mertz 2007). While observing classrooms in eight law schools, Elizabeth Mertz (2007) noticed professors calling on men more often than women. She also saw more men voluntarily participating in classrooms compared with their female peers. What are the repercussions of passive classroom engagement? Mertz speculates that men's overall ease with speaking in class reflects confidence and is a testament to their general positive performance in law school. Further, active classroom contribution exemplifies these men's sense of inclusion in the wider legal community. Women students who do speak up often provide a different perspective, offering legal analysis through a feminist lens. Thus, Mertz found that women students' comments might be dismissed or ridiculed by both professors and peers, especially men. That women students' contributions are not as welcome illuminates Robert Granfield's description of law schools as "provid[ing] a context through which gender identity and experience is 'constructed' in relation to a student's biography and interactions within school" (1992, 100). Women quickly learn either to cease offering comments in the classroom or to adopt their male peers' sense of confidence.

Similarly, law students from working-class backgrounds relate that they make it through law school by faking it, concealing any discomfort they may experience in the law school environment from peers who hail from upper-middle-class backgrounds. While students from working-class families may initially feel happy and proud of their achievements in law school, their confidence often wanes as they recognize that their speech, attire, values, and experiences in the working class are not those of the majority of their peers and their backgrounds are devalued. Working-class students also tend to shy away from class participation and avoid socioeconomic-class stigma by disengaging from more conventional law school activities, such as joining clubs or law journals (Costello 2006; Granfield 1992). Because membership in clubs and journals leads to tangible and symbolic rewards, these students leave law school having accrued less social capital than their middle-class peers.[9] Thus, although most conversation and research about law school portray it as a class- or gender-neutral experience, women and those from lower socioeconomic backgrounds experience alienation and may actually receive less benefit from it. While these topics appear sporadically in works on the legal profession, it is rare for scholars to fully engage with the experience or to interrogate how the experiences matter. As more native-born, second-generation immigrant,[10] nonwhite students enter professions such as law, it is vital to examine how professional school socialization dictates these students' career outcomes and understand the significance of "mainstreaming outsiders" (Blackwell 1987), or the professional socialization of nonwhite professionals. If we, as a diverse and changing society are to prosper, it is crucial for the academic community, as well as legal, political, and mainstream culture, to understand the diverse realities of pedagogical and professional experiences and institutions that only *appear* unmarked by gender, race, or class.

Punctuated moments ripe for critical race investigation abound in legal education. Unfortunately, these moments are often filled with silence, due to a lack of data or participants' unwillingness to engage in discussion around these topics. Students may want to talk about racism or sexism but fear that would redirect classroom conversation and upset peers who want to learn only black-letter law. They might fear, too, that simply engaging with such topics will result in the discussants themselves being perceived as overly left leaning or radical and tied to their personal backgrounds and experiences. It is not surprising, then, that Asian American and Latino respondents, many of whom are second-generation immigrants, understand their schooling differently from their native-born white peers. Akin to the women law students who are often accused of being overly feminist and are therefore dismissed, Asian American and Latino respondents tell me that sometimes their class contributions are similarly marginalized and devalued. Through this understanding, Asian American and Latino law students learn that part of the process of becoming a lawyer involves simultaneously silencing their (pan)ethnic and immigrant identities and experiences.

This book pushes for understanding (pan)ethnicity as lived experiences within an institutional context. I situate panethnicity as the frame of analysis when discussing professional socialization. Doing so underscores the processual nature of race and racialization and elevates the impact of human interactions and social structures on how identities are shaped and reshaped, especially in the context of professional socialization.[11]

"New" Immigrants: Successful Integration and Racialization

What is significant about being an immigrant? Why does this matter for the story of Asian American and Latino legal socialization? Immigrant background anchors racialization and professional socialization. Recall the four prominent Asian Americans and Latinos featured at the beginning of this Introduction. They are all second-generation immigrants, and their ascension to prominence characterizes the quintessential American dream.

Post-1965 immigration changed the American landscape. Unlike previous waves of immigration, post-1965 entrants—mostly Asians and Latinos—benefited from changes in immigration policy that favored family reunification and educational or technological skills (Alba and Nee 2003; Bean and Stevens 2003; Portes and Rumbaut 2006). The demographics of these "new" immigrants, especially Asians and Latinos, spawned numerous studies that focus on whether the incorporation processes of the two groups would mirror that of their European predecessors. Classic theories support a straight-line definition, whereby European ethnics assimilated into the mainstream according to Milton Gordon's (1964) seven-step process: acculturation (immigrants adapt to the host culture through absorbing and adopting language, norms, clothing, etc.); structural assimilation (immigrants enter mainstream clubs and organizations in large numbers); marital assimilation (widespread intermarriage between immigrants and members of the host society); identificational assimilation (immigrants feel bound to the host society and start identifying as members of it); attitude reception (the host society demonstrates an absence of prejudice toward the immigrant group); behavior reception (the host society demonstrates an absence of discrimination against the immigrant group); and civic assimilation (lack of contestation over values and power).

Since then, new theories of assimilation have emerged, challenging and supporting the classic ones based on European ethnics' assimilation.[12] And while some immigrant groups' experiences may superficially resonate with the European assimilation model, their integration outcomes are largely contingent on their socioeconomic status before and after migration, their career trajectories, and their countries of national origin. The two panethnic communities in question in this book have been characterized differently in the American imaginary. Asian Americans—at least, since the second half of the twentieth century—are generally seen as "good" immigrants who bring innovative technology and talents to the United States. Comparatively, Latinos are seen as "bad" immigrants and are stereotyped to be undocumented immigrants who sap government resources. Of course, such broad generalizations do not capture brilliant Latinos or undocumented, low-skilled Asian Americans. But more importantly, such stark comparisons obscure that, as more recent immigrant groups, Asian Americans and Latinos share remarkable similarities in their quest to become a part of the United States of America.

Asian Americans, for example, are often characterized as a model minority, given their relatively high levels of educational and professional entry into the American middle class or higher. Latinos exhibit a slightly different pattern—specifically, a bifurcated population, whereby some take longer to assimilate into the American mainstream while others ascend the socioeconomic ladder rather quickly. The pace of integration, of course, depends on the circumstances under which many of these immigrants enter the United States (Brown and Bean 2006; Hirschman and Wong 1986; Lobo and Salvo 1998; Tang 1993). But whether as a model minority or in a bifurcated assimilation, Asian Americans and Latinos structurally and culturally integrate into the mainstream at a faster rate than other racialized groups, such as black Americans, who are overrepresented in impoverished neighborhoods, or Native Americans, many of whom reside on reservation lands. On the whole, Asian American and Latino residential proximity with white Americans and higher intermarriage rates with them are measures of their more successful integration into the American mainstream when compared with their black American counterparts. But what do these patterns mean?

The shrinking social, economic, and geographic gap between these two racialized groups—Asian Americans and Latino Americans—and white Americans has led some scholars to infer that race is no longer a problem for these populations. In other words, white Americans do not necessarily consider Asian Americans and Latinos to be racial outsiders in the same way that they do black Americans. Some scholars even argue that the integration of Asian Americans and Latinos creates a new black-nonblack racial divide (Lee and Bean 2007, 2012). Using the experiences of European immigrants, some argue that it is just a matter of time before Asian Americans and Latinos also become "white," in the same way as the Italians, Irish, and Jews did.

Native-born, white Anglo-Saxon Protestant Americans discriminated against other ethnically unfamiliar whites initially, making it difficult for white ethnics, such as Italians, Irish, and Jews to be accepted into numerous mainstream institutions, including medicine, law, and education. Over time, the "white" category expanded and the mostly Eastern European ethnics became "white" in large part because of residential proximity, friendships, and intermarriage with members of the Anglo-Saxon Protestant population (Alba 1992; Alba and Nee 2003). Today, European ethnics are mostly subsumed under the "white" racial category, and while some may align themselves ethnically, their identities are overwhelmingly symbolic;[13] phenotypically, European ethnics are seen as resembling the dominant group of white Anglo-Saxon Protestants. By shedding their ethnic identities in favor of a racialized, panethnic white Anglo one, these ethnic groups have assimilated more readily into mainstream America.

In the twentieth century, the panethnic umbrella "white" widened to include non-Protestant Eastern Europeans. Twenty-first-century America consists of numerous racial umbrellas for heterogeneous racialized panethnic groups. For example, Chinese, Filipinos, and South Asians fall under the panethnic umbrella "Asian" or "Asian American," while Mexicans, Salvadorans, and Peruvians fall under the panethnic umbrella "Latino" or "Hispanic." These panethnic umbrellas provide an alternative form of mainstream adaptation that does not mirror the experiences of white ethnics. Whereas for white ethnics, belonging to an umbrella category affords race-based privileges, for nonwhite groups an umbrella category actually results in the opposite. These individuals continue to experience negative implications of race as they undergo racialization (Waters 1999). These processes were in large part modeled within a white sociohistorical framework that is continually sustained and perpetuated.

Panethnic or racial categories persist and remain significant even among middle-class individuals of color. For example, Joe Feagin (1991) finds that middle-class black Americans experience discrimination in public places, despite their structural incorporation into mainstream America as doctors, lawyers, or professors. Middle-class black Americans often receive poor or no service in establishments, hear racial epithets directed at them, or are harassed in other ways. Feagin adds that while middle-class status alone provides some protection from racial discrimination as members of the black middle-class interact with coworkers and colleagues who are less likely to be openly hostile toward them, this armor does not extend into public arenas.

Feagin's analysis reveals how social mobility does not necessarily protect against skin-color-based discrimination. More recently, Feagin and colleagues challenged common perceptions about race and racism by unveiling discrimination directed at Asian Americans and Latinos (Chou and Feagin 2008; Feagin and Cobas 2014). The authors argue that the lack of attention to racism directed at Asian Americans and Latinos results from the narrow conceptualization of racism in the average American's imagination. With regard to Asian Americans, the authors explain, "for many people, *racism* conjures images of extremists associated with the Ku Klux Klan or neo-Nazi skinheads engaging in racial violence. While extreme forms of overt racism have not ceased, they now occur less frequently. Associating these extremely violent images with the idea of racism can mislead a person into thinking that racism is a thing of the past" or that Asian Americans are exempt from it (Chou and Feagin 2008, 29).

Despite race-based prejudice, Asian Americans and Latinos continue to integrate into mainstream America through professions. Pawan Dhingra's (2007) research on Asian American professionals finds their identities to be performative—they must perform their racial identities. Asian American professionals incorporate aspects of their private lives into their work and also intertwine their work and private lives. Although Asian American professionals may not necessarily be concerned with overt racism directed at them in the workplace, they are cognizant of racialization in their professions. At work, these professionals may even deliberately evoke ethnic identities by performing to satisfy their white colleagues' expectations. Dhingra writes, "Race does not necessarily restrict the short-term mobility of Asian Americans at work but may in fact facilitate it, for their use of the model-minority stereotype could help them get certain jobs and connect to the state" (2007, 238). He gives, for example, the strategy of one respondent who wore nonprescription eyeglasses at work to better fit the image of the smart model minority. As these scholars demonstrate, racialization persists among Asian American middle-class professionals who elevate their ethnic identities and bolster racialized stereotypes.

Unlike Asian Americans, who are perceived to be middle class and well educated—in short, model minorities—Latinos are stereotyped as low-wage workers and are often believed to have migrated to the United States without legal documentation. Linda Chavez points out, however, that Latinos, particularly those born in the United States, "are very much like other Americans: they work hard, support their own families without outside assistance, have more education and higher earnings than their parents, and own their own homes. In short, they are pursuing the American dream—with increasing success" (1991, 107). Many second- and later-generation Latinos are quickly ascending the mobility ladder by becoming professionals. Patricia Gándara (1995) finds that Latino doctors, lawyers, and professors value the promise of hard work early in life and share stories of overcoming class, race, and linguistic discrimination to achieve their current careers. Yet continued immigration from Latin America sustains stereotypes of poor and undereducated Latinos, because recent arrivals speak limited English and are often concentrated in urban and rural barrios. For this reason, Latinos' advances into the mainstream seem to be overshadowed by hardened images, and there is a dearth of research specifically examining the experiences of middle-class and professional Latinos.[14] While previous research demonstrates that race still matters for Asian American and Latino professionals and that racism does not cease when one is a part of the middle class (or above), little remains known about racialization in the professions.

The following pages direct attention to the presence and significance of nonwhite panethnicity for individuals undergoing professional socialization. A recurrent argument throughout the book challenges the notion that Asian Americans and Latinos are "whitening." At best, they may be nearing economic parity, but this achievement is superficial in many ways. Delving into law students' stories reveals the recalcitrant nature of racialization and its ability to undermine the capacity of even the most prestigious professions to serve as paths to genuine equality for nonwhite groups.

Multiple Layers of Law Student Socialization: Guide to Chapters

Between 2009 and 2011, I spent most weekdays at either Western Elite or Private Metropolitan.[15] Separated by fourteen miles, these two law schools boast divergent characteristics. While Western Elite is a tier-one law school, meaning it is highly competitive and ranks in the top thirty of all U.S. law schools, Private Metropolitan is in the fourth tier, which means it is ranked in the lower one-fourth of all U.S. law schools and is less competitive for admissions.[16] Through interviews with 106 law students,[17] nonparticipant observation of panethnic student groups, and analysis of their e-mail list correspondence, I find law students' experiences to be rather complex. Asian

American and Latino students experience racialization in and out of the classroom and negotiate stereotype threat surrounding their achievements. At the same time, panethnicity and immigrant background anchor their friendship circles, career trajectories, and cultivation of simultaneous professional and personal identities.

Instead of touting Asian American and Latino acceptance into the mainstream as successful integration, I add meat to the bare-bones metrics of economic and social parity with white Americans. Anyone must contend with layers of socialization when adapting to a new profession. But Asian American and Latino law students must also negotiate "othering" as racial or ethnic deviants in their profession, otherwise known as "outsiders" (Blackwell 1987). I characterize Asian American and Latino law students as both agents of and reactors to their socialization processes. Their racial or ethnic identities may be asserted by them or ascribed by others, and these identities may be used in different circumstances and for different reasons. For instance, law students join panethnic organizations to cultivate, negotiate, and manage their racial or ethnic identities. They also join these organizations to reap academic and professional benefits.

This book examines how racialization and professional socialization happen simultaneously for Asian American and Latino law students. I focus on these two panethnic groups because of their similar historical, political, and cultural experiences with race and racism. I am well aware that each panethnic group is heterogeneous, representing linguistic, ethnic, and religious diversity. But descriptively disaggregating each group would not adequately permit an in-depth analysis of the processes by which members of these groups are racialized in law school. As an entity, Asian Americans and Latinos demonstrate their liminality between black and white and the continued production and reproduction of that status. Knowing this, furthers the need to conceptualize race and racialization beyond our current understandings.

This book also features comparisons among students, across institutions, and between genders. Chapter 1 describes why students choose to pursue law. Some students view law as a path for upward mobility, while others focus on the public interest contributions made possible by those with law degrees. These general reasons do not vary across race or ethnicity but rather evoke immigrant experience with the law. Chapter 2 highlights an ignored (and often unknown) history of discrimination toward these two groups in a nation focused on the black-white racial binary.

Chapters 3–7 delve into the law school experience and document how race becomes salient in Asian American and Latino law students' lives. Chapter 3 features white students speaking about their simultaneous appreciation of and frustration with diversity. It complements Chapter 4, which characterizes law school as an institutional white space, drawing on Wendy

Leo Moore's work (2008), that heightens nonwhite students' sense of racial identity and awareness. Racialized experiences in the classroom, through interactions with professors and peers, and culture shock on arriving at law school propel nonwhite law students to adopt, even if only peripherally, panethnic identities. Chapter 5 examines in depth the role of panethnic student organizations in this racialization endeavor. How organizations operate and welcome new members creates allegiance to not only the organizations themselves but also the wider panethnic communities in question.

Chapters 6 and 7 demonstrate the dramaturgical nature, per Erving Goffman (1959), of legal socialization by focusing on distinct subsamples of respondents. Chapter 6 features the stories of Asian American and Latino law students on a corporate career trajectory and how they use a repertoire of strategies to manage their professional (front stage) and panethnic (backstage) identities. The strategies—marginal panethnicity, tempered altruism, and instrumental ethnicity—are evoked on the basis of Asian American and Latino law students' panethnic affinity. Chapter 7 intersects (pan)ethnicity, immigrant history, and gender to underscore how Asian American and Latina women law students are typecast into particular professional and gendered roles. This chapter places women of color at the center of the discussion and explores the multiple roles expected from them.

Rounding out the book, the Conclusion's "Epilogue" provides a glimpse into a subsample of respondents who have been working for the past two to three years. Their professional, panethnic, gender, and immigrant experiences foreshadow how they continue to negotiate their multiple identities. The most striking feature is the importance and value they attribute to panethnic bar associations, which hints at the place of race beyond law school.

Confessions of an Imposter Law Student: A Personal Note

I am not a law student; I never was and never will be. Although I began my undergraduate degree in political science with intentions of eventually going to law school, I realized that law school appealed to me more as an *object* of study. The students featured in this book, however, thought that I was one of them—at least when we first met. They were intrigued when I came clean and unveiled my actual identity as a doctoral student at the time. This affiliation engendered a sense of familiarity, as they and I were all aspiring to advanced degrees, and this probably helped me to be accepted into their world. I admit that I certainly felt an affinity with them, perhaps even more than they did with me. My husband was a newly minted attorney when I began my fieldwork, so I felt a connection to the law students I met, many of whom are featured in this book. Most of the respondents were second-generation immigrants and many were first-generation college students, and as such, their paths to graduate education paralleled mine in many ways.

When I returned to the West Coast of the United States to conduct follow-up interviews in 2013, I was excited to see my friends. That excitement was short-lived as I realized that this "friendship" has been, and always will be, one sided. I was an imposter.

This book primarily focuses on the stories of Asian American and Latino law students. Interspersed throughout are voices from a number of white and otherwise-racialized students—what the scientific community refers to as a control group. All respondents knew my intentions and permitted me to speak with and observe them. The Asian American and Latino respondents were frequently motivated by the dearth of literature about them, their lives, their families, and their copanethnics. They shared their experiences with me as a way to improve and contribute to inclusion efforts in the legal profession. Many of the white students wanted the same, as they too are members of a changing profession. Thus, all respondents may reflect a slight selectivity bias. But who does not, at least outwardly, support diversity in the twenty-first century?

Why study Asian Americans and Latinos? I am often asked this question. A partial answer begins with my childhood in the United States. I was born in Taiwan, moved to the United States at age seven, and grew up in Corvallis, Oregon—a predominantly white town and state. My parents are high school graduates and owned a small restaurant, which is a different profile from the majority of the Chinese people who lived there, who were college-educated, graduate students or professors (or family to graduate students or professors) at Oregon State University or worked at the local Hewlett-Packard campus as engineers. The socioeconomic gap and identity politics among the Mainland Chinese, the Taiwanese, and the Chinese from Taiwan created enormous divisions, such that my family was marginalized by the overall Chinese community. In other words, we did not have many Chinese friends.

As a result, the majority of my friends were white. I must note that I never felt white, and I experienced covert discrimination even in a "blue" college town where over half the residents are college graduates.[18] I treasure my childhood friendships, but my mostly white friends could not sympathize with the pull between cultures and my marginalization as a racial other. After all, my white friends never experienced being yelled at by white store clerks who assumed I did not understand English; they never had white teenagers ridicule their mother's English (an act that silenced her for twelve years, with me acting as her interpreter until I went to college); they did not watch white families get served at restaurants while we patiently waited our turn, even when we arrived before them.

But there is one particular friendship that occupies a special place in my memory. This friend and I were similar in many ways. We both have much younger sisters whom we often had to babysit. Both our parents owned restaurants, which meant we were obligated to work in the evenings and on weekends when our friends were at football games, movies, or sleepovers. We both had culturally conservative parents, especially when it came to dating. We both immigrated to the United States as young children. As required by our parents, we both spoke different languages at home but English when we were in public. Unbeknownst to our other friends, we often went to a local diner after work for marionberry pie and conversations that made sense in our bicultural world. My friend Heidy is Mexican American, and our friendship has forever shaped the way I think about race relations in the United States.

Similarities between Asian Americans and Latinos extend beyond childhood friendships and into legal history, conceptualizations of citizenship, and belonging. As I advanced in my education, specializing in race and ethnicity, I became ever more annoyed by the (mis)interpretations of these two groups by scholars basing their arguments almost solely on demographic figures. While numbers are important, they do not capture the discrimination I experienced or witnessed as a child. They further underestimate the role of socialization as it intersects with immigrant history and racialization. Asian Americans and Latinos are the fastest-growing panethnic groups in the United States and are expected to contribute directly to the nation becoming minority majority by 2050 (Passel and Cohn 2008). As Eileen O'Brien writes, "Taken together, Latinos and Asian Americans will soon constitute about 35 percent of the U.S. population while African Americans would only be at 13 percent" (2008, 2). Introducing this figure is in no way meant to denigrate the importance of black history or current social conditions but is meant to illustrate the special place occupied by Asian Americans and Latinos in U.S. history, policies, and society. Moreover, members of these two groups experience a different process of racialization that is often omitted from popular discourse on race relations. Their existence between black and white situates them in a liminal space. I use law students as a case to further unpack that space. I invite you to accompany me, in this book, to better understand these experiences.

1

PRESTIGE, JUSTICE, AND EVERYTHING IN BETWEEN

Why Pursue Law?

> I remember telling my mom, "I want to be a lawyer!" I think I really liked the glamor of it with the suits and what the Hollywood portrayal of it was. And I think when you're little, you just kind of fall into that.

This comment from Beatriz Mendoza demonstrates that law students considered the image of lawyers before they decided to pursue the profession. They also considered many other reasons. My conversations with law students revealed two primary modes by which they ended up in law school: practical and accidental. Consideration of prestige is interwoven into these responses too, as it was often the immediate reason provided by law students when asked to explain their choice of study. But there was almost always more to their stories than that. This chapter introduces law students' various rationales for pursuing law. On the surface, it appears that these students sought only to ascend the socioeconomic ladder, but their nuanced backstories reveal the importance of panethnicity and immigrant history in conjunction with experiences before law school.

First, a note on what most of the respondents are not—namely, the modal law student:

> The typical (i.e. modal) first-year law student is a white male in his early twenties, who speaks English as his first language, attends law school full time, expresses high self-confidence, possesses no physical or learning disabilities, is neither married nor has children, plans

0–9 weekly hours of paid employment during the first year, and comes from an above-average socioeconomic background. (Clydesdale 2004, 724–725)

Instead, the law students featured in this book deviate from the modal first-year law student in many ways. Because the majority of the respondents included here are children of immigrants, many did not speak English as their first language and also do not necessarily self-report high levels of self-confidence. Depending on the law school, some students also worked twenty or more hours per week (paid and unpaid), while others did not work outside school at all. And many respondents hailed from below-average socioeconomic backgrounds. The participants in this study may not be modal law students yet, but their rising numbers and the changing demographics of law school suggest that the portraits I present here provide valuable glimpses into the changing face of the legal profession.

Law Is Prestigious

Why attend law school? As previously mentioned, prestige was often cited as the motivating factor. Law students frequently point to the prestigious status of lawyers in American society as their primary reason for pursuing law. It is important to consider the history connected to this profession's widespread image. Law schools used to offer full-time programs for those with intellectual aspirations and part-time programs for those with pragmatic pursuits. This dual system changed in the late 1800s and early 1900s, placing more emphasis on scientific methods and models. Seeking to replicate scientific rigor in the social sciences and the medical field, the dean of Harvard Law School, Christopher Columbus Langdell, sought to reconceptualize law school by, among other things, introducing a rigorous three-year curriculum. Sociolegal scholar Wendy Leo Moore explains:

> Rather than read statutory law to understand what the law was in a particular jurisdiction, he [Langdell] suggested that reading cases written by sitting judges would reveal the correct process by which law was interpreted and constructed. He also conducted his classes, not by lecturing, the method dominant at that historical moment, but by utilizing the Socratic teaching method . . . [which] he argued would enable students to understand the logical methods being applied by the judges who wrote the laws that mirrored those of the great judges at the time. (2008, 40)

Thus, the focus and culture of law was to admit and then nurture the best legal minds. Qualifications for admission to Harvard Law changed, which led to selection criteria emphasizing intellectual prowess (and economic resources). Other law schools followed suit; the American Bar Association (ABA) sanctioned a three-year law school model and other aspects of Langdell's teachings, such as the Socratic and case methods. This law school culture emphasizing admissions, instruction, and selectivity remains to this day, fueling the image of law schools as elite institutions regulated by scientific rigor. Law students, by default, absorb that prestigious image—or at least, hope to do so.

At the same time, law school culture reflects the racial order and framing of the broader society. Moore describes law schools as "institutional white spaces" with a clear hierarchy in which "a fundamental aspect of thinking like a lawyer is the implicit internalization of a white racial frame" (2008, 40). The ways that people are organized, hired and fired, the ways they express deference, and other aspects of human interaction are tightly bound within a white framework. Joe Feagin uses the white racial frame to describe how the sociohistory of the United States is bound within a culture that not only normalizes but also prioritizes European American norms. Law schools thus reflect a broader societal culture that is built on a dominant white political, cultural, and economic history.

Law's prestige and implicit structuration according to societal norms are reflected in the understandings law students themselves have about the profession. Take, for instance, Thomas Cain's response when asked why he chose law. Thomas is a white, working-class, second-generation college student—meaning, his parents were the first among his extended family to attend college. He explained, "[Law] gives some social status to those of us who go to law school. I suppose, I mean, I feel more confident talking to my peers now that I'm in law school because I feel like I'm doing something that is of value." Thomas attended an Ivy League institution for college but, given his socioeconomic background, never quite felt as if he belonged. Thomas recalled his undergraduate days:

> I was truly out of place because many, many of the kids at [my Ivy League institution] grew up in intellectual households or grew up with parents who were doctors, attorneys, professors. Or just, you know, had intellectual conversations, which we didn't. And I sort of feel that way here, but I don't think I'm the only one who had sort of my experience.

At first blush, one might imagine that Thomas is a candidate to fake it through law school. As mentioned in the Introduction, Robert Granfield explains that working-class students often hide their backgrounds by avoiding opportunities that would make their class upbringing evident (Granfield 1992; see also Costello 2006).

Yet Thomas's story did not align exactly with the typical working-class experience in law school either—something potentially due to his attendance at an Ivy League institution for college. While he noted educational disparities among his peers' parents, he also described finding law school to be somewhat more egalitarian than his college experience. In college, he never felt as if he belonged, but law's prestige gave him a new status boost.

Thomas was not the only respondent drawn to the prestige of the legal profession. Other students echoed Thomas with comments such as "The justice system is what makes the rules that we live by, and one decision in the Supreme Court—it's just so powerful!" (Asha Patel), or "When you think 'attorney,' you think 'money'" (Dean Tam). Prestige appears to be an overriding reason for pursuing law—one that then gets coupled with either a practical or accidental explanation. The next section examines how some students pursue law for practical purposes, while others enter law school rather accidentally.

"I Want to Use My Smarts": The Calculated Law Student

As mentioned in the book's Introduction, many respondents aspired to law from a young age. Some decisions were calculated, with the student systematically completing prerequisite courses and joining profession-specific student organizations. Adam Rhee, a first-year, Korean American law student, talked about the practical (i.e., stable) benefits of a degree in law:

> I had some of the more practical goal aspirations. . . . I consider myself decently smart, so I want an interesting and challenging career. I want to use my smarts in some capacity in my job. I also am relatively risk averse. . . . As soon as I was with my partner, [I was] thinking about getting married, having a family. I started thinking about job security. And [law is] one of the more stable job careers.

Kurt Waters, a third-year, mixed-race (Taiwanese and white) law student, recalled deciding to use his undergraduate degree in a practical manner: "I was a political science major, so I didn't really have any career options going directly out of undergrad. And in general, the law has [options]. . . . I mean, like your general notions of the law, like the lofty ideals of the law." Adam and Kurt both described law as a stable profession, one that gave them a concrete way to apply their undergraduate training.

Other respondents drew on the limited knowledge they had about their career options. To them, a stable job meant becoming a doctor, lawyer, or teacher—common aspirations among children of immigrants experiencing immigrant optimism (the advancing of the American dream, which I discuss more later in this chapter). Prestige matters, but for children of im-migrants, their legal-career aspirations intersect practical tools, serendipity, and an immigrant narrative.

Marta Ortiz is a second-year, Mexican American law student at Western Elite with working-class parents who completed only middle school. Marta recalled trying to decide on a career when she was young:

> I was in eighth grade, and I keep remembering . . . that for me, in my mind, *career* meant you were either a doctor or a lawyer. Nothing else was really visible. . . . I think in my mind, I couldn't be a doctor because there was just too much math, too much science, and I didn't want to do that. So I just decided on law.

Marta recalled taking financial calculations into consideration as she thought about her eventual career, but still, the options were only to be a doctor or a lawyer. And since becoming a doctor required "too much math, too much science," law became the default prestigious profession. Similarly, Norman Lin, a second-year, Chinese American student, said:

> I can't pretend it was one of those revolutionary epiphanies. I was in middle school, I think, and for some reason I had this notion that I needed to decide what I wanted to do with my life. And I did a little process-of-elimination game with myself, and I sort of checked off things that I don't think I could do. And I chose law because I thought you get to talk a lot. I like to talk. You get to write a lot. I like to write. And it seems fun enough; it seems stable enough. You get paid enough. . . . And I thought, this is something I can do and enjoy.

Norman went on to major in political science; he also joined a prelaw frater-nity, which allowed him to cultivate a better understanding of and deeper appreciation for law. He met other college students who shared his career ambition, and he also had the opportunity to meet lawyers and law students and visit firms and judges' chambers.

While prestigious and practical for some, law became the default pro-fession for those who lacked the knack for science or math required for the medical field. Yet there were other students who did not fear math or science and, in fact, chose law precisely because of their previous training in those areas. As they assessed their career options, the law students with under-graduate degrees in the natural sciences saw law as an opportunity to *use* their technical skills, while those with liberal arts degrees looked to law as a way to *build* their skill sets.

Mad Skills

Fred Ngo, a Chinese-Vietnamese American, second-year student who completed a doctorate in biomedical engineering before commencing law school, thought law was a good option. Fred's practical reasons to enroll in law school emerged from the bleak career opportunities awaiting him as a biomedical engineer. He intends to use his training and background in science to advance his legal career. Fred explained:

> Going the academia route can be quite challenging. If I had wanted to pursue the academia route, that would have included a postdoc after graduate school. Postdoc is one of the least attractive career options to me, personally. It's an indeterminate amount of time. Can be two to four years, they say—seems to be getting longer. There's no guarantee of job availability after you postdoc; you may have to do multiple postdocs. You get paid very little relative to the amount of schooling you've had—I think 35K is the average that I've heard. There's a relatively high degree of variability and unpredictability as far as the quality of work that you'll be doing and the results that you'll be able to achieve no matter how talented or qualified you are. . . . And then after that, you have to find a tenure-track position, and those are getting more scarce. And just the actual [experience of] being a professor and seeing what my boss went through—the challenges he had to face and overcome—it didn't seem particularly appealing. It was not the life of the mind, where you pursue your scientific fancies, so much as it was running a small business.

The negatives of academia, coupled with seeing his friends with similar academic backgrounds pursue patent prosecution, sparked Fred's interest in law and made it seem desirable—particularly when compared to the perceived alternatives. Moreover, the monetary compensation was more than fair. Fred continued, "Some colleagues from graduate school have pursued that route—prosecution is considered to have the better lifestyle. It's like a 9-to-5 kind of job. You don't have pressing deadlines, necessarily. So that was the good job."

Like Fred, Helen Trieu, a third-year, Chinese-Vietnamese American law student, has an advanced degree in the natural sciences and worked for many years as a researcher. Helen described being steered toward law by an advisor:

> Because I have a science background, I did research for seven years in industry and academics, and when I got into graduate school . . . my

advisor in the biotech company I was working [for] . . . asked what I wanted to do with my graduate degree once I finished. I just said research, because that's all I knew. And then she suggested, "Oh, you should look into intellectual property, specifically patents," . . . and so, while I was in graduate school, I decided to pursue law.

In this way, former engineers, biologists, and scientists described seeing law school as an opportunity to extend and apply their technical skills and knowledge. While law does draw from an array of academic backgrounds, most lawyers have degrees from the liberal arts. There are few with technical training, and because of this, their expertise is highly sought after in the profession. Thus, the lure of job stability and monetary compensation encourages these students to look to law as a career.

Need Skills

Of course, not all students speak of skills in the same way. Instead of applying their skills to law, some students chose law school to expand their repertoire. Lucia Gutierrez, a second-year, Mexican American law student who plans to pursue a career in policy, focusing on health-related issues, explained her motivations:

> I wanted to go to law school because I always wanted to go into policy. So it was kind of either get a master's in public policy or get a JD. And I think the appeal [of law] to me was, after working in the . . . legislature [of a Western state] and interning in Congress, I realized a lot of people making laws had law degrees. So I wanted to be able to come to the table with an understanding of whatever it is you learn in law school. Secondly, I kind of felt, if you're helping create laws, [you ask] what kind of impact those laws can make. So if you pass a law, is this a good law that is actually going to withstand a judicial—when someone protests the law in a court, will it actually pass the test?

As an aspirant to a career affecting laws, Lucia recognized that she needed legal tools to be a better health advocate. At the time of our interview, Lucia was simultaneously enrolled in a public policy program.

Similarly, Andersen Lee, a third-year, Korean American law student, said:

> Before I came to law school I was working at a nonprofit, mainly doing housing discrimination work. I was an advocate to represent victims of housing discrimination and help them mediate through the process or refer them to lawyers and work with them. We investigated

those cases. . . . I actually got certified as a mediator. And while I was doing housing discrimination work, I also volunteered as a mediator for tenant-landlord disputes. Then I realized if I want to make a living as a mediator or make a living really helping out those people in discrimination cases, I better get a law degree.

For Andersen, the drive to advocate on behalf of clients in discrimination cases led him to law school.

As seen in this section, the variability of skills—needing skills versus bolstering one's skill set—influenced students' decisions to attend law school. These students calculated how they would actualize their careers and strategically decided to pursue law. Unlike them, some other students became law students less by planning than chance.

"I Had This Degree in Sociology": The Accidental Law Student

Law students who fell into the practical camp mentioned planning ahead or pursuing law for instrumental purposes, to use their existing skills or to obtain new ones. Others noted the need to switch fields entirely, especially for financial reasons. These students often evinced a just-because attitude that catapulted them toward law.

Recall Fred Ngo, the Chinese-Vietnamese American law student with a doctorate in biomedical engineering. Although Fred mentioned salary as one of many factors leading him to law school, other students prioritized this consideration. This was especially prevalent among students with liberal arts degrees. They wrung their hands about the so-called great recession that reigned from 2008 to 2011, and they fielded questions from family members about career plans. Elena Chaidez is one such example. Born and raised near the Pacific Ocean, Elena, a second-year, Mexican American law student, was always interested in sea life. She began her undergraduate studies at a junior college with the intent of majoring in marine biology. However, on transferring to the four-year institution where she ultimately completed her bachelor's degree, she realized that it would take too long for her to study marine biology:

So I decided to do anthropology, because I thought it was interesting. But when I was done with undergrad, I didn't see that degree being able to support me in any way. At least not just a bachelor's [degree]. I thought, if I go to law school, I could still be involved with animals—animal rights or the environment, which is something I'm passionate about. . . . I would be still working somewhat in this area. That's why I chose law school, and to provide for my family.

Being a lawyer offered Elena the opportunity to continue to work, albeit tangentially, with sea life while also providing a salary sufficient to support her family.

Smriti Kapur, a first-year, Indian American law student, likewise emphasized the importance of financial stability. Equipped with a bachelor's degree in sociology as she considered entering the workforce during the great recession, Smriti was uncertain about her career prospects:

> I had this degree in sociology. I came straight from undergrad to law school, so it was a pretty immediate decision. And with the economy the way it was when I graduated in the middle of all that, everything that happened, it kind of felt like law school was safe. It's a little bit of a guarantee that I would . . . get some kind of good job coming out of school, as opposed to I really didn't know what I could do. I really didn't know what I could do with just a sociology degree.

The great recession certainly influenced students' plans. When the recession hit in 2008, most of the students in this study were finishing college and facing an uncertain economic future. The law students with bachelor's degrees in liberal arts cited law school as a safe haven where they might wait out the financial instability, which lasted until 2009 and beyond.[1]

Just Because versus Seizing the Moment

Other students saw law as a natural next step for their careers. They seized the moment to move forward in their lives with their college majors or existing work experience. Unlike the students who calculated the practical benefits associated with a law degree, these seize-the-moment students simply saw an opportunity to garner skills for their future careers. The decision to attend law school came at varying times for the students who used this reasoning.

Will Decker, a second-year, white student, took a circuitous path to law school. After finishing high school, Will spent years in and out of college while holding full-time jobs at record stores, coffee shops, and retail outlets. At the end of college, however, Will was determined to carve a different career track for himself. He recalled:

> I got done with college, and I continued working at the same job I was working at, and I kind of wanted to do something more. I was working at a record shop, and I loved it! But I wanted to do something more; I wanted to do something that felt more like I was *doing something* other than selling things to people. . . . And I had been involved in various sorts of activism, and also doing volunteer

work. I'd done some volunteer work for the [American Civil Liberties Union]. So [through] that, I was meeting lawyers who were doing work that seemed really positive to me. And it seemed like a place where I could possibly do work that was helpful to other people, to clients.

Will's desire to "do something more" led him to law school. He serendipitously met public interest attorneys and, finding their work interesting, decided to pursue law. As an attorney, he would not be "selling things to people" and could embark instead on a career that allowed him to help clients.

Some law students explicitly credited serendipity with a significant role in their decision to attend law school. This happened most often among those who majored in political science or other social sciences—common undergraduate majors for lawyers. According to the American Bar Association's "Pre-law" webpage (American Bar Association, n.d.), the most common undergraduate majors of law school aspirants are business, economics, English, philosophy, and political science. This trend was reflected at both Western Elite and Private Metropolitan (see Table 1.1).

As seen in Table 1.1, most of the law students earned bachelor's degrees in the liberal arts. More than 65 percent of all respondents majored in the social sciences, including interdisciplinary studies such as Chicano studies and women's studies. Political science, otherwise billed as politics or

TABLE 1.1: COLLEGE MAJORS BY PANETHNICITY AND AGGREGATE AT WESTERN ELITE AND PRIVATE METROPOLITAN

College major	Asian American	Latino	White	Other	Total
Politics/government/prelaw	17	15	9	2	43
Other social sciences (psychology, sociology, anthropology)	8	7	4	0	19
History	5	3	1	0	9
Business/MBA	3	1	0	3	7
Natural sciences/engineering	4	0	2	0	6
Economics	1	2	1	0	4
Interdisciplinary studies (women's studies, ethnic studies)	1	2	1	4	4
English/literature	0	2	1	0	3
Philosophy/classics	1	0	2	0	3
Other humanities (art, film)	3	0	0	0	3

government, was the most represented of all undergraduate majors, followed by other social sciences—sociology, psychology, and anthropology. Only six students majored in the natural sciences or engineering.

So was it the content of these specializations that steered students toward law, or was it something else? For some, the esoteric nature of their degrees made it difficult to pursue other career options. A degree in philosophy, gender studies, or history may seem intellectually fulfilling, but the students who majored in these subjects became nervous as they thought about their career prospects. What types of jobs could they acquire to ensure a fruitful career? This question drove many to consider what they deemed practical choices. Elise Brown, a first-year, white law student, reflected on her path to law school:

> My bachelor's [degree] and master's [degree] are both in philosophy, and . . . in my master's program, I took a lot of Middle Eastern philosophy and primarily Islamic philosophy. And I took medieval philosophy. So not a lot of practical applications today. . . . So I took the LSAT [Law School Admission Test] on a whim. I took no legal classes in my undergrad and grad work. And didn't know how I would do on it. Took it once, did well. Took a gamble, and it's paid off. I'm really enjoying it.

Elise's high LSAT[2] score ultimately led her to law school.

Similarly, Matt Yoon, a second-year, Korean American law student, was a film major in college. Like Elise, he did not foresee using his film degree, although he found the topic interesting:

> I never seriously considered going into film for grad school. I knew that it would be fairly redundant; it would just be useless. It would be better to just go straight into working in that industry, but that is particular to that industry. But I wasn't serious about film by about my senior year—I think I was kind of drifting. For one day at least, I think I considered business school. But I really dislike business concepts. Med school, I never considered it really. Both of my parents are doctors, but they never pushed that on me. Law school is kind of—I had nothing better to do, so that is part of . . . why I went, and I'm really glad that it worked out and that I like it.

With his film degree, Matt considered practical graduate options: business school, medical school, and law school. Postbaccalaureate planning was evident among law students hailing from families in which at least one parent attended graduate school.

Previous research attests to the influence of parental education and children's academic achievement (Davis-Kean 2005; Eccles and Davis-Kean 2005). Parental years of schooling correlate positively with children's educational achievements and aspirations. Pamela Davis-Kean finds that parental education is an important determinant of academic success for school-age children (ages eight to twelve). Controlling for race, parental education remains a steadfast positive factor in children's academic achievement.[3]

Unpacking the significance of socialization underscores the hidden value of education. Davis-Kean further suggests that the amount of schooling received by parents influences the home environment and how parents interact with their children. She states, "It is possible that parents as 'co-teachers' in the home may find a better psychological balance of stimulation and demand for their children when they themselves were successful in academics" (Davis-Kean 2005, 302). Children whose parents expected them to perform well in school typically did so, as opposed to peers whose parents harbored less than encouraging expectations.

In a similar vein, most law students with parents who earned graduate degrees spoke of considering graduate options while still working toward their bachelor's degrees. Thinking about and planning to attend graduate school was not exclusive to law students with parents who had graduate degrees, however. Most of the second-generation immigrant law students, fueled by immigrant optimism, also thought about graduate training while they were still in college. *Immigrant optimism* describes the positive outlook of recent immigrants, particularly those who are first-generation immigrants. This optimism manifests itself through hard work, dedication, and a generally upbeat outlook about their lives and future opportunities in their newly adopted country. Parents then, prime their kids for law school in two ways: immigrant optimism, and cultural capital via professional parents.

Estelle Ngan's parents completed grade school in Vietnam and were never schooled beyond that. Recognizing the value of education, Estelle's parents impressed on her and her siblings the need to excel in school. Estelle understood the message. But it took some time to actualize her parents' wishes. She fooled around her first three years of high school but started to panic during her senior year when she realized her grades were nowhere near what she needed for admission to four-year colleges. So she started at a junior college and worked diligently with a virtually nonexistent social life until she was able to transfer to a prestigious public university. Estelle had aspired to law school ever since entering college: "When I was in undergrad, I was like, 'Oh, some of our professors were also lawyers too!' And, of course, you see [them] on TV and that type of thing. . . . So [law] was something that piqued my interest." Estelle, a political science major in college, seized the opportunity and applied to law school.

It Was Time

Other students with a seize-the-moment attitude made the move to law because, as they tell it, "it was time." Most of these students were in the midst
of careers when they realized it was time for a change. Some were displeased
with their jobs, while others felt they had reached their potential for growth
in their current industries. For example, Aaron Thompson is a mixed-race
(Japanese and white), first-year law student. An economics major in college,
Aaron worked for a brief time following college graduation but did not feel
that his job was sufficiently fulfilling:

> I was working for a while. I guess I didn't really enjoy it. I did some
> sales work; I did some customer service work. I don't think I felt
> very intellectually stimulated. Speaking with people that were either
> current or former law students and [seeing] what they did—it just
> felt like something that I would really enjoy. It felt like something I
> could be good at. The whole process of researching and making an
> argument just really appealed to my personality.

Aaron's story was common among the students who returned to law school
following a different career.

Lydia Kang is another example. A second-year, Chinese American law
student, Lydia decided to return to law school for a career change:

> I went to [Western Elite] for undergrad, and then I worked in man-
> agement consulting for a year, and I was kind of like, "I did bio[logy],
> and I did business, and I don't really know what I want to do." And
> I really disliked consulting. And I think a lot of that was because it
> was, like, my first work experience, and I think it's pretty natural
> not to like work when you first start because it's such a huge change.
> And I felt like I need to get out somehow. And I had taken the LSAT
> already, and then I was like, "I'm just going to apply to law school and
> see what happens." And then I got in, and [Western Elite] has such
> a strong [intellectual property] program that I thought it's probably
> best to go down this path, and I'm lucky that it worked out that I
> have some exposure to that field. But I feel like a lot of how I ended
> up where I am wasn't really any sort of purpose. It just sort of hap-
> pened the way it did.

Law students like Lydia and Aaron described attending law school as not
unlike a successful experiment. They were at a crossroads in their careers—
they no longer felt as if they were intellectually challenged—and decided it
was time for a change. Many of these students had considered law school at

some point in college, going so far as to purchase study guides and study for the LSAT.

Others actually took the LSAT during or after college on the off chance they might eventually consider law school. These respondents were propelled toward law school because their scores were on the verge of expiration and they felt a tug of urgency. Gregory Watts, a second-year, white law student, was one of these people. Gregory and I met on a rainy afternoon in the Western Elite law school café. He hails from a family with three generations of lawyers; not surprisingly, he always considered law as a potential career. He began, however, by first becoming a teacher. Gregory took the LSAT before college graduation but then went on to teach at an urban high school for several years. Although Gregory felt he was making a positive contribution to society as a teacher, he remembered his soon-to-expire LSAT score:

> I took my LSATs my junior year of college and went into teaching with an open mind, not knowing if that's what I wanted to do long term. Sort of what forced the decision . . . was that my LSATs were about to expire. They expire in five years. So I figured, if I was going to do it, then it was the time. So I made myself make the decision and am very happy with it.

As seen here, factors such as career change or an expiring LSAT score led some law students to plunge into law school.

Immigrant Narrative and Optimism

Most law students provided practical and accidental explanations for attending law school, but the Latino and Asian American respondents also drew on an immigrant narrative. This section discusses how the immigrant experience motived these respondents to attend law school. These immigrant narratives often include personal or familial experiences with the law or using the law as a way to achieve justice or social mobility. This was the case for respondents at both Western Elite and Private Metropolitan.

Jennifer Lee (2014) recently wrote in a *Time* article that Mexican Americans are the most successful immigrants because they possess a positive view of the American dream. That dream is not measured by the make of the cars one owns or the zip code where one resides; rather, the power of the American dream is illustrated by the advances made from one generation to the next. Mexican American parents believe strongly in the power of education and encourage their children to succeed academically. Latinos in the United States—approximately 64 percent of whom are of Mexican descent—are entering college and mainstream professions at high rates.

Roughly twenty years ago, Patricia Gándara explored the academic achievements of Chicano youth from low-income families. In *Over the Ivy Walls* (1995), Gándara argued that a sense of optimism and hard work had propelled Chicano doctors, professors, and engineers to succeed academically. Coupled with their parents' encouragement, these students set out for what some may call successful "structural assimilation." Briefly discussed in the Introduction, *structural assimilation* refers to immigrant groups being accepted into mainstream society. In accordance with the straight-line assimilation experiences of European Americans, *structural assimilation* is explained as minorities entering mainstream clubs, organizations, and institutions. Gándara's respondents corroborated this theory.

While structurally assimilating into the mainstream is cause for celebration, it leaves questions about the mechanisms of such acceptance. In other words, aside from the mainstream population (i.e., white Americans) opening their arms and welcoming Latinos, to what extent does the agency of immigrants themselves play a role? How and why? In her study of Caribbean New Yorkers, Mary Waters (1999) found that these immigrants maintain a positive outlook about life in the United States despite racial discrimination.

Grace Kao and Marta Tienda (1995) introduced the term *immigrant optimism* to explain achievement among immigrant youth. Second-generation immigrants assimilate their first-generation-immigrant parents' optimistic outlook on the United States, including their views regarding education. And sure enough, second-generation youth outperform their third-generation and later coethnics and native-born whites. Kao and Tienda conclude, "It appears that immigrant parents' optimism about their offspring's socioeconomic prospects decisively influences educational outcomes. Thus, the second-generation is best positioned for scholastic success by having foreign-born parents and language fluency conferred by native birth in the United States" (1995, 17).

Since Kao and Tienda's introduction of the term, other research, especially in the field of education, has closely examined the role of immigrant optimism and second-generation success.[4] The specific groups of interest may be different (e.g., Chinese youth versus Mexican youth), but the findings remain the same: the second generation are academically successful. This immigrant drive or optimism is apparent among the law students featured in this book—most of whom are second-generation Americans (see Figure 1.1).

In Figure 1.1, roughly 57 percent of the sample is second generation. When including the 1.5 generation,[5] 68 percent of the total sample is composed of immediate-immigrant offspring. For Latinos and Asian Americans, 70 percent are second generation, and over 81 percent (including the 1.5 generation) of this subsample are children of immigrants. How is immigrant optimism relevant for these respondents? Let us hear directly from the students.

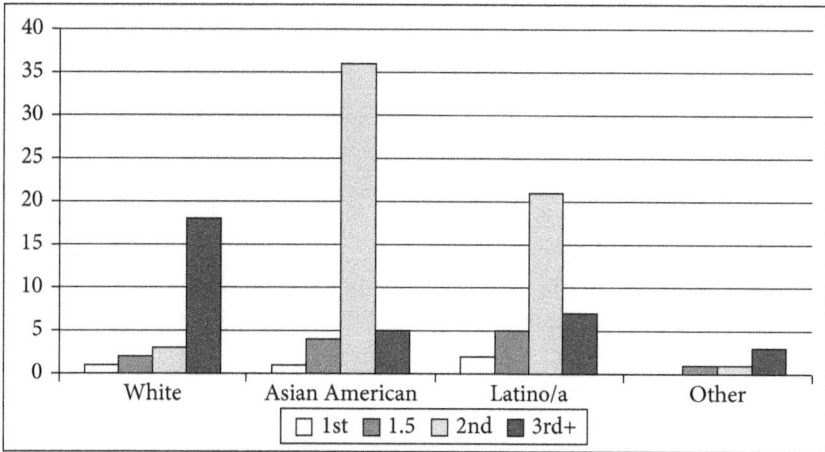

Figure 1.1 Respondents' immigrant generation

Parental Expectations

Second-year student Debbie Kwan and I met on a Saturday afternoon at Western Elite. She had just returned from winter break, and as the chair of the Society of Asian American Law Students,[6] she needed to prepare for the semester. Shuffling through a stack of papers, Debbie explained what led her to law school: "I think part of it has to do with my parents. Growing up, they always told me and my younger brother, 'You have to be a lawyer or a doctor.'" Debbie's parents were computer engineers before retiring, and because of their Chinese-language fluency, their U.S. company sent them to work in China, specifically Hong Kong and Beijing. Up until her family moved back to the United States when Debbie began high school, she was always surrounded by diverse, albeit English-speaking students in international schools. Her time overseas piqued her interest in working for a United States–based firm abroad.

Selena Vallejo, a second-year student, comes from a different background. Unlike Debbie's computer engineer parents, Selena's parents are agriculture workers. They completed high school in Mexico and migrated north in search of brighter futures. Selena described the difficulty of applying to and remaining in law school:

> Growing up, I always had people that served as my counselors because my parents didn't know . . . how to apply to college. To this day, I still have to fill out my FAFSA [Free Application for Federal Student Aid forms]. I'm like, "Did you [parents] do your taxes? I need to do my FAFSA." There's people that I know that are like, "Oh, my

parents do my FAFSA." I'm like, "Oh my god, that's so cool! That's so awesome."

Additionally, Selena's parents do not quite understand law school. Unlike her peers whose parents are familiar with higher education, Selena must explain how her education directly affects her goal of becoming an attorney. She said, "My parents had no idea what I was doing. . . . I told them I was going to law school. They were like, 'Okay, great. Let us know what we can do to help you.' But . . . I don't have anyone like that who can tell me [what to expect]." Selena's frustration was not necessarily directed at her parents but was, rather, anxiety about entering law school without mentors or guidance.

Although Selena's parents did not know the purpose of FAFSA forms or the law school curriculum, they impressed on their children the importance and value of education. Armed with immigrant optimism, her parents saw education as the best tool to attain economic mobility. But their support came with caveats: they would tolerate only certain respectable professions. Selena explained, "I think my parents come from a very traditional Mexican background. . . . You have certain options. . . . I could be a teacher, I could be a doctor, or I could be a lawyer."

Notwithstanding differences in parents' educational attainment, one clear theme emerged among many of the Latino and Asian American law students: their parents wanted them to pursue a respectable profession. While some parents, like Selena's, left the decision making up to their children, others took a heavy-handed approach. These involved parents encouraged their children to attend law school and helped plan accordingly or incessantly "motivated" reluctant children until they relented.

Kevin Gu, a Chinese American, third-year law student, had what one would term stereotypical Asian American parents. Kevin's father is an insurance agent and his mother owns a franchised business in a mall food court. Kevin was a mediocre student at an elite college, making his grades a frequent topic of quarrels. Once he graduated from college, his parents wanted to ensure that Kevin did something practical for a career and decided that law school was his best option. As he related it:

[My parents] definitely stressed education, and my dad, specifically, felt a college degree wasn't—you need something more. So my older sister, she got her master's [degree]. For me, I was a history major, and I knew I didn't want to be a [medical] doctor. And I figured law school—I could do law school. And they really encouraged me to do that. I mean right after college, I didn't go right away. I took a year off. And that year they really encouraged me to start applying and go right away. As soon as you can! So that's why I did it.

For second-generation-immigrant respondents like Kevin, parental influence was instrumental in leading them to law school. Some considered law to be a direct path to upward mobility.

Frequently the first in their families to attend college, first-generation college students understood the pangs of lower socioeconomic upbringing. Recall Elena Chaidez, who possesses a steadfast interest in sea life. In addition to pursuing law as a practical route to supplement her bachelor's degree in anthropology, Elena also stressed the presence of financial burdens:

> Well, I don't have my own family—I'm not married, and I don't have kids. But I eventually want to. And I grew up in a poor family. And so that's always been a driving force—to have something better for myself and for my kids. And also to support my mother, because she doesn't work. She's not married [and] doesn't have any sort of retirement. She needs someone to take care of her.

For immigrant students and those who grew up impoverished, money was a strong force leading them to consider law school. As seen from Elena's comments, she felt pressure to support her mother, who lacks a retirement plan. While the living standards of the United States ensured that these students were fed, had roofs over their heads, and were clothed, they nevertheless could not escape judgmental peers or the pressures of conforming to the norm.

Ernesto Chavez grew up poor and envied peers who had "nice things." His parents, a registered nurse and a price estimator for a sheet metal company, were smitten with the American dream and did all they could to encourage Ernesto's academics. They resided in the district with the better schools and enrolled Ernesto in extracurricular activities. Ernesto proudly told me that he is an Eagle Scout and also a skilled pianist. Ernesto recalled a friend he made when he was an impressionable five-year-old:

> And one of the first friends I made, his dad was an attorney. He always had nice things. When we went to his house, anything we wanted to do we could pretty much do. So . . . [I'm] like, "Wow, your dad's an attorney! Wow, this is the kind of life I want to live. I want to be an attorney!" But then also I recognize that from a young age—I was never hungry or anything like that—but my parents didn't have the means to really live a life like that.

As the first person in his family to attend college, Ernesto is under tremendous pressure to succeed. At the time of our conversation, he had just promised his adolescent sister that he would send her to Harvard if she excelled in her studies. Being a lawyer is more than a career interest for Ernesto; it is also a means for taking care of his family.

Nancy Liang was a first-year law student at the time of our meeting. As the first person in her family to attend and graduate from college, Nancy felt that she needed to continue with her schooling, no matter the subject. Her parents completed high school in Taiwan and come from impoverished circumstances. Nancy said, "My mom's family was incredibly, incredibly poor. Right after high school, she knew she had to work, and all the money had to go home. It was really difficult for her family." Hoping for better work opportunities, Nancy's parents migrated to the United States in their mid-twenties and settled in a major metropolitan area surrounded by coethnics. Both parents are involved in small family ventures—specifically, a language school and a development business. Even so, Nancy intends to financially assist her family through becoming an attorney:

> It's a means to an end for me. It's not my dream to be a lawyer, to be in law school. It's just . . . my family—my parents didn't go to college. And within my extended family, very few people have pursued any kind of graduate degree. So obviously there's prestige involved. And I like school! I like law school. I like studying the things I study. I like learning. . . . But, yeah, it's a means to an end. I want to be able to take care of my parents.

What is the "end" that Nancy spoke of? Financial security—namely, the ability to take care of her parents. If money were not an issue, Nancy would get a doctorate in psychology and become a professor. But as the oldest child from a working-class family, she feels the need to be accountable for not only her parents but also her siblings.

For students like Ernesto and Nancy, family plays an important role in their decision to attend law school. Their parents motivated them to aspire to graduate education, but these students are also cognizant of the financial needs at home. Beyond immigrant optimism, first-generation college students also evaluate practicality in achieving their goal to financially support their family members. A conjoined immigrant optimism and practicality fuels these students' desire to become attorneys. Perhaps, then, a better way to describe these students is to say that they possess a sense of *practical* optimism. Their parents are optimistic about their children's futures, thereby instilling in them a belief in the importance of education. In turn, the children internalize these wishes but do so in a practical manner that considers financial stability.

These practical considerations aside, some students chose to attend law school because of their own histories with the law. These could be in the form of a helpful attorney or experiences that led to desire to make the system better and more accessible to immigrants. Whatever the impetus, these students wished to achieve social justice.

Achieving Social Justice

Edmund Huang was in his final year of law school when we sat down to chat. Edmund's family emigrated from Taiwan to the United States when he was an infant, settling in a large immigrant-Chinese community on the West Coast. Much to his parents' dismay, Edmund, an only child, acted out as a teenager, skipping school and hanging out with the wrong friends. In his own words: "Hanging out with friends. Girls. Drinking, smoking, gambling. Any vice you or I could think of." Nonetheless, Edmund went on to attend and graduate from a prestigious undergraduate institution. He majored in history with the intent of becoming a lawyer. When I asked what prompted his interest in law, Edmund sat back in his chair, sighed, pointed up to the sky, and said, "The stars. As corny as it sounds, I didn't decide on it." He then leaned forward and shared his story.

When Edmund was seventeen years old, he got into a fight. Although not in a gang himself, Edmund had friends who were. He explained:

> Some of my friends were involved with gangs, which I wasn't. But I got into a fight. And after I got into a fight—I was seventeen, I didn't have any weapons—but they charged me with assault with a deadly weapon, because, they said, I'm Chinese, so I know karate. That was the first thing. The second thing, because my friends were gang members—even though I had no criminal record, I was never affiliated—but there's this thing called "gang enhancements," which doubles the sentence. So now they were charging me with assault with a deadly weapon, with gang enhancements, as an adult. At seventeen! I just felt like I got screwed over triply in that situation.

The harsh repercussions of Edmund's adolescent fight left him with a distinct sense of resentment against the criminal justice system. He served several months in custody and became determined to right for others the wrongs he felt were done to him:

> I just felt so, so wronged. There's no other way—there's no other way to describe it. Just wronged! Like, man, this just isn't fair! So I became convinced that I had to change it—to make sure another good kid caught in a bad situation wouldn't be [wronged as I was]. . . . They were trying to give me seven years, Diana! I was seventeen! For a fight! They chose to throw the book at me. So after serving three

months in juvenile hall and one month in county jail, you could say
I became both driven and bitter.

At the time of our conversation, Edmund envisioned himself becoming a
district attorney, intending to "make sure that another good kid caught in a
bad situation" would have justice.

The motivations for seeking justice varied from learning about inequalities to witnessing injustice in courts, to experiencing them personally in
some way as children. For these law students, then, law becomes a tool to
achieve some semblance of equality. And that alone motivates them to complete law school.

Many law students report altruistic leanings before commencing law
school. Robert Stover's (1988) study of University of Denver law students
speaks to this phenomenon. Stover found that 33 percent of the entering
class at University of Denver Law School intended to pursue public interest
work upon graduation. This percentage would then decrease significantly
over the next three years—to 16 percent—as professional leanings begin to
align with law firm ambitions, causing a drift away from public interest law.[7]
The repercussions of this drift are discussed in Chapter 6, but for now let us
focus on the sense of justice that directs many students to law school in the
first place.

Perhaps unsurprisingly, many Latino and Asian American law students
spoke of righting wrongs, altruism, and justice when recalling their motivations to attend law school. Take for example, Margaret Cha, a third-year,
Korean American law student. Margaret's parents emigrated from South
Korea to the United States because her father worked for the U.S. military.
Once on these shores, her parents toiled in factories for many years before
saving enough money to own a dry cleaning business. Although she grew up
in a seemingly successful middle-class American family, Margaret cannot
shake memories of her parents being unable to communicate with English
speakers. Margaret explained her route to law school:

Everyone thinks I was pressured into it because I'm Asian—[they]
assume my parents said that] I have to be a doctor or a lawyer. That's
really not the case! When I was growing up, . . . my dad spoke English
sufficiently. But he couldn't read or write that well. . . . You know, he
could write, but you could tell that someone who wasn't schooled
here wrote it. My mom still has real problems communicating—
reading, writing. For her, it's just really difficult. So I, as the oldest kid, who was most sufficient in English, I was always the one
who was doing all the paperwork and communicating with people
and just all the official stuff. And I think growing up, I just could
feel their frustration. And I could feel how difficult it was for them

to operate day to day when they couldn't really understand the full process or communicate effectively. And the fact that they couldn't communicate effectively—there was a certain way they were perceived. They were perceived as being deficient or subservient or not functioning—incapable of being in society. Because I was constantly trying to make up for that with my parents, I think that's what really inspired me to go into the field [of law]. To help people who can't fully function.

For Margaret, her parents' difficulties were the impetus for her to pursue law, to provide assistance to those who need it. Even though her parents seem to be doing quite well now as business owners, Margaret wants to help others in similar situations.

Luis Pérez, a second-year law student, recalled why he decided to pursue law. Luis is a second-generation immigrant; his parents are from Mexico and El Salvador, and he claims a Latino identity. Growing up, Luis witnessed firsthand how members of the Latino community were mistreated or scammed:

Growing up, there were really no Spanish-speaking or affordable attorneys, and so I saw how that disadvantaged my family—my extended family. And so that kind of influenced me to wanting to be that resource to communities like this. . . . So my dad wanted to help one of my uncles also immigrate—he was trying to do it the legal way. And so to file whatever visa, papers you need to file, it's, like, really complicated. And attorneys are, like, super expensive! And they speak [only] English. . . . Because my parents didn't know anything about attorneys, my dad ended up giving an "immigration expert" $3,500 to do the paperwork. And so the paperwork was given, the money was given, and a week later, when my dad contacts him, the guy leaves the office! He just leaves, never to be found! I think it is important to have attorneys that speak Spanish. And this is what I saw, what I liked in legal aid. I worked in legal aid for two and a half years, [and I] saw what the Spanish-speaking person in an attorney position can do for communities . . . , being that resource for these communities. I liked it a lot. So, big story, I guess, that's why I came to law school.

For Luis, the combination of witnessing familial hardships and the opportunity to work in legal aid solidified his desire to become an attorney. This type of justice, he explained, can be achieved, especially as a Spanish-speaking attorney. Indeed, for a number of Latino students, the role of a specific attorney made a profound impact. Fortunately, not all the stories were as depressing as that of Luis's father getting swindled out of $3,500.

Marco Saldaña, a Mexican American law student, has a positive per-spective on attorneys, and this is what inspired him to pursue law. Marco explained, "The law has always been a presence in my life and that of my family's. We immigrated to this country, and the only reason we were able to stay here legally was with the help of a lawyer, and that kind of left a deep impression on me." Similar to Marco, Ahn Tran, a Chinese-Vietnamese American student, spoke about the importance of law in his life: "My parents were placed in concentration camps and then came to the U.S. So the law represented a kind of justification . . . and [the law] would provide benefits for the masses. So . . . the law was potentially very powerful, at least for changing society." Binh Nguyen, a second-year Vietnamese American stu-dent, recalled:

> When I was young, a few years old, I lost my father. He owned a fam-ily jewelry store, and it was robbed, and he was shot. It was a criminal case, so the DA [district attorney] had to come in, and they caught the guys, prosecuted them. And at the time, my mom knew very little English, so it was kind of hard, my mom being on her own. And the DA just kind of came in, took care of it, reassured us everything was going to be all right, prosecuted the guys, got them a maximum sentence. And it was hard, but it definitely made an impression on me of what the law can do.

For Marco, Ahn, and Binh, lawyers and the law affected them personally, and they admired a profession that had benefited them. The law students represented in this book come from varied backgrounds, yet a recurring theme was that many saw their own and their family's success stories re-flected in the laws that helped them get to and stay in the United States. The power of the law and the power of one who is knowledgeable about the law made a lasting impression on these students.

Most Latino and Asian American law students included justice in their rationale for pursuing law. What was surprising, however, was how this var-ied across Latino students at Private Metropolitan versus Western Elite. Only 20 percent of the Private Metropolitan Latino respondents spoke of justice reasons leading them to law school, whereas 50 percent of their Western Elite peers did so. One possible explanation for this discrepancy is the immigrant background of the students. While half the Latino Private Metropolitan re-spondents are second-generation immigrants, over 80 percent of the Latino Western Elite respondents are second generation. Fewer second-generation immigrants may also mean fewer immigration-inspired motivations.

The other explanation is that of socioeconomic background. Latino law students from Private Metropolitan typically come from solid middle-class backgrounds, whereas Western Elite students had concentrations at the higher and lower ends of the socioeconomic scale. It is more likely for students from lower- or working-class families to speak about the power of the law and how it affected their families. It is also more likely for Latino students from highly educated families to replicate their parents' educational achievements and expectations.

The aforementioned interests, like most human interests, are neither stagnant nor mutually exclusive. For example, students such as Felicia Álvarez decided to pursue law thanks to a spate of interrelated events and realizations:

> I never wanted to go to law school. Then I decided to do an outreach program [during my master's program] that targeted minority students, [a] law fellows [program]. Just to see what's up. . . . I realized I wanted to go to law school because I was in a peer group that seemed like they were very moderate and status-quo-like and very ill-equipped to deal with the societal problems that face a diverse demographic and diverse changing demographic. So I was frustrated. And I decided that if I wanted to be in charge and be the boss, I needed to go to law school because that was something they wouldn't have. And if I were choosing to invest in law school, I wanted to go to [one of the] best law schools that I could go to. So, essentially, graduating with a master's [degree] wasn't sufficient as a Chicana. I felt like if I graduated [with only a master's degree], I would be giving someone copies or giving them coffee. And I didn't want that!

Felicia, a proud Chicana with strong roots in the American Southwest, had a just-because reason given the law fellows program in which she participated. But she was further influenced by the lack of racial awareness among her peers in her master's program, which, in turn, activated a desire for justice as a reason for pursuing law. She also spoke about her own racialized identity and the types of job opportunities available to her. Because all these factors aligned for Felicia, she does not consider one or the other to be her main motivator. Other respondents listed more than one factor encouraging them to pursue law, but the majority provided one core motivation.

This purpose of this chapter is twofold: to introduce a sampling of the law students featured in this book and to delve into the reasons they provided for selecting law. The reasons are practical and accidental, with the immigrant narrative anchoring their explanations. We saw that some students perceived law to be the most practical and versatile degree; others made concerted career shifts to become attorneys. Still other respondents majored in traditionally law-feeding fields and naturally applied to law schools. The second-generation-immigrant respondents, however, also cited the role of immigrant optimism—their own and that of their parents—in leading them down the law path. And finally, prevalent among the law students of color, justice was cited as a driving factor: many students witnessed the potential of law and wanted to harness it for social justice. Motivation for attending law school does not equal a definitive career trajectory, however. Many shift their ideals while in law school, and some even realize that their original altruistic reasons to pursue law will not financially support them. What remains, though, are the stories told by students. The stories of how their lives were transformed through the law or through learning about the law's impact. These stories of justice and transformation were far more common among Latino and Asian American law students, who exist in a liminal space in law school and society at large. The next chapter historicizes this space and illuminates presumed citizenship (or lack thereof) as a part of racialization.

2

"THE SKIN OF A FOREIGNER"

*Asian Americans and Latinos
in Liminality*

As a Chinese American, I feel some sense of being somewhat in between cultures. I'm not exactly Chinese because I don't speak Chinese. I'm much more Americanized, as you can see. I'm not exactly
American because I have the skin of a foreigner, even though I was
born and raised here. I'm a citizen.

Michael Cheng, quoted here, is a second-generation Chinese American
law student in his second year of law school at Private Metropolitan.
He and I met on a rainy day at a café in a busy neighborhood. Michael
was about five minutes late to our appointment and arrived wearing a hat,
jersey, and shorts celebrating a professional football team. He shook my
hand, sat down, and immediately started talking about the team represented
on his outfit. Michael's monologue about sports and his attire represented
the prototypical sports-obsessed American. His comment about race and
citizenship, above, however, underscores his sense of belonging—or rather,
lack thereof. Michael possesses the "skin of a foreigner," which directly ties
to how Asian Americans and Latinos routinely experience race-based prejudice premised on their perceived foreignness. Today, most Americans are
familiar with overt racism directed at black Americans but are relatively
ignorant about the way that laws, culture, and semiotics marginalize those
between black and white, such as Asian Americans and Latinos, who exist
in a space of liminality.

This chapter focuses on the historical racialization of Asian Americans and Latinos and how that has become reified through laws, cultural

practices, and social interactions. These two groups have undergone similar processes of sociohistorical racialization. The shared experiences of prejudice and discrimination among Asian Americans and Latinos underscore their liminal position within a society that remains fixated on a black-white racial dichotomy. Yet it is precisely this in-between position that also reaffirms their status as racial outsiders, similar to black Americans but with added foreignization through legal, cultural, and social nonrecognition.

This chapter contextualizes the sociohistory of racialization for the two groups and their impression of their unique location within U.S. racialized history. It begins with a brief introduction of the history and significance of Asian Americans' and Latinos' "outsider racialization" (Ancheta 1998, 64) and then describes the ways that these two groups experienced panethnic exclusion. Their unique location between black and white muddied their treatment by the law, by American culture, and within social interactions. Their experiences in the racial middle—in liminality—warrant special attention to further understand the complexities of racial othering. Then, to illustrate how historical processes of exclusion still affect members of these two panethnic groups today, I draw attention to three types of citizenship as ways of belonging in the United States: legal, cultural, and social. This chapter concludes with a discussion of how critical race theory permits a more holistic understanding of race relations in general and underscores the importance of master and minor racialized narratives.

Outsider Racialization

Recall Michael, quoted at the beginning of the chapter. Although an American in every way, including wearing clothing that celebrates an American football team, Michael describes himself as having the "skin of a foreigner." This comment is laden with meaning. It connotes historical discrimination directed at Asian ethnics. It conjures descriptions such as "inassimilable," "Celestials," and "Orientals." It further reminds us that while black and white Americans can assert an American identity with little or no questioning, Asian ethnics cannot. Latinos face a similar lack of acceptance and are similarly regarded in the mainstream imagery as not authentic Americans. For Latinos, immigration reform rouses suspicions about their status in the United States (documented versus undocumented) and elicits assumptions about their language abilities. Asian Americans and Latinos face unending challenges to their citizenship and belonging. Incessant reminders abound of their ascribed foreignness, otherwise known as "outsider racialization."

Angelo Ancheta defines "outsider racialization" to frame Asian Americans and Latinos as foreign-born "outsiders." This process works in two ways: (1) by being racially categorized as foreigners via racialization that operates through "psychological cognition and learning, social and political discourse, and institutional structures" (Ancheta 1998, 64), and (2) through race-neutral categories, such as immigrant or foreigner. The first way assigns racial categories, while the second evokes racelessness and color blindness and uses code words to denote otherness. Of particular importance for this comparative sociohistory, Asian Americans and Latinos experience outsider racialization, in part, because discourse on immigrants tends to focus on these two panethnic groups.

Being "raced" as an immigrant also translates into perceptions of foreignness. As "foreigners," Asian Americans and Latinos are perceived to not be real Americans in the same ways as their white peers and, to some extent, their black peers as well.[1] With regard to the Chinese in particular, Bill Ong Hing writes, "they were believed to be immutable, tenaciously clinging to old customs, and recalcitrantly opposing progress and moral improvement. Nonwhite and non-Christian at a time when either trait alone was a serious handicap, the Chinese looked different, dressed differently, ate differently, and followed customs wholly unfamiliar to Americans" (1997, 16). The racialization of citizenship equates all Asian Americans, regardless of their actual status, with foreigners and with immigrants.

Outsider racialization contributed to the devastating internment of over 120,000 Japanese Americans living on the West Coast during World War II—two-thirds of the internees were U.S. citizens (and the majority of them were children). Latinos also endured similar racialization based on assumptions about citizenship and belonging. For example, in many historical U.S. legal cases, Mexican Americans were designated as "other" despite their acquired citizenship through U.S. expansion. Seen as foreigners, both panethnic groups continue to contend with overt and covert forms of discrimination and hostility.

Questioning whether antiforeigner sentiments are branches of racism, René Galindo and Jami Vigil (2006) argue that nativism is a form of acceptable discrimination because it conjures notions of patriotism. Railing against foreigners who speak different languages (though accepting those who arrive from Western European countries), nativists oppose bilingual education, advocate securing our borders with extreme measures, and instill fear that American culture will be lost with the entrance and integration of immigrants from Latin America. But because nativism is almost always directed at those who are racialized as foreigners, it operates as coded racism. With regard to the fear of English erosion, Galindo and Vigil write:

> While society frowns on discrimination based on race, discrimination based on nationalism and fueled by nativism is not always recognized as discrimination. The symbolic-indexical function of a language to represent a national or ethnic group is not always recognized and that makes discrimination on linguistic grounds publicly

acceptable, whereas discrimination on ethnic or racial grounds would not be. (2006, 167)

Juan Perea adds that it is naïve to think of language as merely a utilitarian means for communication. He argues, "Language is the carrier and vessel of culture, which in turn shapes language and perception. Language constitutes a primary symbol of cultural identification. For Mexican Americans and other Latinos, the Spanish language is an emblem of their culture" (Perea 2011, 599). Discrimination based on linguistic differences is yet another form of racism.

Linguistic discrimination occurs only for certain ethnic and panethnic groups—namely, Asian Americans and Latinos and other marginalized and nonwhite immigrant groups. One rarely hears a hullabaloo about immigrants who speak "exotic" tongues such as French, Italian, or German. Despite how they might have been characterized historically on arrival to the United States, those who speak these languages are today understood as reflecting white Americans' phenotype and ancestry.

Exploring how race works in the everyday lives of Asian Americans and Latinos—as members of the racial middle—Eileen O'Brien reminds us that it is important to not dismiss the nuanced ways that these two groups experience racism and discrimination. Because "conceptualizations of what discrimination is have often been shaped by the cultural understandings of what African Americans have experienced in the past . . . there are types of discrimination unique to the racial middle that such a popular conception of discrimination might miss" (O'Brien 2008, 207). And even while those in the racial middle may fall under the spell of discrimination on the basis of black American history and assert that they have not experienced racism, they continue to create new languages that make sense of their unique "phenotypism." Barred from legal, cultural, and social citizenship, Asian Americans and Latinos historically experienced race-based discrimination.

Contours of Legal Citizenship

Legal citizenship safeguards belonging (with more or less tangible results). The purpose of this section is to detail how obtaining legal citizenship was and continues to be a racialized endeavor. Most Americans are familiar with the struggles of black Americans and their quest for civil rights. While the black civil rights movement represents a watershed in U.S. history, civic and popular discourse surrounding race relations couched within the black-white framework inadvertently obscures the story of unequal treatment of other racialized groups. Asian Americans and Latinos underwent a long history seeking equal treatment as legal citizens of the United States. Asian Americans, in particular, sought to be defined as white persons. Ostensibly,

Asian ethnics seem to have thought of themselves as white. But their reasons for asserting whiteness are far more nuanced than mere feelings of racial superiority in relation to black Americans—indeed, members of the panethnic Asian group knew well their social position between black and white.

In terms of legal citizenship benefits, one might wonder why Asian ethnics sought naturalization as white persons rather than black, especially given that they encountered discrimination similar to that experienced by the latter. Ian Haney López explains, "The 1870 act [Naturalization Act] referred to persons of 'African nativity, or African descent,' rather than to 'black persons.' By way of comparison, the naturalization statute referred to 'white persons,' rather than to 'persons of European ancestry'" (Haney López 1997, 37). As interpreted, then, there were fewer restrictions to identifying oneself as white versus black, leading Asian Americans to claim whiteness in their quest for legal citizenship.[2] Table 2.1 is a sampling of nine cases in which various Asian ethnics sought citizenship as white persons because of ambiguous language in the 1870 Naturalization Act.

TABLE 2.1: SELECT RACIAL PREREQUISITE CASES

Case	Holding	Rationales
In re Ah Yup, 1 F. Cas. 223 (C.C.D. Cal. 1878)	Chinese are not white.	Scientific evidence; common knowledge; congressional intent
In re Saito, 62 F. 126 (C.C.D. Mass., 1894)	Japanese are not white.	Congressional intent; common knowledge; scientific evidence; legal precedent
In re Yamashita, 70 Pac. 482 (1902)	Japanese are not white.	Legal precedent
Petition of Easurk Emsen Charr, 273 F. 207 (W.D. Mo. 1921)	Koreans are not white.	Common knowledge; legal precedent
Ozawa v. United States, 260 U.S. 178 (1922)	Japanese are not white.	Legal precedent; congressional intent; common knowledge; scientific evidence
United States v. Thind, 261 U.S. 204 (1923)	Asian Indians are not white.	Common knowledge; congressional intent
United States v. Javier, 22 F.2d 879 (D.C. Cir 1927)	Filipinos are not white.	Legal precedent
De La Ysla v. United States, 77 F.2d 988 (9th Cir. 1935)	Filipinos are not white.	Legal precedent
Kharaiti Ram Samras v. United States, 125 F.2d 879 (9th Cir. 1942)	Asian Indians are not white.	Legal precedent

During this time, when the law clearly stated that individuals of white (i.e., European) or African ancestry were permitted to become U.S. citizens, Asians were seen as neither. Stuck between racial polarities, Asian Americans were designated as inassimilable and thus could not become real Americans.[3] They remained in this legal limbo until the 1940 Nationality Act, which amended and clarified previous naturalization laws that clarified the status of immigrants and their children born in the United States and those groups eligible for citizenship. The 1940 Nationality Act permitted some immigrants to naturalize, but particular Asian ethnics, such as the Chinese, were not granted eligibility until the Magnuson Act of 1943, which repealed the Chinese Exclusion Act of 1882.[4]

In 1943, Congress extended citizenship eligibility to immigrants from China and in 1946 to those from India. Finally, in 1952, the United States abolished the last of its racist citizenship laws that excluded Asian ethnics from legal citizenship. Hiroshi Motomura explains, "Section 311 of the Immigration and Nationality Act now provides: 'The right of a person to become a naturalized citizen of the United States shall not be denied or abridged because of race or sex or because such person is married" (2006, 75). Asian Americans' road to legal citizenship was long and hard fought—one that lasted nearly an entire century. But unlike the quest for black American freedom and citizenship, which was supported by liberal white Americans, there were few advocates on behalf of these Celestials.[5] In part, this was due to the invisibility of Asian Americans within a nation that perceived race relations to be narrowly defined as black versus white.

Lawsuits brought by Chinese, Japanese, Asian Indian, and Filipino ethnics seeking citizenship were dismissed on the same grounds: the plaintiffs had darker skin, possessed a phenotype that deviated from Europeans', and were "inassimilable" peoples. As a result, Asian ethnics' shared history of citizenship exclusion not only contributed to the formation of a panethnic Asian American umbrella but also racialized them. Legal citizenship does not always equate to citizenship parity, however. The next section describes how Mexican Americans, as legal citizens, sought belonging through cultural citizenship.

White in Name Only: Latinos and Cultural Citizenship

While Asian ethnics yearned to be white legally, their Latino counterparts, especially Mexicans, were considered white when the United States extended its territory into Mexico after the signing of the Treaty of Guadalupe Hidalgo in 1848. The Mexican experience in the United States demonstrates how racialization loses ethnic significance among the mainstream populace. The panethnic category Latino includes various South and Latin American ethnic backgrounds. Given Mexican Americans' sociopolitical history and that

Mexicans are the largest Latino ethnic group in this country, I use Mexican Americans' history as proxy to understand processes of Latino racialization and immigrant integration.[6]

Whereas Asian ethnics fought for the privileges of legal citizenship, colonized Mexicans were granted legal rights. As Suzanne Oboler reminds us, the Treaty of Guadalupe Hidalgo, signed at the end of the Mexican-American War, "ensured Mexicans, unlike African Americans, the full privilege of U.S. citizenship . . . making them the first non-Anglo-Saxons to have the rights and privileges previously reserved only to white, European men" (1995, 32). The treaty extended U.S. citizenship to Mexican citizens residing in Arizona, California, Texas, New Mexico, Nevada, Utah, and parts of Wyoming and Colorado before any other nonwhite racialized group in the United States, including black Americans. Despite the indigenous mixing of Mexicans, most of those who became U.S. citizens were designated as racially white by U.S. law.

Although the majority of Mexican Americans who resided in newly acquired U.S. territory were thus deemed citizens of the United States, they were not necessarily treated as such. Alejandra Castañeda refers to the "culture of citizenship" that continues to be denied to Mexican Americans: "'Culture of citizenship' refers to the social practices and understandings of membership in a given community—at either the national or local level—in the arenas in which citizenship is negotiated and constituted. In this sense, belonging, law, and politics are inextricably related to one another" (2006, 143). Although considered white by law, Mexican Americans encountered historical discrimination similar to that encountered by their Asian American counterparts—and similarly turned to the courts to seek fairness and equality.

As example, *Hernandez v. Texas* (1954) demonstrates the liminal space occupied by Mexican Americans and by extension Latinos. Pedro Hernandez was a farmworker convicted for the murder of a fellow Mexican American man. His team of attorneys argued that only a jury with a mix of whites and nonwhites could be impartial. Although legally white, Mexican Americans were treated as a secondary class in Jackson County, Texas, where the case was tried (see Olivas 2006).

Ian Haney López describes the treatment of Mexicans in the county at that time:

First, residents of Jackson County, Texas, routinely distinguished between "white" and "Mexican" persons. Second, business and community groups largely excluded Mexican Americans from participation. Third, until just a few years earlier, children of Mexican descent were required to attend a segregated school for the first four grades, and most children of Mexican descent left school by the fifth or sixth grade. Fourth, at least one restaurant in the county seat prominently displayed a sign announcing "No Mexicans Served." Fifth, on the Jackson County courthouse grounds at the time of the underlying trial, stood two men's toilets, one unmarked, and the other marked "Colored Men" and "Hombres Aquí" ["Men Here"]. Finally, with respect to jury selection itself, a stipulation recited that "for the last twenty-five years there is no record of any person with a Mexican or Latin American name having served on a jury commission, grand jury or petit jury in Jackson County," a county 15 percent Mexican American. (Haney López 2011b, 374)

Supreme Court Chief Justice Earl Warren wrote in a unanimous ruling that the Fourteenth Amendment protects all individuals from discrimination and does not narrowly treat only "white" and "black" racial groups; he concluded that Hernandez should be retried with a different jury.

As illustrated above, citizenship, whether legal or cultural, can be difficult to acquire for Asian Americans and Latinos. They do not neatly fit into the historical black-white dichotomy and have struggled, both personally and through legal means, to make sense of their in-between positions. Even when afforded legal citizenship (and considered legally white), they still faced discrimination as phenotypic "others," as seen in *Hernandez*. Asian Americans and Latinos who experience discrimination remain in an ill-defined racial gray zone formed by resilient assumptions about language proficiency, presumed nationality, and phenotype. The next section details the lack of social citizenship through the exclusion of Asian Americans and Latinos in education.

Social Citizenship and Educational Exclusion

The simultaneous inclusion and exclusion of Asian Americans and Latinos is a familiar story, especially as it pertains to histories of nonwhite Americans. To examine nonwhite inequality and exclusion within American society, let us turn to the basic social right of education. Asian Americans and Latinos traveled a long road to educational equality. Yet as with legal and cultural citizenship, dominant discourse surrounding school segregation—a form of social citizenship—ignores how those in the racial middle understood their second-class citizenship (or as one might argue, second-class *nonwhite* citizenship).

We begin with *Tape v. Hurley* (1885), decided eleven years before *Plessy v. Ferguson* (1896).[7] Mamie Tape, an eight-year-old child born in the United States of Chinese parents, was denied admission to Spring Valley Elementary School in San Francisco, California, because she was not racially white. Her lawyers argued that the San Francisco Board of Education violated the

California Political Code by denying Mamie a place at Spring Valley Elementary School because of her Chinese ancestry. At the time, the U.S. Constitution and the California Political Code required schools to be "open for the admission of all children between the age of six and twenty-one years of age" (California Political Code, §1667). Judge James McGuire ruled in favor of the Tapes, granting Mamie admission to Spring Valley. The victory, however, was short-lived. Following the ruling, the San Francisco school board began planning a separate school system for "Mongolian" children and, in the wake of *Plessy v. Ferguson*, established a separate Oriental School solely for students of Chinese, Japanese, and Korean descent.[8]

Plessy established segregation as permissible and legal, so long as an "equivalent" alternative existed for nonwhite individuals. *Plessy* also affirmed that buses, hotels, restaurants, and public schools could be legally segregated for white and black Americans. Under this binary racial climate of separate but equal, Martha Lum, a nine-year-old Chinese American born in the United States, could not attend a public school meant for white students in Bolivar County, Mississippi, because of her ethnicity. In *Lum v. Rice* (1927), Martha's father, Gong Lum, argued that, because there were no separate schools in the county for children of Chinese descent and because Martha was of school age and was mandated by law to attend school, the denial of her admission to a public school meant for white students resulted in a violation of her civil rights under the Fourteenth Amendment. The case made its way to the U.S. Supreme Court after the Mississippi Supreme Court ruled against Martha. Writing for the majority, U.S. Supreme Court Chief Justice William Howard Taft noted that Martha could normally attend segregated schools for children of color, but no such schools existed in Bolivar County, where the Lum family resided. Taft wrote:

> The case then reduces itself to the question whether a state can be said to afford to a child of Chinese ancestry, born in this country and a citizen of the United States, the equal protection of the laws by giving her the opportunity for a common school education in a school which receives only colored children of the brown, yellow, or black races. The right and power of the state to regulate the method of providing for the education of its youth at public expense is clear. (Gong Lum v. Rice, 275 U.S. 78 [1927])

The U.S. Supreme Court thus affirmed the Mississippi Supreme Court's ruling that Martha Lum could not attend the school in Bolivar County meant for white children. Instead, she had to travel out of district to attend a school designated for colored children.

The above two cases exemplify the discrimination endured by Chinese Americans because they were deemed nonwhite and inassimilable—lacking social citizenship. Mamie and Martha were both born in the United States and thus were citizens jus soli, or by birth. Both also endured treatment that simultaneously mirrored black Americans' experience with school segregation. Such stories are rarely, however, considered when discussions arise regarding the history of educational segregation in this country.[9]

In a similar case, *Mendez et al. v. Westminster et al.* (1946), ten years before *Brown v. Board of Education*, five Mexican American fathers challenged school segregation in several cities in Orange County, California. The fathers argued that forcing their children to attend schools designated specifically for students of Mexican heritage violated their children's equal rights under the Fourteenth Amendment. As discussed earlier, Mexicans were legally white per the 1848 Treaty of Guadalupe Hidalgo. In *Mendez*, a federal court held that it was unconstitutional to relegate children of Mexican descent to separate schools. Judge Paul McCormick of the Ninth Circuit summarized the plaintiff's case:

> The [trial] court found that the segregation as alleged in the petition has been for several years past and is practiced under regulations, customs and usages adopted more or less as a common plan and enforced by respondent-appellants throughout the mentioned school districts; that petitioners are citizens of the United States of Mexican ancestry of good moral habits, free from infectious disease or any other disability, and are fully qualified to attend and use the public school facilities; that respondents occupy official positions as alleged in the petition. (Quoted in Westminster School District v. Mendez, 161 F.2d 774 [9th Cir. 1947])

The Ninth Circuit Court of Appeals held that as both citizens and persons deemed legally white, the children were permitted to attend free public schools. The court further concluded the children were "free from infectious diseases or any other disability"—a backhanded endorsement that belied the belief of white racial (i.e., hygienic) superiority and the inferiority of other racial groups. The then existing legal distinction between the racially white Mexicans and their nonwhite (and nonblack) Asian counterparts was made abundantly clear later in the summary with reference to the availability of public schools for all children:

> There are no exceptions based upon the ancestry of the child other than those contained in Secs. 8003, 8004, Calif.Ed.C., which [excludes from integrated schools American] Indians under certain conditions and children of Chinese, Japanese or Mongolian parentage. As to these, there are laws requiring them in certain cases to attend separate schools. (776)

Although *Mendez* resulted in a positive legal outcome and dealt a blow against school segregation, the fact remains that the Orange County School District historically segregated students on the basis of deviation in phenotype, race, and culture.

This section demonstrates how social citizenship dictated who could experience educational rights. Mexicans, integrated through geopolitics, were considered legally white and legal citizens, yet treated as "others" with regard to public education. Similarly, Asian ethnics, especially the second generation, were U.S. citizens yet were not treated as citizens socially, as exemplified by segregated schooling. As these cases show, Asian Americans and Latinos experienced a nonwhite racial framing but were also relegated to a liminal space between black and white, which contributed to their racial ambiguity among scholars and the American public. Unlike a clearly demarcated black-white binary, these individuals at times existed on the periphery but mostly in the middle, where questions abounded as to their legal, cultural, and social belonging. Sociopolitics influenced Asian American and Latino history in the United States. And this history remains significant today as Asian Americans and Latinos continue to contend with race-based discrimination complicated by their more recent immigrant roots. Examined through critical race theory, this history underscores how all forms of racialized discrimination should be considered holistically.

The Legacy of Racialization

Racialization refers to categorizing ethnic groups as panethnics, putting them under racial umbrellas. An intricate part of American history is dividing, merging, including, and excluding particular groups of people based on race. Critical race theory emerged in the 1980s to examine the intersection of power, law, and inequalities in relation to race. Its sociohistorical frame of analysis centers on the omnipresence of racism as a phenomenon embedded in American culture and institutions and manifested in myriad ways via individual interactions. Critical race theorists assert that race is dynamic and processual, considering phenotypic differences, histories, identities, and experiences of *all* communities of color. This line of reasoning challenges dominant discourses that relegate race to static variables and thus neglect how it is actually experienced in the lives of nonwhite individuals (Delgado and Stefancic 2001; Peller 1995).

While changes in social and public policy have created opportunities for Asian Americans and Latinos to be embraced by mainstream white America, to what extent are they actually included in the mainstream? That is, while Asian Americans and Latinos take the reins as CEOs of major companies or become partners at major law firms, do they feel white? Are they fully accepted into the elite country club, or are they merely caddies? If the latter, what forces keep them there? Critical race theory offers a way to explore such questions that challenge, rather than reinforce, existing racial categories. Operating within a critical race framework, for example, Devon W. Carbado and Mitu Gulati examine whether nonwhite individuals can achieve success without being charged with acting white (2013). The message received by all nonwhite groups, they find, remains the same: nonwhites are social and institutional "others."

This chapter provides the foundation necessary to understand the racialization of Asian Americans and Latinos. Sociohistorical events racialized Asian Americans and Latinos as simultaneously undesirable and unwelcome minorities. Stuck between a black-white racial binary, Asian Americans and Latinos negotiated their racial, ethnic, and national identities alongside legal, cultural, and social citizenship. To borrow from Michael's comment at the beginning of this chapter, Asian Americans and Latinos possess the "skin of a foreigner." The next chapter examines how phenotypic difference becomes salient in law school. Although most are legal citizens, Asian American and Latino law students cannot escape continued racialization that makes them cultural and social outsiders. Further, their white peers imagine them in noninclusive ways that reinforce their otherness in this elite profession.

3

DIVERSITY IS GOOD IN A GLOBALIZED WORLD, AND IT'S NEAT

White Students, Diverse Peers,
and Privilege

In May 2015, the *Washington Post* ran a guest article titled "Law Is the Least Diverse Profession in the Nation, and Lawyers Aren't Doing Enough to Change That." Written by the law professor Deborah Rhode and supported with reams of data, the article presents a disjuncture between support for diverse job candidates and actual practice in the profession. Rhode's surveyed attorneys are concerned that 88 percent of attorneys are white but nonetheless cite challenges to overcoming this underrepresentation of nonwhite lawyers. A host of cultural, social, and political obstacles prevent improvement, but Rhode concludes the article with sound suggestions:

> Most important, lawyers need to assume personal responsibility for professional changes. They can support workplace initiatives and expanded efforts to increase the pool of qualified minorities through scholarships and mentoring. To make all these reforms possible, they must not be seen as "women" or "minority" issues, but as organizational priorities in which everyone has a stake. The challenge is to create that sense of unity and to translate rhetorical commitments into daily practices. (2015)

Rhode's call for more concrete action is supported by scholarship examining the resilience of contemporary racism. In *Racism without Racists*, Eduardo Bonilla-Silva (2014) reminds readers that racial discrimination is now "colorblind." Now that a mixed-race president has served two terms, white Americans often suggest that racism is a thing of the past. Yet racism manifests in

institutional and personal ways, and lip service to diversity without committed actions and improvement serves as but one example.

As discussed in Chapter 1, the law is a prestigious profession that historically barred any who came from nonelite backgrounds. The culture of law
was framed through the lens of white Anglo-Saxon Protestant mores and
continues to be bound to that history. While numerous traditions, cultures,
and histories built (and continue to sustain) the United States, the white
racial frame feeds our collective imaginary. Our institutions, policies, and
education prioritize a white standard while dismissing other practices and
principles. A white framework is thus conventional, simply accepted as the
unmarked norm, the standard.

But as our nation becomes more racially diverse, it is impossible not
to question these norms, especially within institutions of education. "Law
school is white" was a comment I often heard from both nonwhite and white
law students. But as I discuss in this chapter (and the next), most students
did not enter law school thinking about, let alone prioritizing, race. They
thought about becoming attorneys and the three years of schooling required
to achieve that professional dream. They did not think about sitting next to
a copanethnic in the classroom or befriending only individuals of their respective racial or ethnic backgrounds. But on campus, attending classes and
interacting with peers, these law students gained an increasingly heightened
racial awareness. Notably, both white and nonwhite students reported feeling this way, yet their specific reactions to the space of law school, the place
of race, and their own panethnic affiliation differed.

The overall numbers of nonwhite law students have dramatically increased, without regard to the specific racialized group. Ostensibly, this increase in racial diversity suggests that the legal profession has become more
tolerant of lawyers of color. To corroborate this assumption, law students
point to Sonia Sotomayor as Supreme Court justice or Barack Obama as
president—both of whom trained as attorneys and have gone on to become
highly successful and visible to the public. And among law students it is
widely understood that there are numerous other successful lawyers of color
who are not household names. But how students process and make sense of
this fact and its continued disjuncture with the white face of law varies.

This chapter focuses on white students' perspectives on race and diversity in law school. I argue that white students practice what I call *paternalistic exoticism* to talk about changing legal institutions, their nonwhite
peers, and professors. Their positive take on this exoticism is genuine and
honest but also a part of the larger white racial framing. White students
express outward support for diversity. They often use progressive tropes of
"diversity is good in a globalized world," "diversity is neat," and "law school
could use more diversity" to demonstrate their recognition and problema-
tization of the pervasive whiteness of law school. As we see in the following

pages, however, such comments and ways of thinking about race and its place are complex. And like the lawyers cited in Rhode's *Washington Post* article, these white students' enthusiasm for diversity rarely extends beyond politically correct lip service.

Go, Team Diversity!

White law students regularly affirm that diversity is important. By far the most common means of doing this is to refer to globalization and the necessity for intercultural cooperation and communication in our increasingly connected world. Businesses have become more international, often with clientele spread across the globe. Some white students, like Ben Brightmore, feel that the legal profession has begun to reflect this change. A third-year law student, Ben is from a cosmopolitan area on the West Coast, but he grew up in a homogeneously white suburb. When asked whether being a white male has affected his experiences in law school, Ben immediately responded, "At least I know I didn't get in here because I'm black or Hispanic or because I am of a culture that they want." He paused, looked sheepishly down at his hands and attempted to answer my question again: "It's been nice to observe and get to know people of other cultures. One of my best friends here [in law school] is Punjabi, and learning about his culture is absolutely amazing. It's really neat! Another one of my really good friends here is Filipino, and learning about Philippine culture is really neat."

Ben's immediate comment about his own ostensibly nonracialized admission to law school, coupled with his characterization of ethnic and cultural difference as "neat," reveals much about how he perceives the place of race in law school. On the one hand, it muddies the waters around admission, but on the other hand, it enriches the environment and education available for white students. Law school, in short, becomes a place to befriend nonwhite friends and gain valuable intercultural knowledge and skills. Ben further explained the significance of diversity:

> We have to know where other people come from and the difficulties that other people face, and I, especially being white, if I went to a 100 percent white law school, I understand where other people come from when you're kind of sitting there going through the same experience yourself [as a fellow white person]. I'm sitting there [in class at Private Metropolitan], and two of my very good friends—one of them is Indian, and the other is Filipino, so I guess understanding who they are and where they come from helps me understand how to approach my legal career with people who are that type of race [Asian American]. So for my Indian friend, I know that family is a really big deal for him. I understand the dynamics of Indian culture

now that I have been able to talk at length with him about his culture and their core values.

Interacting with nonwhite law students has helped Ben realize that diversity could be good for business. With an eye to becoming an estate lawyer, Ben will likely come into contact with nonwhite clients. One could argue that his understanding of Indian culture remains essentialized; nonetheless, his knowledge in this area may well benefit him in the future if and when he interacts with Indian clients.

Beyond purely instrumental benefits, Ben also stressed that interactions with nonwhite peers have helped him appreciate (pan)ethnic diversity. He continued:

> I think diversity is a big deal, and it should be stressed more. I wish it wasn't a big deal, at the same time, because I wish we wouldn't have to make an effort in order to be diverse, and it was just the status quo. And especially with some of my friends back home [in a conservative, predominantly white town], or some of my friends that I went to college with who are racists . . . it just unnerves me. So I just want to be like, "Shut up! You're a moron!" It's not that they're bad people, but I think if they had a chance to be in a diverse setting, I think their attitudes would change immediately. It's easier to be racist if all of your neighbors are white.

Ben relishes that law school has allowed him to interact with people from different walks of life, people—and in turn, cultures—to which he might not otherwise have been exposed. As he mentioned his hometown and college friends, he became visibly angry. He curled his fingers into fists and spoke as if his friends were present: "Shut up! You're a moron!" Ben feels that law school broadened his horizons—it was the first occasion he had met so many people of different racial backgrounds. And it has been a good experience, one totally divergent from his hometown. Ultimately, Ben characterizes law school as more than learning the basics of the law; it is a space ripe with opportunities to associate with culturally diverse peers.

Scott Fahy, a third-year, white law student at Private Metropolitan, comes from a background similar to Ben's but prides himself on his preexisting knowledge of Latino communities. Scott grew up in an area of the American West that was predominantly white but had a sizable Latino population:

> My high school and college were very similar. We had a very significant Hispanic population. . . . But African Americans and Asians were not represented at all in my high school. . . . Being involved in

student groups and classes and having more exposure to those other minority groups [in law school] that I never had in high school or college . . . has changed and affected my career, but in a positive way.

Scott credits law school with allowing him to interact with "other minority groups" in classrooms, student organizations, and informal exchanges in the hallways. When asked why these interactions have affected him positively, Scott explained:

I'm not going to say I was intolerant, but I was just sort of unaware of cultural differences and a lot of what other cultures consider important and what they value and what their needs and desires are in the community. I come from [a rather large Western city], which is primarily whites and Hispanics. So there was no chance for me to ever know what the background of an African American kid growing up in an urban neighborhood was like. Or Pacific Islanders immigrating here, and their parents don't speak English. I never experienced any of that. So I think putting a more global perspective on people, on community needs, has opened my eyes to the reality that not every community is like the community that I grew up in. There are a lot of other issues that can be addressed and need to be addressed that directly affect and involve those other minorities and ethnicities.

Scott, like Ben, credits the law school environment for his new comprehension of nonwhite individuals and cultures. Both students value friendships with nonwhite students for the knowledge they impart in preparation for working in a diversifying profession.

Ben and Scott share the perspectives of most of the white law students represented in this book. They celebrate law school for the opportunity to interact with nonwhite peers, they underscore the importance of diversity for their future careers, and they appreciate the organic lessons learned in the halls of law school. But some select students, such as Ben, still harbor the stereotype of affirmative action advantage in admittance when speaking about students of color.

Nonracist Racists in Law School?

In *The White Racial Frame*, Joe Feagin explains that a pervasive, dominant framework normalizes collective sociopolitical memories at the expense of those who deviate from whiteness. For most white Americans, then, "the white racial frame is more than just one significant frame among many; it is one that has routinely defined a way of being, a broad perspective on life, and one that provides the language and interpretations that help structure, normalize, and make sense out of society" (2013, 11). Similarly, Eduardo Bonilla-Silva identifies a new U.S. color-blind racial climate in which everyday racism exists but is rarely acknowledged. Bonilla-Silva explains that the "principle of equal opportunity, central to the agenda of the civil rights movement and whose extension to people of color was vehemently opposed by most whites, is invoked by whites today to oppose affirmative-action policies because they supposedly represent the 'preferential treatment' of certain groups" (2014, 76). Color-blind racism, he notes, is located at the intersection of four insidious frames: abstract liberalism, naturalization, cultural racism, and minimization of racism. The white law students in this book represent two of the frames: abstract liberalism (a belief in meritocracy) and cultural racism (essentializing stereotypes).

Affirmative Action Is Unfair: Abstract Liberalism

Abstract liberalism refers to belief in equal opportunity and the idea that students of color should not be given preferential treatment. All law students take the same LSAT and all law schools have minimum criteria for admissions. Many white students believe that those who do not meet a school's requirements should not be accepted by the school. To do otherwise, they argue, violates the principles of fairness. Take, for example, Spencer Fagan's discussion of how he felt he was slighted because of his race:

> I know if you're a minority it is easier to get a scholarship. But I understand why they're doing it, and it makes perfect sense. . . . But it [being white] hasn't affected my law school or anything. . . . I mean, socioeconomically, it's weird because my parents got divorced, and . . . my mom is literally insane, so she lives kind of really poor, and my dad lives really rich. So I don't know. I mean, I had to go and live in some pretty bad places; my dad gave her money, but she blew it all.

Spencer is a first-year law student at Private Metropolitan; he is actively involved in sports and has many nonwhite teammates. Although he appears to understand why there are "preferential" scholarship opportunities for minorities, he explains that he too has experienced disadvantage. This reasoning is problematic because he uses an individual analysis without taking into consideration how racial disparities are structural. Moreover, he neglects to fully consider the privileges he had through his father (with whom he lived for most of his high school years). Superficially, Spencer appears liberal, but his explanation makes that progressive ideology seem abstract. In this way, the abstract liberalism frame veils structural inequalities.

It Is in Their Blood: Cultural Racism

Bonilla-Silva's second frame, cultural racism, is so engrained in American lives that individuals struggle to recognize that they are, in fact, racist. Attributing particular characteristics to certain groups essentializes that group, and that act alone can lead to insensitivity or even blatant racism. Stereotypes, such as the belief that most welfare recipients are black Americans or that Asian Americans are inherently math whizzes, are examples of cultural racism. The belief that law schools admit cultures that they want is an outcome of this frame.

Many of the white students who express frustration with affirmative action or the awarding of financial aid do so through a critical lens. They are, on the one hand, upset, because they assume some peers of color might not have been admitted based on merit, implying that they, themselves, studied harder and outperformed their peers of color by leaps and bounds on the LSAT to secure a spot in law school.[1] On the other hand, they also recognize and are bothered by the overwhelmingly white culture that characterizes law.

White law students negotiate their place within a society framed by white history and their own more racially diverse experiences. They may also recognize that they have certain racial privileges. Lori Rasmussen, a third-year student at Private Metropolitan, offered a sociological analysis of her privileged upbringing:

I guess, just because I'm white, I was lucky to attend good schools. I grew up in a white suburb of a city in [a midwestern state]. . . . [T]he public schools I went to were the best in the area because my parents could afford to live in the area where the property taxes were highest and the schools were the best. And my parents had enough money to send me to camps and buy books and do all the things that money affords. From the beginning—nutrition, all those things. That elevated me to the status [of being] privileged educationally and financially. . . . And my parents helped me so much with money through undergrad. I knew the door [to law school] would open. It would be easy. Not that I don't work hard, but there's not the same barriers that other people have.

Lori's candid description of her privileges as a result of her race and socioeconomic class is enlightening, and most white students recognized their privileges in relation to their nonwhite peers. Even so, white students still struggle at times with how race-based privilege does not always benefit them. Thomas Cain, the white, working-class law student who had attended an Ivy League institution for his undergraduate studies and whom we met in

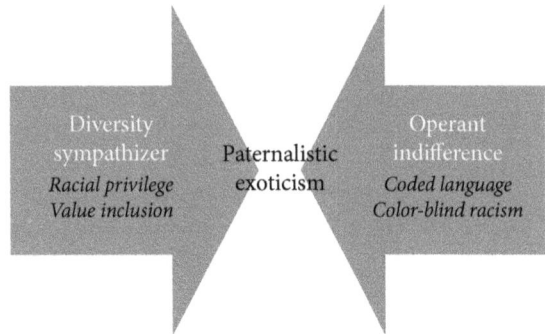

Figure 3.1 Paternalistic
exoticism

Chapter 1, intends to work with nonprofit organizations, most of which serve communities of color. Interviews for internships often left him frustrated because the interviewers invariably asked how he would reconcile his race and that of his potential clients. He shared his perception of the disadvantages facing a white male entering the nonprofit world:

> I mean, in this particular context, I had a disadvantage. I think that it's not something that bothers me that much because I recognize where the people I interview with are coming from and what they're looking for, and I agree with what they're doing. So for me, I think I do need to take an extra step for myself in that context because I've lived my life, pretty much up to this point, taking advantage of all kinds of advantages. Looking at it from that perspective, I don't have much to complain about. . . . I didn't have to worry about my race. To a certain extent I had to worry about how I differed culturally from people, how I was different, sort of, socioeconomically. But as a straight white male, I didn't have to worry about a lot of things.

Thomas takes an introspective approach to examining his own privileges. Although he finds some interview questions difficult to answer, his reflexivity demonstrates that he does not subscribe to one-dimensional color blindness. This type of reflection and negotiation was common among the white students, especially *paternalistic exoticism* (see Figure 3.1). White law students value diversity and recognize their own privilege, yet they may also seek instrumental rewards and complain about their perceptions of racial inequality. Thus, a typology emerges, and I analyze this typology in the following sections.

Diversity Sympathizers

To understand diversity sympathizers, let us turn to Will Decker, whom we met in Chapter 1. By way of a brief reintroduction, Will worked in retail and other service industry jobs for roughly ten years before returning to school. He pursued law because he felt that he could connect with potential clients and serve as their advocate. Will comes from an upper-middle-class background and attended elite private schools for primary and secondary education. When asked how being a white man affected his experiences in law school, Will responded:

> My high school was 95, 99?, almost a 100 percent white. . . . [Being a white man] affects every experience. Really, I guess it's just something that I am negotiating, with the privilege and the advantages I've had my whole life and will continue to have, even in the most basic ways. . . . I mean, it's white dude culture.

Will's childhood was racially homogeneous, but ten years in the real world, interacting with diverse populations in Chicago, Boston, and other major metropolitan areas exposed Will to his race, gender, and class privileges.

Intending a future in public interest work, Will is critical of the legal profession and of American culture in general, describing it as "white dude culture." When asked to say more about this culture, Will did not hesitate:

> It's a lot of white guys. Law school, lawyers, it's a lot of white guys thinking about white guy issues a lot of the time. . . . You do see, when issues have come up about social justice or racial justice issues come up, you hear a lot of really ignorant and thoughtless comments . . . that I wouldn't say are explicitly or on their face racist. But certainly . . . you see that. I think *I* see that more . . . in some of the comments I've heard and seen, and I'm not saying I'm hearing people make explicitly racist comments. But I'm hearing just a lot of things that don't involve a lot of critical thinking or compassion or anything like that—where people consider where they came from and how they got to where they are. And I'm not trying to exempt myself from this either. I do try to be critical of myself because a lot of work I want to do is going to be directly tied to issues of race. And I am and will be working with lots of people of color. And I try to sort of interrogate the way that I'm thinking about these issues and the way I'm positioning myself in what I want to do.

Will recognizes the structural and complex nature of racial inequality. Rather than subscribing to the idea that the United States is now a postracial society, he is reflective about his law school experiences, and life more generally, and openly shares his criticism.

Will's description of the legal profession and law school as "a lot of white guys thinking about white guy issues a lot of the time" echoes the work of race and ethnicity scholars. Over the past two decades, critical race scholars have actively called for the consideration of nonwhite experiences in research (Carbado and Gulati 2004; Gómez 2004; Wilkins 1997, 2000; Wilkins and Gulati 1996). While some sociolegal scholars may include racial diversity by presenting data on crime rates or domestic disturbances, these descriptions lack substance. Laura Gómez calls on scholars to think and write about the experiential nature of race. She notes that sociolegal scholars have "rarely . . . made racial inequality, racism, or racial identity the central focus of their inquiry (the dependent variable), and thus a certain lopsidedness characterizes law and society scholarship on race" (2004, 455).

For diversity sympathizers, diversity is not just a quota to be met. Like critical race scholars, diversity sympathizers understand the importance of examining the processes by which racial inequality is effected and endures. Because Will anticipates a public interest career, relative to his law-firm-bound friends, he notices comments made about race. To Will, the unthoughtful comments made by his peers that lack "critical thinking or compassion" illuminate racial privilege.

Within the white racial framework, diversity sympathizers often first recognize the racial diversity of the United States in a context such as law school. Once made aware of this diversity and, at the same time, their privileged place within it, they are often even apologetic for their position or ignorance. Such was the case for Lori, who earlier described her privileged upbringing and then reflected on her relatively sheltered upbringing in the American Midwest:

> In [the Midwest], diversity means there's black people. Here, it's actual diversity. To be honest, there's not a lot of Asian people in [my Midwest state]. And it was kind of a culture shock when I came out here. Just being honest. I was like, what?! I had no idea! Even though I was raised with equality and that it's very important, there's going to be things, because . . . I was not raised in a diverse community. And it's really been something that I have to constantly check myself [on] and educate myself purposefully to overcome being raised with such little diversity. So, yeah. I definitely noticed; I just hadn't been around Asian people that much. Sad, but true. Embarrassing.

Another way that diversity sympathizers understand racial dynamics is through their classroom experiences. That law school classrooms often lack critical discussion of race is not shocking. After all, the white racial frame persists throughout U.S. cultures and institutions. As previously explained, it describes the institutional, cultural, and historical processes that normalize whiteness at the expense of those who are not white. Feagin explains that this hegemonic frame "rationalizes and structures the racial interactions, inequalities, and other racial patterns in an array of societal settings. It routinely operates in both the micro (interpersonal) and macro (institutional) areas of society" (2013, xi). This framing elevates a national sociohistory based on facts created, nurtured, and propelled by European Americans and, in doing so, relegates nonwhite racialized experiences to being abnormal. Although many white law students presented in this book recognize how little law school attends to race, their lives remain situated within a white racial frame. They refer to diversity as infinitely important and sorely needed to create a just and fair society. And yet underlying this understanding is the taken-for-granted assumption that, sans diversity, whiteness is the unspoken norm. We return to Will, who spoke about experiencing the white racial frame inside and outside the classroom:

> People from different racial and ethnic backgrounds bring different points of view to the table and can challenge students to think about things in different ways. Or think about why they're looking at something the way they are. I mean, that's where my biggest sort of wake-up calls came in undergrad—listening to students of color and professors of color. And having to sort of think about how institutional racism works, how white privilege works. . . . In high school, all I got was "racism is bad, and there was a civil rights movement," you know? That was the education. And I think those professors and students [of color] made those issues clearer to me.

For Will, the presence of professors and students of color challenged his perspectives on race and racism as a college student. The modal framework casts race as a binary—black-white, pre-1960s–post-1960s—without attention to the processes that shape and reshape it. These processes structure people's lives (and affect their livelihoods). Disappointed by the dearth of professors and students of color at Private Metropolitan, Will argued that a diverse educational setting organically teaches students from perspectives usually confined to the periphery. Many other white students echoed Will's sentiments. Most also lamented the few faculty of color at their respective institutions.

Before we examine comments on the lack of racial diversity in law school, let us take a look at the faculty numbers for Western Elite and Private Metropolitan, presented in Tables 3.1 and 3.2. These numbers are the reason law students believe there is a lack of racial diversity in law school.

We see from these tables that less than one-third of the full-time faculty at both Western Elite and Private Metropolitan consists of minorities. Although these figures may not be surprising, what is interesting is that while the total number of full-time faculty declined at both institutions between spring 2013 and fall 2013—a decrease from 59 to 55 at Western Elite and

TABLE 3.1: FULL-TIME MINORITY FACULTY AT WESTERN ELITE

Spring 2013		Fall 2013	
Minority	Total	Minority	Total
13 (22%)	59 (100%)	11 (20%)	55 (100%)

Source: Data are derived from the American Bar Association's 2013 *Standard 509 Information Report*, which is generated annually from university-reported data. For purposes of maintaining the anonymity of the specific institutions included in this study, I cannot disclose the URL from which I acquired these data.
Note: "Minority," as used by the American Bar Association, refers to Asian Americans, black Americans, Latinos, and Native Americans. See, for example, American Bar Association Commission on Racial and Ethnic Diversity in the Profession 2012.

TABLE 3.2: FULL-TIME MINORITY FACULTY AT PRIVATE METROPOLITAN

Spring 2013		Fall 2013	
Minority	Total	Minority	Total
6 (19%)	32 (100%)	7 (26%)	27 (100%)

Source: Data are derived from the American Bar Association's 2013 *Standard 509 Information Report*, which is generated annually from university-reported data. For purposes of maintaining the anonymity of the specific institutions included in this study, I cannot disclose the URL from which I acquired these data.
Note: "Minority," as used by the American Bar Association, refers to Asian Americans, black Americans, Latinos, and Native Americans. See, for example, American Bar Association Commission on Racial and Ethnic Diversity in the Profession 2012.

from 32 to 27 at Private Metropolitan—the minority faculty saw a small increase at the latter institution. This could be due to conscious recruitment or coincidence.

Because law students interact with a host of individuals in law school, including administrators and part-time legal clinic staff, it is also worthwhile to examine the demographics of staff and administrators. Tables 3.3 and 3.4 display the numbers and percentages of minority and total staff at each institution.

Here, too, minorities represent less than one-third of the combined faculty and administrators at both institutions. Interestingly, however, Western Elite trails Private Metropolitan by 3–6 percentage points for minority staff. As noted previously, respondents from both institutions stressed the need for more diversity in law school. And the numbers in Tables 3.1–3.4 show that there are, indeed, far fewer minority faculty and staff than nonminority. But how and why does this matter for legal education? Does it change how students learn to read and interpret the law? Let us hear from some students.

Thomas Cain, whom we have met a few times, is a first-year law student. He grew up in a predominantly white, suburban neighborhood on the West Coast of the United States. His parents, however, were born and raised in urban centers on the East Coast and instilled in him an understanding that

TABLE 3.3: TOTAL FACULTY AND ADMINISTRATORS AT WESTERN ELITE

Spring 2013		Fall 2013	
Minority	Total	Minority	Total
34 (17%)	198 (100%)	22 (14%)	160 (100%)

Source: Data are derived from the American Bar Association's 2013 *Standard 509 Information Report*, which is generated annually from university-reported data. For purposes of maintaining the anonymity of the specific institutions included in this study, I cannot disclose the URL from which I acquired these data.

Note: "Minority," as used by the American Bar Association, refers to Asian Americans, black Americans, Latinos, and Native Americans. See, for example, American Bar Association Commission on Racial and Ethnic Diversity in the Profession 2012.

TABLE 3.4: TOTAL FACULTY AND ADMINISTRATORS AT PRIVATE METROPOLITAN

Spring 2013		Fall 2013	
Minority	Total	Minority	Total
24 (20%)	119 (100%)	23 (20%)	100 (100%)

Source: Data are derived from the American Bar Association's 2013 *Standard 509 Information Report*, which is generated annually from university-reported data. For purposes of maintaining the anonymity of the specific institutions included in this study, I cannot disclose the URL from which I acquired these data.

Note: "Minority," as used by the American Bar Association, refers to Asian Americans, black Americans, Latinos, and Native Americans. See, for example, American Bar Association Commission on Racial and Ethnic Diversity in the Profession 2012.

the demographics of his home community were not necessarily representative of the rest of the world. Thomas, a second-generation college student, felt sorely marginalized at the Ivy League institution he attended. When asked about diversity in law school, Thomas candidly spoke of the importance of having professors of color in law school:

I've had six professors. . . . One was a [white] woman, one was an Asian American male, and I have had four tall white men, and [these four] weren't necessarily comfortable talking about questions of, you know, race, sex, and gender. [The white woman professor] is super comfortable, and she does a good job of engaging in those subjects, but the others [white male professors] struggle with it. And that is really frustrating in class sometimes, not just for me, and probably less so for me than it is for [white] women and people of color who are more conscious of the way that the subject matters. . . . I . . . think that [white male professors] don't always really think about it or . . . have anything useful to say because they don't think about it a lot. . . . I love my professors, but I think that, as they retire, hopefully some of them will be replaced by faculty who I think will help enlighten or [give a] green light to other issues that we deal with outside of class, outside of just black-letter law.

Thomas criticized the limitations of classroom instruction imparted mainly by "tall white men" who have not confronted issues of race, sex, and gender and thus "don't . . . have anything useful to say because they don't think about it." Professors of color, on the other hand, think about these issues and present them in meaningful ways to their students. Under the spell of the white racial framework, it appears that law school instruction is "bleached out," or professionally neutral. A bleached-out curriculum would entail materials on law that have no consideration for how race, gender, and class affect individuals' experiences in and with it.[2] A bleached-out curriculum works as a part of white racial framing and is easily seen in U.S. legal and political institutions. Feagin explains that this framing is actually racist because it involves "hiding or sanitizing racist realities and entices those operating out of that frame to generally view societal inequalities as normal" (2013, 146).

Although in his first year at Western Elite, Phillip Mattson was in his early thirties at the time of our interview. A musician, he spent the better part of ten years focused on his music, but he eventually pursued what he perceived to be a more intellectually challenging career. After considering his options, Phillip decided to join the family business by becoming an attorney.[3] Phillip was raised in the American Midwest and attended religious schools before enrolling at a public college. He described his high school as "the whitest place on earth." But like Thomas and Will, Phillip also learned to recognize his race and gender privilege:

Some of the experiences I've had have made me aware of a privilege [white males] have. And I see that playing out in the law school. I can raise my hand and talk about something, and people will be like, "Oh, you made a really good point! That was really smart." And I don't think they would've thought the same thing had I said it in a slightly different way. With a little bit less confidence. Or the fact that I was not a deep-voiced, six-foot-five white guy. There's, I think, sort of a physical thing about me that I've noticed in my life that [leads] people [to] overattribute some sort of confidence or capability [to me]. . . . And being a white guy . . . I look like the judges in the case-books! You know what I mean? I see myself reflected a lot in these sorts of traditions. And for a lot of people in the class, I can see that they wouldn't have that same experience.

Phillip embodies the same physical characteristic as the judges in casebooks. And he attributes his perceived confidence to his race, gender, and physical appearance.

Cognizant of his privilege and the modal race and gender of the legal profession (white man), Phillip considered the types of role models his white female and nonwhite peers have in law school. When he looked around the halls of Western Elite, he realized there are not that many professors of color:

> Trying to think of my professors' backgrounds, they've been primarily white. I had one African American criminal law professor, a woman. And I know there are a lot of women I spoke to in our class, especially women of color, [who] talked about what a role model she was. And she was very active. She would go out and get lunches with undergrads who were thinking about going to law school. . . . And so I heard about what an inspiration she was! And I thought to myself, "It's good there's somebody like her here."

This professor was mentioned in many of the interviews with Western Elite students. Not only did law students describe her as "a ridiculously brilliant" woman, but they also admired her compassion for students. Her office door was always open for meetings—indeed, one Asian American law student feared that he monopolized too much of her valuable research and writing time. Sadly, professors like this one are few and far between, especially at a place like Western Elite. Phillip poignantly described how professors of color serve as role models, particularly to black women in this case. Phillip realized, in contrast, that he will always be able to find a role model on his road to success—all he has to do is look at a panel of judges, law firm partners, or the majority of his law professors.

Operant Indifference

Operant indifference refers to the white law students who claim a color-blind ideology but use codes to denounce what they perceive as unequal treatment between white and nonwhite students that benefits the latter. The white law students we have met so far spoke positively about the value of diversity for both the legal profession and their individual development. They appreciate faculty of color and laud their abilities to connect with students. But this does not mean that white students always favor diversity in law school. Indeed, some students turn to a more neoconservative form of commentary to argue that too much diversity may not necessarily be a good thing. According to some white students, student organizations based on racial or ethnic affinity further divide the student body and distract students from their primary purpose: learning the law. These white law students also argue that law schools should not be preoccupied with the race or culture of their faculty; rather, they should work to ensure that the *best* professors (regardless of race or gender) teach their students. They believe that issues of race and ethnicity have no place in core law classes where students are paying money to learn black-letter law and not a semester's worth of civil rights. These perspectives harken back to our earlier examination of how racism is enacted in a society without self-proclaimed racists (à la Eduardo Bonilla-Silva).

Diversity and Financial Aid

Some white students say that being white is actually detrimental, putting them at a disadvantage relative to their nonwhite peers, especially when it involves paying for law school. This neoconservative critique of affirmative action and assertion of reverse racism came up frequently among these otherwise progressive law students. White students from Private Metropolitan, in particular, lamented their lack of eligibility for financial aid opportunities available to their peers of color. Hollie Jackson, a first-year Private Metropolitan law student, had this to say:

> As far as financing law school, it seems like there are more opportunities for people who aren't Caucasian, and that can be kind of frustrating. . . . Just, there's more scholarships for people who are minorities. In undergrad, I did have a good [grade point average], but I wasn't qualified for a lot of [law school] scholarships just because I [am] white. And there's nothing about my religion or my race or where my parents are from that's anything special, I guess, according to people who write scholarships, to make me eligible for anything.

Burdened by the financial costs of law school, Hollie believes that her peers of color have more scholarship opportunities because they possess special traits. But Hollie being a woman bestows on her a modicum of specialness in the eyes of white men. For example, Nick Morgan, a third-year, white law student at Private Metropolitan, commented, "Yeah, I'm not eligible for as many scholarships because I'm white, and I'm a male, which I can't complain about." Aware of his race and gender privilege, Nick nevertheless also expressed discontent about the lack of scholarship opportunities available to him.

Hollie's and Nick's frustrations are not unwarranted. Nonwhite law students *are* more likely to benefit from race-based scholarships, including those offered through professional panethnic organizations, such as the Hispanic National Bar Association or the Asian American Bar Association. These organizations provide financial assistance to advance the presence of traditionally underrepresented racialized groups in the legal profession (e.g., Latinos and Asian Americans). Additionally, large law firms will often reserve diversity internship opportunities for first-year law students who hail from underrepresented racial groups or socioeconomic upbringings or are not heterosexual. Such scholarships and internships target nonwhite law students (especially at Western Elite), and white students know themselves to be excluded from such opportunities. And even though they understand the reasons for race-based scholarships and internships, they feel frustration at being excluded.

Too Much Diversity: Panethnic Student Organizations

Putting aside structural initiatives, such as scholarships, that lead to perceptions of unfairness among some white law students, others express frustration about the exclusivity of panethnic student organizations. While law students in general agree that panethnic organizations are necessary to sustain a diverse student body, some white students view the presence of these organizations as an obstacle to friendships. Brett Larkin, a third-year, white student at Western Elite, said:

> I think [panethnic student organizations] are good in that they serve as a place of solidarity for groups to get together [and], you know, enjoy their traditions and things that make them unique and provide a space for them to feel comfortable where they wouldn't feel completely comfortable elsewhere. At the same time, though, I feel like some [panethnic] groups tend to be a little bit more exclusive to the extent that I don't feel comfortable going to their events. Sometimes, I feel like I'm imposing, and the last thing I want to do is impose on anyone or suggest that I don't care or that I'm not sensitive to race or ethnic issues. . . . So it makes me hesitant sometimes, and I feel like the existence of these groups sometimes creates more racial divide than it does anything else.

Brett is a first-generation college student who hails from the American South. As the first person in his family to attend college, he remained close to his parents by enrolling at a large state school for his undergraduate degree. After scoring well on the LSATs, he was admitted to four tier-one law schools. He chose Western Elite because he believed it was the most elite of the schools to which he was admitted. He appreciates his move from the South and believes it changed him for the better. Since leaving, he has had the opportunity to interact with people from different ethnic and racial backgrounds, establish enduring friendships, and learn to embrace diverse politics.

And yet, for Brett, the existence of panethnic groups at law school creates "more racial divide than it does anything else" because these organizations serve as a one-stop shop for social, academic, and professional needs. Brett told me that he is an active member of a particular panethnic student organization at Western Elite only because he has many friends who are in the organization. But he explained that he does often feel like an outsider since he does not identify as a member of that panethnic group.

Black-Letter Law and Hiring the Best Professors

Some white law students activate what Eduardo Bonilla-Silva calls a "diminutive trope" to disguise prejudice or biases. Bonilla-Silva explains that many white individuals use "diminutives" to "soften their racial biases" (2014, 114). In other words, their prejudice is coded as a quest for equality. Some white law students emphasized that they were in law school to learn about the law and that issues of diversity should be reserved for classes that focus on race, class, or gender. They wanted to learn black-letter law—technical legal rules and regulations—and believed other topics to be superfluous, even frivolous. Spencer Fagan, introduced earlier, was one such student. Spencer and I met at a cramped Starbucks on a dreary day. We both arrived early for our appointment, identified each other, and began our conversation right away. He grew up in a predominantly white state and community but attended racially diverse schools that also included students from neighboring ethnoracial enclaves. Thus, Spencer's high school friends were white, Latino, and black, and he went on to befriend many black teammates while playing college basketball. He is cognizant of the economic and social disparities between him and his peers of color and is aware of structural inequalities. But he does not see how these issues are relevant to the study of law. In other words, issues of diversity matter to him—just not in the classroom:

> I mean, actually, I don't know how much diversity really matters because you're not really teaching anything. [*Pauses.*] Well, I could see maybe more in substantive classes. But I don't know how much race really matters the first year because [professors are] just following the ABA guidelines and just teaching the black-letter law. So it's not like they would have too many insights. But I mean, obviously, in a civil rights class, I can definitely see that being an important thing.

To Spencer, short of classes on civil rights or other topics directly related to race, all other classes should focus solely on teaching black-letter law. For white students who also think like Spencer, issues of diversity—whether related to race, gender, or class—have no place in constitutional law, torts, contracts, legal writing, or criminal law classes.

Such an understanding aligns with the traditional image of professional schools as providing socialization devoid of human experiences. These students' expectations to learn black-letter law and *only* black-letter law stem from their understanding of the socialization (and education) necessary to become an attorney and specifically of the neutral nature of that process. David B. Wilkins (1998) describes how this normative, or bleached out, professionalization does not, however, adequately characterize the experiences of nonwhite attorneys. Wilkins explains:

> The bleached out view of professionalism assumes that it is possible for people to "check" their identities at the door once they become lawyers. Just as important, it assumes that the rest of society can do the same; i.e., that lawyers and non-lawyers alike will treat individual lawyers as generic ones, without reference to the contingent features of a given lawyer's identity. There is, however, very little support for either proposition. (1998, 153)

Wilkins further addresses how the profession and society more generally expect black lawyers to possess particular allegiances, such as becoming civil rights attorneys. To become an attorney, then, is not a value-neutral, cut-and-dry experience. Yet many white students expect it to be so in a white racial framework.

While some white students desire only to learn black-letter law, others use coded language to speak about assumptions surrounding nonwhite professors' educational pedigree and legal training. For some, hiring the best professors trumps having a diverse faculty. We return to Nick, the third-year law student at Private Metropolitan. Nick boasted about his graduation from a liberal college and questioned whether a diverse law faculty would add value to his legal education:

> We need to have the best-quality teachers we can get, regardless of race, ethnicity, and gender. And unfortunately we have a lot of bad teachers that are white males. We have a lot of bad teachers that are Asian males. And I don't think we have many Latin [sic] teachers at all. We need some. Maybe they'll do better. So I don't see law as a place where you need this different type of background. For the most part, they're teaching us for a test [the bar exam]. It's not a legal studies class, or it's not sociology. We're not studying the impact of law on society; we're studying how the law operates, not how the mechanics affect society.

From this description, Nick desires good teachers who can effectively convey course materials, and race, as he sees it, is irrelevant to such considerations.[4]

Still, even students like Nick recognize a need for diversity. He allowed that sociology, legal studies, and other fields that examine how "mechanics affect society" warrant diverse faculty. And diversity, he argued, should be reflected in the student body. Following the above commentary, he added that it is "interesting to have that different background" but that "it's more important to have that in the student body [than among faculty] because then the students can discuss aspects of the criminal justice system on their own—its laws, the impacts it has on society. But I'm not paying for that." It appears that, under a white racial framing of law school, Nick desires what Wilkins would describe as a bleached-out, neutral law school experience.

Nick's sentiments illuminate similar responses from many white respondents at Private Metropolitan. I should emphasize here that all students, without regard to panethnicity, talked about the value of having a diverse law school and profession. But among white students in particular, there was a striking difference: more students from Private Metropolitan than from Western Elite regarded diversity as something that has no place in the classroom. On the surface, it seems as if these students are only interested in the standard law curricula. But when we unpack these comments, we see nuances beyond just a commitment to the white racial frame.

Diversity within a White Racial Framework

Private Metropolitan is a lower-tiered law school. The students who attend Private Metropolitan typically had scores on the LSAT that were less than stellar.[5] The median LSAT score for Private Metropolitan students in this sample was 156, and the median LSAT score for Western Elite was 165. Recall that self-reported data from the respective schools' websites lists the median LSAT score as 150 at Private Metropolitan and 167 at Western Elite.

Aside from lower LSAT scores, most respondents from Private Metropolitan also attended less prestigious educational institutions and graduated with mediocre grade point averages (GPAs). The median undergraduate GPA for Private Metropolitan respondents was 3.3, and the median undergraduate GPA for Western Elite respondents was 3.8.[6] For the former, becoming a lawyer is contingent on test scores. They experienced this firsthand with their undergraduate GPAs. These students understand that surviving law school necessitates securing good grades. First, they need to do well in their classes to acquire high GPAs, which are required reporting on most law-firm job applications. Second, they have to pass state-specific bar exams or they are not permitted to practice law in that state. Law students from Western Elite appear to possess additional cultural and social capital that many Private Metropolitan students lack. A student from Western Elite may have a lower law school GPA than a student from Private Metropolitan, but Western Elite has a pedigree that Private Metropolitan lacks. And employers take pedigree seriously when considering applications. Practical considerations thus appear to muddle color-blind racism within a white racial framework. White law students from Private Metropolitan are in a competitive race wherein their starting points already lag their higher-ranked counterparts. While white students from Western Elite have the luxury to speak on behalf of diversity and complain that they need more professors of color as good role models, their Private Metropolitan counterparts are in effect hustling to get the best legal education they can so that they can pass the state bar exam and find jobs. It is not that the white students from Private Metropolitan do not care about issues of diversity. They do. They just cannot afford to care *too* much.

Paternalistic Exoticism among White Law Students

This chapter examines how white law students at Western Elite and Private Metropolitan understand diversity in relation to the legal profession and their legal training. In their paternalistic exoticism they are generally aware of structural racial inequalities and recognize their racial privilege even as they complain about not benefiting from affirmative action policies. At the same time, they are paternalistic to their peers of color, expressing sympathy for the lack of cultural understanding among most white persons. They also exoticize nonwhite panethnic communities as "neat" groups that add diversity to white students' law school experiences.

White law students appear to hold a host of perspectives about diversity: it is good for business, it is important in the changing legal world, and it has its place *outside* the classroom. But their perspectives generally fall into one of two categories: diversity sympathizers or operant indifference. As we see in this chapter, diversity sympathizers recognize their own racial privilege and speak about the need for diversity inclusion. They see nonwhite peers and professors as welcome and necessary to change the "white dude" culture of law. On the other hand, some white students embody operant indifference, valuing diversity primarily for instrumental, practical reasons and limiting its relevance to a small number of arenas.

Both diversity sympathizers and those who express operant indifference are captured within the overarching category of paternalistic exoticism. White students tend to exoticize what little diversity there is in law schools and remain paternalistic toward nonwhites. Take Brett's comment about how ethnic minorities need their space or Spencer's perspective on preferential treatment. While such students may want to be allies, they continue to operate within a white racial framework in which the legal, cultural, and institutional standards remain white. And they feel sorry for their peers of color but do little to change the law school culture. This paternalism derives from a considerate and conscious place but nevertheless marginalizes nonwhite law students. And although white students may not necessarily engage in unprompted conversations about race with nonwhite students, the latter make assumptions about the former, and vice versa. These assumptions then further influence how white and nonwhite students think about race and the legal profession. In the next chapter we explore how Latino and Asian American law students understand the place and value of diversity in law school. As we will see, they not only learn to appreciate the significance of what it means to be a racial "other" in law school but also begin to cultivate panethnic allegiance.

4

THE SET AND STAGEHANDS

*Challenges of Being Nonwhite
in Law School*

Beatriz Mendoza, a third-year law student at Private Metropolitan, comes from a Salvadoran immigrant family. Growing up near a major metropolitan city, Beatriz attended diverse primary and secondary schools composed of students from all racial and ethnic backgrounds. She proudly noted that her high school friends were "African American, Asian, and Latino." While college proved to be different—she had mostly Latino friends—once in law school, her friendship circle expanded again. Her two closest friends are white and Chinese. Using an assimilation measure, some may say facts such as these reveal Beatriz to be becoming white or only symbolically Latino. Yet Beatriz expresses acute awareness of her panethnic affiliation. She joined the Society of Latino Law Students almost immediately after setting foot on campus. When asked why, she explained:

> It's like when you go into a room and you're kind of conscious of who you are, I guess, when you're the only one in the room. But then to expand on that, to say also, when you're in that room, people are already breaking into racial groups. And so you have a lot of white groups together, and Asian groups together, and then African American groups together. And it's just so weird to see that breakdown, but it happens . . . in classrooms, even where people choose to sit. If you observe a law school classroom, people are sitting in those groups. I think it's just maybe that everyone's new and they don't know each other. Instinct?

Beatriz attributes the panethnic groupings to "instinct"—some innate desire to be among those deemed more familiar. In this case, that familiarity is based on phenotype. But do familiarity or instinct explain why some students group panethnically? Previous research implicates discrimination as the force behind Beatriz's declaration of "instinct" (Tatum 2003). Other research points to social networks and homophily as the cause (McPherson, Smith-Lovin, and Cook 2001). But is the decision to sit among copanethnics based solely on instinct or homophily? Or do other forces affect the choice of who one sits next to in an unfamiliar sea of faces? The reason for this grouping appears to be far more complex than instinct or simply cultural allegiance. Instead, the answer reveals an unintended—what I term *incidental*—form of racialization that takes place during law school.

Chapter 3 examines white students' perspectives regarding diversity in law school. This chapter turns to the racialization processes that shape Latino and Asian American students during their three years in law school. This racialization takes place in the midst of a legal profession and culture that remain stubbornly white and male. It is a process I describe as front-stage racialization. The stage is the law school itself, and the stagehands are the professors and white law students. Students of color are cast as actors. Because front-stage racialization is veiled and nuanced, I divide this chapter into three sections. In the first section, "Prelesson: Becoming Minorities," I examine a prelesson whereby Latino and Asian American law students learn that they are racial minorities in law school. This happens as they visually scan classrooms and find few copanethnics or as they participate in conversations with other law students about the dismal numbers of nonwhite peers. In the second section, "Racial Lessons: Omissions, Interactions, and Assumptions," I describe three lessons learned by Latinos and Asian Americans as they undergo racialization in law schools. The third section, "Three Lessons of Not Belonging," provides a conclusion. This chapter and the three chapters that follow delve deeper into the perceived race-neutral climate of professional schools and invite us into a world that teaches black-letter law but also unknowingly and unintentionally emphasizes the delimited cultural place and value of panethnicity.

Prelesson: Becoming Minorities

Like their white peers, most Latino and Asian American law students describe law school as a numerically white place. This perception of whiteness may be elevated for Latinos and Asian Americans because they are panethnic minorities. As racialized immigrants who grew up or frequented ethnic enclaves, many Latino and Asian American law students find themselves in new racial and cultural territory. For many, law school is the first place where they interact with so many white peers. Being immersed in law school's sea

of cultural and social whiteness evokes a feeling of marginalization. Thinking about their schooling, these law students remark on the stark racial contrast among their high school, college, and law school classmates.

Binh Nguyen was a second-year law student at Private Metropolitan
when he told me about the dearth of people of color in law school. Binh,
who is Vietnamese American, grew up near coethnics and attended a predominantly Asian American and ethnically Vietnamese high school. He
compared how he felt in that context with how he felt on entering law school:

> High school in [my multiethnic county], specifically [in my pre-
> dominantly Vietnamese enclave], I would say 70 to 80 percent of the
> students are Asian, specifically Vietnamese, so, my ethnicity. So it's
> kind of close-knit and you kind of blend in because there are a billion
> other Asian kids around you. So in a sense it's fun, you meet a lot
> of friends, blend in. [In law school], it's different. You do stick out a
> little more. If you're, like, only one of two Asian guys in the class, [the
> other students and professors] notice that. I wouldn't say they single
> you out but they notice that. And for me, I notice it more.

Binh considers himself "Americanized," as he was born in the United States,
does not speak English with a Vietnamese accent, and has befriended non–
Asian Americans. Even so, he noticed a striking difference between his high
school and law school. Most students in law school do not look like him, so
he "stick[s] out a little more" in class; as he put it:

> It's easy for [professors] to spot you in the crowd of students. More
> Caucasian students here, so they can kind of blend in. But as far as
> an Asian [American] student, when [professors and peers] look up,
> they're like, "Oh, he's an Asian [American] student." Nothing bad.
> Your looks just kind of stand out as an Asian person in law school.

Most other Latino and Asian American students similarly described feeling
that they stuck out in law school, emphasizing this as a change from their
high school or college experience.

Estelle Ngan, a second-year, Chinese-Vietnamese American student,
recalled her first day of classes at Private Metropolitan: "I remember sitting in my first day of class, kind of looking around. . . . In a room full of
seventy-five people, [there were] maybe four Latinos, one black person, and
six or seven Asians, and that includes South Asians." Because she was raised
in a predominantly white community, Estelle told me that she often feels
conscious of her surroundings, and that on entering a new environment,
she identifies other nonwhites, especially Asian Americans. When she attended a prestigious public university for college, she saw and interacted

with numerous nonwhite college students. Going back to a predominantly white environment—law school—was thus a shock, albeit a familiar one that reminded her of her high school.

Felicia Álvarez, a first-year, Chicana law student, expressed her discontent with the number of Latino and black students at Western Elite:

> [In] law school, there's no black students. There's a lot of mixed-race students. There are very few Chicano—native, domestic Chicano—males; there's like four, which is ridiculous. But there are a lot of [white] women; there are a lot of Chicanas and a good, significant Asian Pacific Islander population, but definitely there's a lot of white people.

Similarly, Ernesto Chavez, a third-year Mexican American student at Private Metropolitan, offered his reaction:

> I've got to believe there are more minorities out there that can attend law school, you know? I've been a peer mentor the last two years for [Private Metropolitan], and I feel like, from the first year to the next, [fewer] minorities were admitted. I mean, even from my year! I feel like there were [fewer] black people from my year—from three years ago to now. I understand, with the economy the way it is, they have more applicants that probably were qualified applicants, but I don't think it's reflective of the people that are applying, the people that are getting admitted. Personally, I don't have solid data to back that up. But I just feel like we don't even have that many black people or Mexican people being admitted, and now it's like almost none!

Ernesto's frustrations stemmed from witnessing fewer first-year black and Latino students admitted to Private Metropolitan each year. His supposition that the depressed economy made attending law school more difficult for minorities appears to be complicated.[1] Figures 4.1 and 4.2 present data collected by the American Bar Association showing the number of total and minority JD enrollees at Private Metropolitan and Western Elite over a four-year period. The total number of nonwhite enrollees did not increase significantly between 2010 and 2013 and decreased in some years. Nonwhite enrollment at Private Metropolitan decreased from 2012 to 2013.[2] Ernesto likely observed this decrease in nonwhite law student enrollment, of which black and Latino students were already a minority.

Where Are the Asian Americans?

Black and Latino students were not the only faces missing in law school. Several students expressed concern over the seemingly small number of

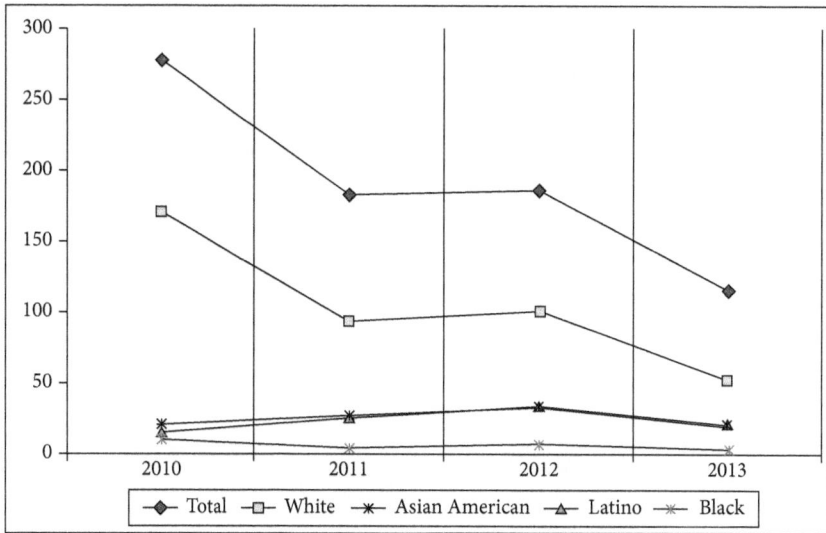

Figure 4.1 Private Metropolitan first-year JD enrollees, 2010–2013

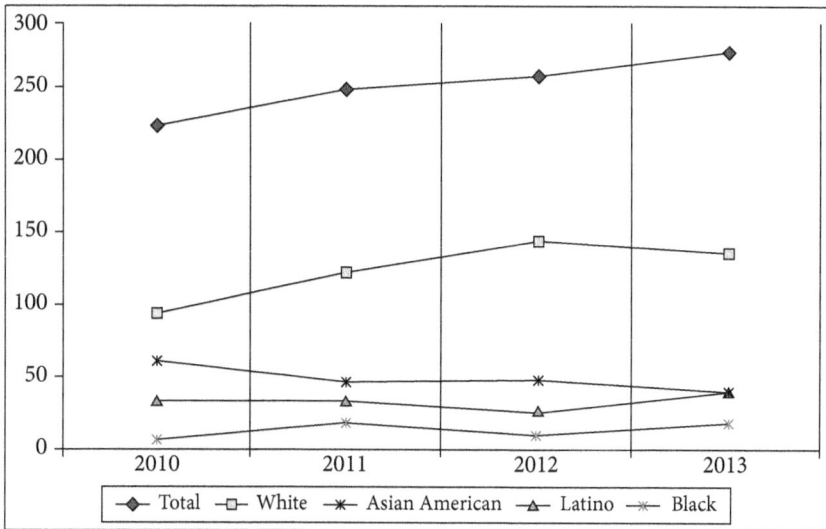

Figure 4.2 Western Elite first-year JD enrollees, 2010–2013

Asian American students. When speaking about diversity in law schools, most Latino students at Western Elite mentioned the small black and Latino presence, but many also pointed to a perceived decrease in Asian Americans. These students, like most at Western Elite, grew accustomed to being the cream of the crop in high school and college. They took advanced placement classes and enrolled in honors courses. A number of these students noted and remarked on the seemingly low numbers of Asian Americans, particularly when they compared these numbers with those they saw in their high school or college. Lucia Guiterrez, a second-year, Mexican-American student at Western Elite, recalled that Asian Americans were a constant presence for her in high school and college, making up a majority of the students in her advanced classes. But Lucia said that, compared to her high school and college experiences, Asian Americans appeared to be underrepresented in law school:

> I think the one difference for me is, I was used to being in advanced classes [where] the majority of the students were Asian [American] in high school and college. Not so much in law school. So I think that's a difference. The ethnicity—or the majority of the students are white. And I've never been in an environment where the majority of the students are white. So that's a little different for me, personally. . . . I'm [so] used to being exposed to a certain Americanized Asian culture in high school that I just kind of always assumed that there would be an Asian [American] population. . . . It's so strange to me that there is a really big population of educated Asians and yet in law school there isn't a lot. They're definitely a minority in law school, just like Latino and black students are, which is not something I was used to.

Likewise, Evellia Moreno, a first-year, Mexican American student from Western Elite, commented, "There are minorities, but I would say there are other minorities that are very not represented: the Asian American community, I don't see much representation." And Elina Reyes, a third-year, Chicana student, said, "Usually there were a lot of Asian [Americans] and whites [in college and high school classes]. At [Western Elite], I see more white than Asian [American], actually; . . . mainly white."

To see so few black and Latino students in law school is one thing, but Lucia, Evellia, and Elina expressed surprise regarding the small number of Asian Americans. Gilda L. Ochoa's (2013) research conducted at one Southern California high school offers insight on why these students might have expected more Asian Americans. Ochoa finds that although Latinos and Asian Americans represent 43 and 46 percent, respectively, of that particular school's population, they are not enrolled equally in advanced placement courses. Over 80 percent of Asian American students are in advanced placement classes, compared with a mere 10 percent of Latino students. This trend may hold at other high schools in portions of the American West. The majority of the Latino law students who took advanced placement courses in high school sat next to, worked on projects with, and befriended Asian

Americans. For them, this trend continued in college. Thus, the few Asian Americans in law school was a change.[3] In the words of Elina, law school is "mainly white. Not that [many] people of color."[4]

Role Models, Scholarship, and the Pipeline: Professors of Color

As we have seen, Latino and Asian American law students perceive law school as lacking racial diversity. From these students' perspectives, fewer Latino and Asian American students attend law school compared to their high school and college experiences. These students also advocate for more faculty of color. Like the white students discussed in Chapter 3, Latino and Asian American law students mentioned the need for mentorship and role modeling, especially for students of color. One student said:

> I don't think we can have enough minority professors in law school. We do have one Asian American female that I can recall right now and one African American male professor—who was awesome! Recently, we had an Asian American male professor joining us. That was about it. I think it would be helpful to have more minority professors for the minority students because I think they see the bright light out there. I think it will be helpful for students to think, "It's not so bad being a minority in this field because there are professors out there for minorities who are Asian American or African American." But when you have just one for a token . . . .

The above observations were made by Andersen Lee, a third-year, Korean American student at Private Metropolitan who was juggling an internship, law school, and responsibilities as a new parent. Andersen saw a pressing need for faculty of color to mentor students of color and serve as role models. As a nontraditional, older-than-average student, Andersen worked before turning to law school and felt disappointed by, in his words, the "token" professors of color at Private Metropolitan.

Natalia Melendez, a second-year, Mexican American student at Western Elite, spoke candidly about the dearth of nonwhite faculty at Western Elite. Natalia expressed her frustration regarding the dismal representation of faculty of color:

> I think for Latino students, it's important to see somebody in a position of authority and somebody they can admire and has done scholarly work, like them. And I think there is something wrong when there's a significant number of Latino students, but for some reason, in the position of power, they're missing. The implications from that, I think, are what's serious. I don't know what the implications may

be—just that Latinos don't pursue that route? They think [they are] not qualified for that route? Whatever it may be. I think that's what's problematic.

Natalia captured an institutional problem with the low number of Latino professors: law students assume that Latinos are not qualified to become lawyers or law professors. This perceived deficiency may deflate Latino and other nonwhite students' belief that they could succeed as attorneys.

This defeatist thinking reflects research on status anxiety or imposter syndrome. *Status anxiety* refers to the fear of underperforming because of one's marginal status—this could be because of gender (being a woman among men), socioeconomic status (being poor among wealthy peers), or race (being nonwhite in a predominantly white environment). Pauline Clance and Suzanne Imes (1978) pioneered the term *imposter phenomenon* to characterize the anxiety experienced by high-achieving women. Other research since has chronicled the imposter phenomenon and anxiety among university professors' assessment of their evaluations (Brems et al. 1994), employees who feel undeserving of their jobs (McDowell, Boyd, and Bowler 2007), and women engineering students (Cech et al. 2011).

Research suggests that nonwhite students immersed in a predominantly white setting experience a heightened sense of inferiority complex. For example, black math and engineering students must overcome expectations about their underachievement to successfully complete their academic programs; these expectations foster a sense of inferiority (McGee and Martin 2011). This inferiority extends into the professional world, where Mary Blair-Loy and Gretchen DeHart (2003) find that black women attorneys turn to community support in order to manage apprehensions and anxiety about their careers. In other words, without such support, they would find it difficult to manage their insecurities among white male colleagues.

Some students, such as Binh, whom we met earlier, were uncomfortable in law school classrooms, where they feel as if they stick out. One could argue that many people stick out from time to time: the student who chooses to dye her hair a flamboyant blue or the working-class student faking it to acculturate in law school. But Latino and Asian American law students embody racial differences that follow them beyond law school. As explored in Chapter 3, Joe Feagin describes the white racial frame as society's norm, presenting a particular version of history, politics, and culture as universal:

Whites do not have to say explicitly to other whites that "I am white like you and need to use my racial capital to gain privileges" to get privileges. Symbolic capital enables whites to avoid many interactive problems, such as police profiling and similar official harassments, and it facilitates positive interactions among whites in many settings, such as in party settings, job interviews with interviewers, or gaining access to white political officials. (2013, 139)

Bringing attention to white racial privilege illuminates why nonwhite students feel ostracized in law school. While their law professors do not necessarily engage in race-based harassment, Latino and Asian American law students do experience racial profiling. They are readily identified as "other" law students, not the norm or modal law student, who is presumed to be white, middle class, not working for pay during law school, in her or his early twenties, and childless—to name just a few of the characteristics described by Timothy Clydesdale (2004) and in Chapter 1. Wendy Leo Moore's characterization of law schools as "institutional white spaces" resonates with the understanding of nonwhite students in this book. Moore writes, "The visual messages at the law schools, the messages sent by the physical structure as well as the racial demography of the people in the space and the positions they held, revealed tacit assumptions about whiteness, privilege, and power" (2008, 58). Thus, contrary to Binh's assertion that standing out is "no big deal," it often limits Latino and Asian American students' overall sense of belonging in law school. The recognition that one deviates from the norm of law school serves as a prelesson that sets the stage for the three lessons that follow.

Racial Lessons: Omissions, Interactions, and Assumptions

Continuing from the prelesson that teaches Latino and Asian American students that they and faculty of color are numerical minorities at law schools, I now unpack the unscripted, subtle lessons learned by these students about their appropriate place in law school as nonwhite individuals. The lessons—conveyed via the omissions of race in the classroom, interactions with professors and peers, and assumptions about merit—play out in three domains where students absorb what it means to be nonwhite in a predominantly white profession. Table 4.1 lists the three methods of conveyance, their domains, and their implications.

The subject of race is omitted in the color-blind classroom, compelling complex negotiations for students of color. They are led to think about race hypothetically rather than acknowledging the experiential nature of each student's actual racial identity. Perceptions about race, merit, and admissions to law school leave Latino and Asian American law students feeling as if they do not belong, that law school is a foreign territory. Through these interactions, these students are reminded that they are different, or they undergo what Angelo Ancheta (1998, 64) refers to as "outsider racialization" (described in Chapter 2). Latino and Asian American law students also sense that their experiences with race in law school are dismissed in a color-blind

TABLE 4.1: RACIAL LESSONS IN LAW SCHOOL

Medium	Domain	Lesson
Omissions	(Color-blind) classroom	Paradox: experiential versus hypothetical race
Interactions	(Color-blind) law school	Foreignize and trivialize experiences that deviate from the norm
Assumptions	Law school; virtual legal world	Race-based, nonmeritocratic admissions

classroom. Finally, assumptions about race frequently surface within the boundaries of the broader legal culture, including public blogs on the Internet. Questions about nonwhite students' qualifications for law school admissions and debates regarding affirmative action policies characterize virtual and verbal assumptions about race. I devote the remainder of this chapter to elucidating each of these lessons, detailing their domains and the types of inferences that students make about their own race and place in law school.

Racial Lesson 1: Awareness through Omissions

As described in the prelesson, one of the first things that students of color recognize is that, unlike the majority of their peers, they are not white. They also soon encounter their first racial lesson: racial awareness through omission. Some students read case law that they believe to be prime for racial analyses, but this view is often dismissed by law professors or peers. Esperanza Macias, a second-year, Mexican American law student, majored in sociology. Coming to law school, she identified numerous courses that she felt were ripe for using her sociological imagination. But she was disappointed and discouraged when her peers were reluctant to engage in these topics. She recounted insensitive and hurtful comments made by her peers and her professors' failure to properly mediate. Remembering a particular moment in property class during her first year of law school, Esperanza became incensed:

> We were talking about, like—I don't remember what principle we were talking about. But it was a video about housing issues. Like, people think that too many people living in an apartment is not okay. Or the fact that a landlord is saying, "I'm not going to fix your place because . . . ." It was just—we were watching this video about tenant issues. . . . So it was more just to highlight, look, here's how housing can really be a problem in a community. And it was just tenants fighting with their landlords, so they would go to city council meetings,

and they were just talking about, "Look, they don't fix the stairs when they're broken" and this, and this, and that. And so the lights are kind of off [in the classroom], but everyone's on their laptops, and we're watching this video, and everybody's just paying attention. And there's this scene where this landlord goes up, and she's like, "Look, I'm tired of people telling me to fix their places. I'm tired of people trying to tell me that I need to paint their apartment. I'm tired of people telling me that they need a new refrigerator." And she's just complaining. She says that her tenants are too needy. And then she's like, "Besides, they act like I don't know that they got, like, twenty Mexicans in there." And half the class kind of laughed. And I was like, "That's really—it was so weird, because it made me feel strange. Because they were laughing at this idea of, like, twenty Mexicans living in this apartment. But I was like, "I'm a Mexican! I'm sitting right here! You just laughed. I'm sitting right here." And I just remember for some reason it was, like, really personal to me. That they would laugh at this woman being really ignorant. That they laughed at a very ignorant comment when we're supposed to be this classroom [full] of very enlightened and intellectual people. . . . It was, like, this out of body experience. I was like, "I thought we were all supposed to be smart." And it made me feel weird, because then I also realized I was one of two Mexicans in that ninety-person class. So it was, like, of course it would be personal to me. Maybe it's personal to [the other Mexican American student]. There are only two of us in here.

In this brief moment, Esperanza negotiated racial omission through a white racial framing of Mexican Americans. As mentioned previously, the United States is built on white racial framings. Media pundits portray Mexican Americans as a drain on social and financial resources, despite research discrediting this assertion. Further, Mexican Americans are stereotyped to be poor, thus needing to share living quarters with many family members. This framing then spurs a racist understanding of members of this community.

Crucially, however, perpetrators are unlikely to express their prejudice openly when or where such attitudes may be shunned as politically incorrect. Instead, they save their racism or racist stereotyping for when they can commiserate with fellow copanethnics. Referring to white Americans in particular, Joe Feagin says:

> If whites do not articulate racist ideas in public, if they keep them to themselves or just express them in the backstage, then they or their white friends and relatives frequently do not see them as serious "racists." Articulating blatant elements of the racist frame in private

settings seems to be at least acceptable, probably because in their view no one is "really hurt" by that tactic. (2013, 124)

Tucked safely in the dimly lit, color-blind classroom, Esperanza's classmates openly laughed in response to the landlady's framing of her "Mexican" tenants. Although the students were not necessarily in a class of copanethnics, they nevertheless felt sufficiently comfortable to laugh with one another through a shared perception about Mexican immigrants. The dark classroom provided protection for these students to react in a way that might not have been acceptable had the lights been on. There was camaraderie among those who laughed, as they could not be identified in the dark (unless peers knew each other's laughter). These students may be progressive and "smart," but the white racial frame is so much a part of American history and society that they are more than likely unconscious of the meaning behind their actions. It is almost certain that if confronted, these students would have expressed regret at laughing.

For Esperanza, however, the moment revealed a clear divide between, on one side, herself and the other Mexican American student and, on the other, everyone else who laughed or was complicit in the laughter. Esperanza was uncomfortable and astounded that her supposedly smart peers could be so insensitive. It is possible that the laughter was directed at the landlady and not necessarily indicative of a negative perception of Mexican Americans. The key, however, is that the professor did not offer students an opportunity to reflect critically on the video or the moment of laughter, thus dismissing a sensitive event in the classroom. Esperanza had hoped that her professor would devote time to address the laughter and discuss its inappropriateness. But this did not happen. Moments of omission like this lead to a heightened sense of panethnic awareness.

Classroom Lessons in the Daylight

The classroom plays a significant role in the life of a law student: they learn there, interact with peers and professors there, and internalize lessons that help them become good attorneys. Elizabeth Mertz's research focuses on the linguistic nature of the legal classroom. She notes that students read and decipher the legalese in their casebooks, they form analyses in the legal-linguistic frame, and they make arguments using law-specific frames and voices (Mertz 2007, 215). These techniques reflect a traditional white, male, upper-middle-class approach to learning, and law students outside it are excluded. White women, students of color, and students from lower socioeconomic backgrounds are often assessed negatively compared to their white, male, upper-middle-class peers because the former are seen as including—inappropriately—emotions and personal experiences in their analyses. Mertz's observations at eight differently ranked law schools across the United States shed a sobering light on this phenomenon. She finds that white male students tend to talk more and take up more class time at elite institutions where the majority of the professors reflect students' race and gender. When white women and students of color speak in classrooms at elite law schools, their mostly white male professors often fumble to incorporate their comments or, in a more offensive gesture toward the students, dismiss their comments entirely. In instances in which white women and students of color present emotionally charged responses to cases, other law students, especially white men, display disagreement or annoyance by rolling their eyes or engaging in side conversations with one another. Comparatively, white women and students of color voluntarily speak in classes at nonelite institutions, especially in courses taught by women professors.

Thus, Wendy Leo Moore (2008) eloquently characterizes law schools as "institutional white spaces" that reproduce systemic racial inequality by silencing and ignoring the experiences of nonwhite law students. Law professors are hesitant to incorporate "extraneous" material into their lessons outside black-letter law and, thus, keep the classroom "color blind." Moore argues that using a color-blind approach to interpret the law replicates a structure that is bound to an institutionally racist society because "color-blind racism operates as an ideological framework that allows whites to espouse views that normalize systemic racism, minimize the relevance of racism, and denigrate the cultures of communities of color, while at the same time denying that they themselves, are racist or responsible for racism" (2008, 84). This color-blind approach trains students to interpret legal cases and engage in classroom politics in an acceptable manner. Adia Wingfield finds that rules surrounding black professionals' expression of feelings are not neutral but rather follow a white, masculine script. She argues, "African American professionals find the feeling rules are not neutral, but are in fact racialized in ways that deny them areas of emotional expression accessible to their white colleagues" (2010, 265). Law students are trained to possess certain emotions—not their racialized and gendered ones but white and masculine ones.

Additionally, controlling images become an important factor in daily interactions. Otherwise known as stereotypes, controlling images affect the way that peers perceive Latino and Asian American law students. With regard to black women in particular, Patricia Hill Collins argues that controlling images derive from ideological justifications of race-based oppression. The black mammy, or matriarch, signals the black woman as the "other," who is deviant from the white middle-class woman. Controlling stereotypes extend beyond the black population to any nonwhite racialized group. Latinos are often portrayed as undereducated or undocumented immigrants, while Asian Americans are assumed to be model minority overachievers.

Individuals at times internalize these images and begin to believe the stereotypes actually do differentiate them from the standard American. This is an insidious effect of the white racial frame. Patricia Hill Collins asserts, "These controlling images are designed to make racism, sexism, and poverty appear to be natural, normal, and an inevitable part of everyday life" (1990, 68). Law students recognize and act on these controlling images in both obvious and covert ways.

Jessica Laus, a third-year, Filipina American law student at Western Elite, recounted an experience in her criminal law class that left a deep impression. She told me that several of the criminal law cases they read involved rape or domestic violence, and students were expected to read the facts of each case without taking into consideration how intervening circumstances could be interpreted and evaluated before making a judgment.[5] As a shy person who did not want to draw attention to herself, Jessica normally avoided volunteering to speak in class. On one particular day, however, she could no longer contain herself after none of her peers addressed possible gendered dynamics in a particular domestic violence case. As a woman of color, Jessica believes that one's gender and race inevitably affects one's interpretation of a case.[6] In other words, it was not possible for students to be purely objective in their readings of the case. Speaking to the entire class, she argued that it was important for them, as law students and budding attorneys, to recognize that the law was written by men and interpreted to favor men. And just because there was case law precedent did not mean that every case should be interpreted the same way. Immediately following her remark, Jessica was greeted with negative comments, sour expressions, and eye rolling on the part of the white men in the class. And although she did not remember verbatim what the professor said in response, she did remember feeling as if her professor and peers found her to be overly biased because she was a woman and even more so as a woman of color. Feeling hurt after this incident, Jessica thought about how being a woman of color shaped her understanding of the case and that if she were a man, especially a white man, she would have used a different approach to evaluate the case. And if she were a white male attorney arguing the case, she probably would have just reported the facts, as she was trained to do in law school.

The omission of race and gender in the classroom draws awareness to the inadequacies of a fact-reporting exercise. Race is injected into but simultaneously denied in the classroom through the insistence on a color-blind agenda. Latino and Asian American students often report that they do not expect race to play a central role in case law, but they nevertheless find it problematic that classes on constitutional law, criminal law, and others lack racialized discourse. To these panethnic law students, personal backgrounds are intrinsic to understanding how the law affects particular communities, especially those from which they hail or with which they are familiar. The omission of such considerations is conveniently couched as "emotional neutrality" and "color blindness" in formal legal education. This approach to classroom instruction thus delivers a lesson for students of color—namely, that their race and any emotions they might have attached to it are unwelcome and inappropriate considerations that should be effectively shelved as they learn to become attorneys. Additionally, students begin to also think about how they, as budding attorneys, need to negotiate their gendered and raced understandings alongside expected professional neutrality. Their non-modal identities already contribute to how they understand and read cases, which suggests that they may continue to do so once they begin working.

Racial Lesson 2: Interpersonal Interactions
and the Assumption of Race Values

Conversations among law students in the classroom are often tinged with racial undertones. Latino and Asian American law students note that the law classroom *could* be a dynamic place to exchange different viewpoints, but most professors do not foster such an environment. Far from simply delivering lessons, professors play a crucial role in shaping classroom dynamics. Occasionally, professors make deliberate and perhaps unintentionally hurtful comments directed at particular students. This can set the tone for an entire class session or, worse, the remainder of the semester. Esperanza Macias, introduced earlier, had another story seared into her memory, involving an exchange between herself and one of her professors. This experience led her to reevaluate how her professor perceived her (as a Latina law student) and also to question her position among her fellow law students.

During the first week of law school, Esperanza attended an 8:25 A.M. torts class that consisted of only the thirty students from her section. As the class began, the professor retrieved the class roster and asked each student to introduce her- or himself. Esperanza wanted to enunciate her name clearly for her professor, as many people have had trouble pronouncing her name in the past. When her turn arrived, Esperanza very slowly articulated her name, but the professor still mispronounced it—omitting a vowel—and made no effort to correct his pronunciation. While she was upset that it seemed as if the professor had no interest in learning to pronounce her name correctly, Esperanza decided to let it go. It was the first day of class and she hoped the professor would eventually learn to pronounce her name, especially given the small-class setting.

Unfortunately, Esperanza's optimism dissipated during the next class meeting. The professor presented a hypothetical case involving football and then used the Socratic method to call on Esperanza, again mispronouncing her name. This time, Esperanza decided to proactively correct his pronunciation, but again he made no effort to correct his pronunciation or to apologize. He then asked her a question regarding the hypothetical case but immediately followed with the clarification, "Wait, I am talking about American football—are you familiar with it?" Esperanza was surprised by this comment and described herself as feeling "weird" and "numb" that he questioned her familiarity with American football, because she was born and raised in the United States. The class consisted of mostly white students, and the professor did not ask anyone else if they were familiar with American football. It appeared that the professor thought that, because Esperanza had an ethnic name, she would be familiar only with *fútbol* (soccer). Further, given the unbalanced power dynamics, Esperanza felt bullied, which left her feeling "numb."

After class ended, several classmates expressed their surprise that the professor had directed a subsequent question *only* at Esperanza. She remembers saying to them, "Yeah, I get it. He thinks I just got here. I get it."[7] For law students who are children of immigrants, race is intertwined with immigrant status to further highlight difference and inequality in the classroom. Professors draw attention to Latino and Asian American law students' perceived foreignness through "benign" actions, such as mispronouncing their names or assuming they are recent immigrants. Mia Tuan's work on later-generation Asian Americans demonstrates that members of this panethnic group straddle a liminal space between "honorary white" and "forever foreigner." Tuan notes, "In subtle and not so subtle ways, Asian ethnics continue to find themselves excluded from the racial and cultural center, denied their rightful sense of place in this nation. Although longtime Americans, they fail to be perceived as such. Instead, they remain 'model minorities,' the best of the 'other' bunch but not 'real' Americans" (1998, 161). Despite the depth or breadth of their American roots, Asian ethnics are forever answering questions about their "real" countries of origin or demystifying assumptions that they know how to speak Asian languages. This puts Asian Americans' identities in limbo, because they might be accepted as "honorary white" in one context yet perceived as "forever foreigner" in another. This conflicting identity applies to the Latino population as well. Esperanza's story is one of many in which Latino and Asian American law students felt slighted because of their ethnic-sounding first or last names, their perceived recent immigrant history, or assumptions about their lack of familiarity with American culture.

Throughout the history of the United States, immigrants have been assigned to racial groups on arrival—a process that continues to the present day. The ascribed racial categorization of immigrants leads to social and political consequences for members of particular immigrant groups. Mary Waters (1999) finds that West Indian immigrants may align themselves with other West Indian coethnics (e.g., Jamaicans, Grenadians) but are racialized as "black" in the context of the United States. Speaking about the immigrant experience more generally, Alejandro Portes and Rubén Rumbaut (2006) report that second-generation immigrants generally identify racially, or pan-ethnically, while their first-generation counterparts evoke ethnic identities.[8] But as Steven Cornell and Douglas Hartmann write, "With the exception of whites . . . the society at large generally has either ignored or minimized these [ethnic] identifications throughout much of its history, emphasizing more comprehensive racial distinctions" (1998, 26). Parallel to this phenomenon by which Latinos and Asian Americans are assigned to racialized groups, they are additionally framed as foreigners.

It is also important to note that not all professors and peers treat Latino and Asian American law students as if they are foreigners, and only a handful of law students recount one or two such incidents during their law school tenure. However, these few events bear tremendous significance and become central to how law students think about their place as racialized immigrants in law school and in the broader legal profession.[9] Latino and Asian American law students thus find themselves occupying a unique space at the intersection of race and perceived immigrant background—negotiating both a racialized identity and a foreignized one. And despite most of the students in these pages being native-born, second-generation immigrants, they are sometimes treated as recent arrivals by their professors and peers. As shown in Chapter 1, the majority of the Latino and Asian American respondents are 1.5- or second-generation immigrants, which means that they either immigrated to the United States as young children or were born and raised on U.S. soil. In other words, the vast majority of the Latino and Asian American students represented in this book are not foreigners.

Other forms of in-class instruction, especially talks by guest speakers, also conjure racial awareness and immigrant distinction. Often, instructors in clinical classes (experiential classes often taught by practicing attorneys) will invite experts or practicing attorneys to lecture on their expertise. These presentations demonstrate to students the range of career possibilities and specializations and also pique student interest in a particular field. However, these positive intentions can turn sour, as in one of Marie Chiang's classes. Marie, a Taiwanese American law student who emigrated from Taiwan as a young child, was a first-year law student at Western Elite with an interest in environmental law. In a workshop on the subject, the professor invited a guest speaker whom Marie was extremely interested to hear. The speaker, "an older white man," as described by Marie, had retired from the Bureau of Reclamation and had a wealth of professional knowledge. After the speaker's presentation, Marie was bursting with questions, especially with regard to the connection between water use and agriculture—an issue she feels passionate about given her time working for an environmental nonprofit organization. She recalled asking the speaker about the best way to integrate the water needs of farmers on a national scale but being interrupted by the speaker before she could finish:

> And he interrupted me and said "So would you rather see a bunch of dry cleaners?" And at the time I was so focused on my point that I didn't even realize how that was racist. But upon retrospect, it came out of nowhere! There was no reason for him to become so angry and defensive with me, because he had not done that with any other student. There was no reason for him to pick out dry cleaners aside from any other business considering we're talking about the use of water and how it compares with agriculture uses and urban uses—it makes a lot more sense to say something like high-rises or suburban development or anything else that uses a lot of water. I don't even know how much water dry cleaners use or don't use! I mean, it just made no sense! Why would he say that except for the fact that I was one of the few Asian [American] people in the room? And it may be, unconsciously, that just came to his head. I don't know until you ask him, right? But also the force with which he responded and the way in which he disregarded my point, the way that he was almost angry with me even before I got my point across completely, completely affects me.

The guest speaker's assumption about Marie may have been based on her visible phenotype as an Asian American—an identity she cannot hide. And many Asian immigrants do own dry cleaners, among other small businesses, especially in urban centers. Min Zhou (2009) reports that Asian-owned businesses make up roughly 4 percent of total U.S. non-farm-related businesses. Dry cleaners, greengrocers, nail salons, and fish markets are typically family-run and rely on intergenerational, intrafamilial support. For many Asian immigrants, these types of family-owned businesses provide financial security and also require minimal education (and less in English-language ability) while employing low-skilled laborers, concentrated in ethnic niches.

Given this, it is not entirely surprising, and may be even understandable that the speaker associated Marie with dry cleaners. Nonetheless, this form of essentializing located Marie firmly at the intersection of immigrant background and race. By looking at Marie, the speaker identified her as Asian American—again, an accurate assessment as she does, indeed, identify as such—but he also assumed a connection between Marie and recent immigrants from Asia. One might say that the speaker made an assumption about Marie's Americanness by connecting her to a type of business commonly owned by Asian Americans. This conjoined foreignizing and racializing is particular to Latinos and Asian Americans—and speaks directly to the outsider racialization mentioned earlier.

Classroom interactions thus heighten racial awareness in two ways: the brushing aside of critical racial analyses (lesson 1) and verbal and nonverbal exchanges with other students and with professors or invited speakers (lesson 2). While professors may not intentionally avoid racial analyses of particular cases, many Latino and Asian American law students see the omission as problematic. Yet when Latino and Asian American students muster the courage to bring attention to this oversight, they often feel that their peers are annoyed and their professors dismissive. These instances not only marginalize Latino and Asian American perspectives in the classroom; they also heighten their foreignness and their status as outsiders in law school and, eventually, the profession.

Lesson 3: In the Shadows of Affirmative Action—
Assumptions about Law School Admissions

Race is injected into the classroom through a lack of focus on racial analysis but also through comments that Latino and Asian American students receive from their peers and professors. One way this happens is through discussions or offhand comments regarding law school admissions. Many law schools claim to consider each application holistically, assigning weight to life experience, personal background, undergraduate GPA, and undergraduate institution, in addition to the LSAT score.[10] Despite these efforts to affirmatively admit truly diverse individuals, the criterion of race, like a wound that refuses to heal, infects how some law students think about admissions.

The legacy of affirmative action policies haunts many nonwhite students and fuels white law students' speculations about the former's admissions to law school (Moore 2008). Marco Saldaña, a first-year, Mexican American student at Western Elite, explained his sense that "there are some people out there who may feel that because [Latinos] are minorities, there may have been a lower standard for us to have gotten into a school like [Western Elite]." When asked to elaborate, Marco said that he visited many online blogs before applying to law school and that the discussions on these blogs sometimes were hostile, especially on the topic of race and admissions at top-tier law schools.

A recent search on a well-known blog, *Above the Law* (http://abovethelaw .com), yielded interesting comments from readers with regard to the U.S. Supreme Court upholding Michigan's state ban on affirmative action–based admissions at public universities.[11] One commenter wrote, "Good. Now people will be admitted on their merits rather than their race. I have absolutely no sympathy for minorities whatsoever. It's time for them to stop making excuses and get off their assess." Another commenter had a similar sentiment:

We either accept equality or we don't; and admitting students of any persuasion or race into a highly competitive school from which they will graduate knowing that they didn't "really earn it in their heart of hearts" doesn't help anyone. A very strong argument can be made that it is a better situation in which a student is admitted to a school based on their own accomplishments. I know all the arguments, but at the end of day we have to either be equal or we are never really out of kindergarten.

And there was the sarcastic "OOOOHHH NOES!!! scUM is now admitting students who qualified through achievement rather than skin color. Whatever shall we do???!?!?"

Such comments are but the tip of the iceberg; other overtly racist examples included differentiating between "dot" and "feather" Indians and crafting grammatically incorrect sentences on purpose to represent nonwhite individuals' sentiments about the decision. This is the type of virtual hostility experienced by many Latino and Asian American law students. They begin to experience microaggressions and subsequent anxiety even before stepping foot on campus when they read blogs such as this.[12]

Reflecting on his own admission into law school, Marco said:

I had this amazing GPA, but I didn't have the amazing LSAT score, and I hear people say, "Oh, the only people that get into the schools with low LSAT scores are minorities," so I feel like that is a common sentiment out there. I guess that may be true, but I'm thinking that the schools that let me in, they took everything [into consideration] and didn't just look at my numbers. I think they looked at my story, my whole life, to see what constitutes merit.

In addition to Western Elite, Marco was also offered admission at University of Notre Dame and Columbia Law Schools. Marco faced tremendous adversity in his educational pursuits. He is from a single-parent home with an absent father he never met. His mother completed middle school in Mexico and makes tortillas for a living. Marco attended a prestigious public university for undergraduate studies while working several jobs to pay rent and living expenses. Despite potential differences in upbringing and undergraduate achievement, race remains prominent in how white law students think about admissions to law school, which in turn affects student interactions with one another.

Race and speculations about "affirmative action admits" may preoccupy some white and nonwhite law students, but they rarely engage in conversation with each other about it (unless it is on a public blog). When such discussions do happen in person, however, the experience is often a highly unsettling one for nonwhite students. Jenna Ito, a third-year, mixed-race

(Japanese and white) student at Private Metropolitan, was shocked when another law student questioned her admission to law school. Being from Hawaii, a majority Asian American state, Jenna had not previously encountered such racial stereotyping or racism. The following exchange between Jenna and me captured how pointed conversations about law school admissions heighten the role of race for law students:

> JENNA: I definitely had a lot of comments made to me during orientation—when I came to [Private Metropolitan] for first-year orientation, one student asked what it felt like to be the product of affirmative action.
>
> ME: Was this another Asian American student?
>
> JENNA: No, this was a white student.
>
> ME: What did you say to that?
>
> JENNA: I didn't say anything. I was shocked! I was like, "I'm sorry? What?" And he was like, "Yeah, because there aren't that many of you here." And by "you," I'm assuming he meant people of color. So he's like, "There aren't that many of you here, so I'm assuming that you're here because of affirmative action, so that must have been really interesting for you. And I'm sure you'll love to learn about it in con[stitutional] law" or something like that. He said something along those lines.
>
> ME: And this was another first-year student?
>
> JENNA: Mmm hmm. So I just didn't say anything. I wasn't sure what to make of it. I'm not sure if he was being rude or if he was truly stupid. Really ignorant.

We may never know whether the white student's query stemmed from animosity for affirmative action policies or from pure curiosity. Either way, the story reveals the important place of race in the minds of white and nonwhite law students. The exchange between the two new law students illuminates how the legacy of educational inequality taints some white students' perception of their nonwhite peers. It is worth noting, too, that during a follow-up interview, five years later, Jenna again used this particular encounter to describe how she still feels as if she is posturing as an attorney. The incident, while brief, continues to fuel her sense of being a racialized imposter. As mentioned earlier, these types of person-to-person exchanges, although not necessarily common, leave lasting impressions on students of color.

Three Lessons of Not Belonging

The three lessons in this chapter reveal the oddly prominent yet problematic place of race in law school. These lessons characterize law school as a white space and culture where Latino and Asian American law students feel marginalized. In the first section of the chapter, we see the prelesson for Latino and Asian American students, who learn to recognize and understand themselves as minorities within the law school context. They see fewer students of color at law school compared with their high school and college experiences. They come to feel as if they stick out in their classrooms, and while they do not necessarily characterize sticking out as negative, they do emphasize that they feel strange in the overwhelmingly white environment.

The second section introduces the three lessons assimilated by Latino and Asian American law students in law school. These lessons are conveyed via the omission of race in the classroom; interactions among faculty and assumptions made about foreignness and immigrant status; and peers' assumptions that particular law students of color benefited from affirmative action policies. Taken together, these lessons haunt Latinos and Asian Americans in all avenues of law school—in the classroom, during casual conversations, or even in pointed accusations (as in Jenna's case). These forms of front-stage color-blind racialization do not necessarily engage race but are implicitly loaded with racist notions. These assumptions reflect American society's preoccupation with color blindness and may certainly affect how the law is applied to different racialized groups. Latino and Asian American law students come to recognize their deviance from the law school norm and anticipate further alienation once they begin working. However, color-blind racialization is not the sole culprit for this line of thinking. The next chapter examines the role of panethnic associations as a part of professional socialization. Latino and Asian American law students join panethnic organizations for various reasons, and even among copanethnics, these students still experience racialization, albeit on the backstage.

5

BLOCKING THE BACKSTAGE

*Panethnic Student Organizations
and Racialized Affiliations*

A hn Tran and I met during spring break, at a café near Western Elite. It was a chilly March day as I arrived at the café and found Ahn typing furiously on his laptop. As an editor of the *Law Journal of Asian Americans*,[1] he was using his reprieve from school to catch up on a backlog of manuscripts. He saw me as I approached, waved me over, and signaled for me to sit down. Ahn identifies as Chinese, although his family are refugees from Vietnam. In law school, he took an active role in the Society of Asian American Law Students (SAALS), serving as a board member when we first met. When I asked why he joined a panethnic organization, Ahn immediately responded with a giggle:

> Basically because the people there look like me [*laughs lightly*]. I started going to meetings, and also people in [SAALS] kind of reached out and said, "Oh, come join [SAALS] or come to a meeting!" So I think seeing that people were involved and that they are always trying to recruit—that's really helpful. And I joined the [Western Elite] technology law journal last year. But I definitely did not stay—not because the people were not nice, but I just didn't connect with them on a personal level. I kind of felt like an outsider in that journal. . . . I don't know if it's that important, but maybe it's subconscious. I think some people just don't try very hard to talk to you. One thing is that I didn't realize . . . how much beer that [white] Americans drink, which is something that [the students in

the technology journal] engaged in a lot last year, and it's something that I don't really do.

Ahn's explanation for joining SAALS is multifaceted. He desired a sense of personal familiarity, which led him to quit the technology journal when he was unable to relate to the members and their preferred social activity of drinking beer. He was, however, able to relate to the members of SAALS. Actively recruited to join the organization, he felt immediately at home among the SAALS members. It helped that the people in the organization "look[ed] like" him, and the organization was a refuge from the culturally and socially alienating environment of law school. In this way, panethnic organizations differ from other student groups formed through common legal interests or political affiliation. Panethnic organizations offer social support along with copanethnic familiarity.

The previous chapter examines how front-stage racialization—interactions with professors and peers, the environs of the law school classroom, and assumptions made about merit and admissions—signal the relevance of panethnicity. This chapter peeks behind the set to focus on backstage racialization, where benign actions such as joining panethnic organizations heighten racial awareness in law school. The purpose of the chapter is to examine the intergroup nature of racialization. Why do students such as Ahn join panethnic organizations? How does this environment foster panethnic allegiance? I first explore the forces that propel students to join panethnic organizations—namely, the search for cultural familiarity and shelter from the storm of law school socialization. I then examine how these organizations provide relief from the front stage of law school classrooms and peer interactions, while heightening panethnic allegiance backstage.

All law students often say that law school is the hardest thing they have ever done.[2] Law school veterans Scott Turow and Martha Kimes caution that law school requires mastering legal language, learning how to analyze cases and make coherent arguments, and adopting proper decorum (Kimes 2007; Turow 1977). Both authors vividly recall marked moments in law school that left a lasting impression, such as peers' or professors' commentary. Scott Turow quotes a professor characterizing law school:

> About now . . . law school begins to become more than just learning a language. You also have to start learning rules and you'll find pretty quickly that there's quite a premium placed on mastering the rules and knowing how to apply them. But in learning rules, don't feel as if you've got to forsake a sense of moral scrutiny. The law in almost all its phases is a reflection of competing value systems. Don't get your heads turned around to the point that you feel because you're

learning a rule, you've necessarily taken on the values that produced the rule in the first place. (Turow 1977, 89)

Turow's classmate Gina reacted viscerally to this. Turow describes Gina with friendly words: she had just graduated from Barnard and was "full of the bristle of New York City. She was big, feisty, outspoken, and glitteringly bright" (1977, 82). According to Turow, the professor's suggestion struck a chord: "'They're turning me into someone else,' she said, referring to our professors. 'They're making me different.' I told her that it was called education and she told me, quite rightly, that I was being flip. 'It's someone I don't *want* to be,' she said. 'Don't you get the feeling all the time that you're being indoctrinated?'" (82).

The students represented in this book, like Turow's Gina, are anxious about their legal education. They rely on family members for support, decompress with their law school friends, or frequent the gym to handle the stress of being indoctrinated into the profession. For Asian American and Latino law students, they must further contend with front-stage racialization that happens in classrooms and in interactions with professors and peers. Some Asian American and Latino law students find refuge in panethnic student organizations filled with their racial and ethnic compatriots.

Shelter from Deviance

Membership in panethnic organizations permits students to speak openly about cultural practices of others (both Asian American and Latino law students and their white peers) that they perceive as deviating from theirs. And when they do, they find their peers nodding in agreement. Copanethnic peers share cultural practices and will often commiserate with those who feel that camaraderie is lacking elsewhere in law school. Nancy Liang, a first-year, Chinese American student, related a story about the Korean American law student she was dating:

> He told me once, he said, "My mom goes to a fortuneteller once a year to see how this year is going to go." And my mom [does] the same thing! And I just think it's ridiculous. Not that I think it's bad, but I think it's funny. And he thinks it's funny too. And a lot of my Asian [American] friends—their parents do this too! And it's something we laugh at all together. But when I think of someone else of some other racial background saying, "That's weird. You're weird," I'd be offended. Stuff like that. Or the fact that we eat chicken feet.

Nancy finds camaraderie among copanethnics who are a part of the Western Elite SAALS. Copanethnics can relate to one another about their superstitious moms, about the cuisine served at home that diverges from the usual Western fare. But this is an in-group experience, and Nancy notes that she would not afford a non-Asian person the same liberty to make fun of those practices. A sense of proprietary poking fun is common among cultural groups. Aside from this cultural familiarity, other motivators drive Asian American and Latino law students to join panethnic law student organizations.

History of Affinity Groups

Affinity groups have played an important part in U.S. immigrant history, serving as a valuable resource to facilitate new immigrants' adaptation to their destination countries (Lamphere 1992). For example, Chinese immigrants in the late nineteenth and early twentieth centuries turned to their respective *huis* and *tongs*[3] for ancestral and community support upon arrival to the United States (Takaki 1998; Wong 2004), and Vietnamese immigrants continue to rely on community-based institutions to settle into their host country (Takaki 1998; Zhou and Bankston 1998). Central American immigrants to Southern California depend on coethnics to maneuver the multiethnic composition of the region (Hamilton and Chinchilla 2001), and transnational Mexicans turn to United States–based village-specific youth groups to help children adjust to life on both sides of the border (Smith 2006).

Panethnic law student organizations function similarly to these ethnic affinity groups and indirectly influence the experiences of Asian American and Latino law students. While each law school offers an array of professional organizations (such as the technology journal mentioned by Ahn), many identity groups cater to law students of color, including the Society of Asian American Law Students (SAALS) and the Society of Latino Law Students (SLLS). These student organizations are composed mostly of law students who are a part of minority groups that have incorporated at different rates into mainstream American society (Lee and Bean 2007). Nearly all of the respondents from Western Elite are members of SAALS or SLLS. In comparison, about 80 percent of Asian American students and 60 percent of Latino respondents from Private Metropolitan are members of either SAALS or SLLS.[4]

One might be tempted to assume that such high participation in these organizations continues from college, that these students joined panethnic organizations then and naturally continued their membership in law school. Some scholars of immigrant adaptation use college as a proxy for panethnic mixing, describing students as finding and aligning with persons of similar ethnic heritage or panethnic ancestry (Alba and Nee 2003; Kibria 2000; Rumbaut 1994).

TABLE 5.1: GROUP AFFILIATION AND EXTRACURRICULAR
ACTIVITIES IN COLLEGE

Affinity group	Top three extracurricular activities
Asian American	
Western Elite: 20%	Work
Private Metropolitan: 35%	Prelaw association
	Mentoring or volunteering
Latino/a	
Western Elite: 33%	Work
Private Metropolitan: 17%	Department-specific organizations
	Mentoring or volunteering
White	
—	Work
	Prelaw association
	Sports

But as shown in Table 5.1, the majority of Asian American and Latino respondents were not involved in affinity groups while in college. Of the Asian American students from Western Elite, 20 percent were involved in ethnic or panethnic organizations while in college, compared with 35 percent of Asian Americans from Private Metropolitan. The majority of Latino students at both schools were also not involved in affinity groups in college: 33 percent from Western Elite and 17 percent from Private Metropolitan were in ethnic or panethnic organizations in college.

Looking at the table, we further see that Asian American and white students joined schoolwide prelaw associations, whereas Latinos tended to participate in clubs that resonated with their majors of study. This is not to say that none of the Latino students were involved in prelaw associations or that Asian American and white students were not a part of department-specific clubs. All students were involved in extracurricular activities included on the three lists, as well as sororities or fraternities, student government, honors programs, performing arts (choirs, bands, orchestras), fine arts (photography, poetry, etc.), theater, and many more. But that prelaw associations were disproportionately represented among the three most cited extracurricular activities could signify a sense of familiarity and belonging for Asian American and white students or could represent the types of student activities available at the undergraduate institutions.

As mentioned earlier, the majority of the law students involved themselves in panethnic associations while in law school, citing three main reasons for doing so: (1) "it's like a second family," (2) "I wanted to be with people who shared my background and understand where I am coming from," and (3) "[panethnic associations] have excellent resources." On the surface, these reasons may not seem influential to students' law school tenures, and one can imagine students providing similar rationales for joining other organizations, whether based on political affiliation (e.g., the Western Elite Democrats or the Private Metropolitan Federalist Society), gender/sexuality (e.g., the Western Elite Women's Association or Private Metropolitan's Queer Students Association), or professional interest (e.g., the Western Elite Society for Sports and Entertainment Law or the Private Metropolitan Association for Intellectual Property Law). However, other forces besides simple affinity compel Asian American and Latino law students to join and remain in panethnic law student organizations: academic opportunities, refuge and support, and professional networks were all reflected in organization mission statements.

Aside from providing academic support and professional resources, connecting law students with community issues is central to the mission of panethnic law student organizations. Members of these organizations make concerted efforts to contact prospective members (i.e., copanethnics) before, during, and after the beginning of the academic year. They specifically target copanethnics. For SAALS, this may mean getting in touch with Chinese, Korean, Pakistani, or mixed-race (Asian and white) students, among others. For SLLS, the students contacted may be Mexican, Salvadoran, Argentinian, and from mixed-race ancestry, among others. Members of respective student organizations then reach out to prospective members through organized activities or informal conversations. These efforts, while casual, bring together students of varying ethnic backgrounds under one panethnic umbrella. Immediate friendships are offered to law students as they navigate a new set of rules and expectations. They can also safely gossip about professors and talk freely about assignments among familiar faces.

We Are Family: Finding Refuge in Law School

Why *do* Asian American and Latino law students choose to join panethnic student organizations? Unequivocally, students expressed a desire to associate with those of their own racial or cultural background in a search for familiarity and comfort. Debbie Kwan, a second-year, Chinese American student at Western Elite, compared law school to war—one wants a "war buddy, someone who understands you. We're in the foxhole together, so you want to have a trustworthy war buddy." Debbie aspires to a future in international business law, so she initially joined Western Elite's *Journal of Business Law*. However, she quickly abandoned that endeavor because she got a "sorority feel" from the organization. When asked to elaborate, Debbie simply said that the organization was all white members and she did not feel comfortable. Instead, she chose to join the *Journal of Asian American Law* and SAALS, where she found some great "war buddies" with whom she could not only take classes and study but also socialize when she needed a break from law school.

Daniel Rincón, a third-year, Mexican American student, did not know what to expect in law school and joined the only organization, SLLS, that seemed familiar upon arriving at Western Elite. He explained:

> I was totally confused [about] what was going to happen [in law school]. So I needed someone who has a similar background as mine [and] was going to be here and tell me what they went through and how they got through it. I received good advice from a lot of people. . . . [Other students in SLLS] shared the bad and the good . . . and how to make sure to take advantage of the good. There's a lot of sacrifices that go on in law school, [and] they kind of cope with those situations and how to get through them and make the best of it. . . . Having someone with a similar background as yours—they will understand where you're coming from.

Daniel is from the Midwest, and chose to attend Western Elite over Columbia Law because he has family near the law school. Given his apprehension about law school, he surmised it wise to be near family for support. He used this same logic to join SLLS—familiarity, he reasoned, would help him succeed in law school. The organization helped link Daniel to more advanced Latino students who served as mentors, helping him understand how to read casebooks and study for exams. The advanced students were regarded as trailblazers for Latino students in the legal profession.

Belonging to panethnic organizations does not guarantee successful law school completion, but it does provide a safe place within a context that often feels hostile to students of color (Moore 2008). Aside from support and services, Asian American and Latino law students rely on these organizations for mentorship and assistance navigating law school, since most of them lack attorney role models. In fact, the parents of only three Asian American and Latino respondents held JD degrees.[5]

SAALS and SLLS at both law schools offer mentor-mentee programs that match second- and third-year students with incoming first-year students to provide support and guidance. Even if this relationship does not survive their entire law school tenure, most students remember their assigned mentor and greatly appreciate the help offered to ease them into law school. Luis Pérez, a second-year student at Western Elite of Salvadoran and Mexican descent, reflected on the SLLS mentor-mentee program:

> There aren't that many people of color in law school, and so I think it's pretty common for people of color to feel more comfortable with other people of color. And so those 2Ls and 3Ls,[6] they helped me a

lot, whether just talking about classes, studying strategies, summer work advice. And so, mentors-friends-mentors. And I think that's one of the beauties of [SLLS]. We all care, and we all try to help each other. We're all in the same classes, we all compete for the same jobs, but it doesn't matter. We're all friends, and we're all trying to support each other. It's a beauty.

In the same vein, Whitney Hong, a second-year, Chinese American law student at Private Metropolitan, told me how her mentor-friend served as a nonjudgmental ear: "There is one [student] who is a 3L right now, and he's always just available. We'll talk; he'll talk to me. Like when we're stressed, we'll go out. He'll smoke a cigarette; I'll drink some coffee. And we'll just rant on about our day. Things like that." To have someone available to listen can be important to maintain a positive outlook on law school. Some second- and third-year law students even remain in contact with mentors who have transitioned to being practicing attorneys. The mentorships can thus also serve as a gateway into the real world of law.

One Stop Shop: Professional, Academic, and Social Support

Organizations like SAALS and SLLS feed into professional organizations such as the National Asian Pacific American Bar Association or the Hispanic National Bar Association. Law students often use panethnic groups in law school instrumentally by networking, thereby building their social and human capital. SAALS and SLLS provide many opportunities for their members to interact with alumni and other practicing attorneys. Alumni events, such as formal panels, law firm receptions, and informal mentor-mentee activities, introduce members to the profession. Aside from professional networking opportunities, panethnic student organizations also provide academic support, such as archived class outlines and notes, advice on which professors to take or avoid, or general survival tips for how to navigate law school. And given the inherently social nature of these associations, there is no lack of happy hours, soccer games, or even weekend retreats.

The functions of these organizations differ between Western Elite and Private Metropolitan. SAALS and SLLS at Private Metropolitan are extracurricular in the truest sense of the word: students do not report strong allegiances to the organizations, though they do attend occasional meetings, review sessions, and panel discussions. In contrast, members in SAALS and SLLS at Western Elite see each other daily, frequently eat meals together, engage in social activities, and study together. Some even room together.

Why the divergent attitudes toward panethnic organizations between the two schools? There are two possible explanations. First, the students at Private Metropolitan are typically older than their Western Elite counterparts.

Most Private Metropolitan students worked in the real world between college and law school and join panethnic organizations for the practical purpose of networking. Second, students at Private Metropolitan may also have less time to incorporate panethnic organizations into their lives. Most of them work or take on internships (paid and unpaid) to boost their legal skills and to network for their future careers. The culture at Western Elite is different. Save for the advanced third- and second-year students who may intern for credit during the school year, most of the law students postpone such work opportunities until the summer break. Thus, the sole responsibility of Western Elite students is to attend classes—this likely frees them up to invest more time, energy, and commitment to their panethnic organizations.

Professional networking opportunities abound for students involved in SAALS and SLLS. For one, law firms cosponsor events with these organizations to recruit minority associates. Firm-sponsored events range from small meet-and-greet hors d'oeuvre hours to events focused on providing interview and résumé tips. Take, for example, a big law firm's invitation to Western Elite's SLLS members for an all-day résumé and cover-letter writing workshop. The attorney who organized the event is a Western Elite SLLS alumnus who coordinated the workshop with his office and Western Elite SLLS board members. The students were fed lunch in addition to receiving feedback on their résumés, cover letters, and interview techniques. An ethnic lawyer association based in the same city as Private Metropolitan likewise sponsored an event for new Private Metropolitan students held at the local office of a large firm. Andréa Rodriguez, a second-year student of Guatemalan and Mexican heritage from Private Metropolitan, reflected on such opportunities:

> I've noticed lately we've [at SLLS] been trying to do a lot of law firm mixers, and they're mostly with Hispanic judges or lawyers. And I feel like that's important because the more and more that I meet people of my [panethnic] background in this profession, I feel like they'd be willing to help me. And not that other people wouldn't. But I feel that there's more of an unspoken bond. . . . I think that's probably one of the things that I'm going to gain by being a part of the organization.

The kind of professional events referred to by Andréa link Asian American and Latino attorneys with Asian American and Latino law students. The opportunity to meet copanethnics who survived law school and are bona fide attorneys provides students with role models and a status to which to aspire. Further, as Andréa remarks, there is an "unspoken bond" for Latinos—in this instance, to assist others from similar backgrounds, thus creating networks for employment prospects.

Aside from professional support, SAALS and SLLS also offer academic services to their members. An outline bank and exam review sessions are perhaps the second reasons (followed by panethnic familiarity) mentioned by students when I asked why they joined panethnic student organizations. Take, for example, Jillian Wong, a Chinese American, third-year student who talked about joining Private Metropolitan's SAALS: "I heard [SAALS] provided good review sessions on midterms and reviews for midterms and finals for 1Ls. And they gave out good outlines." Final exam assessments are overwhelmingly used to determine students' course grades, which directly impact job opportunities. Exam grades also affect how students perceive their own abilities as aspiring attorneys. Outlines, some exceeding a hundred pages, consist of notes about topics, cases, and rulings. Students who build a course outline from scratch spend a considerable portion of their semester at it. Members in panethnic organizations share their course outlines and notes with one another, and the organizations meticulously manage outline banks to ensure that each course and professor is represented, often with multiple versions.

Consider the contents of a post on the Western Elite SAALS e-mail list at the beginning of the semester in preparation for final exams:

Dear 1Ls, 2Ls, 3Ls,

Please send me your outlines from the past semester so I can update the [SAALS] outline bank! Any and all outlines are welcome—we are in particular need of outlines for 2L/3L classes. Please provide information on: (1) Class, (2) Professor, and (3) Semester for each of the outlines—you can include this information in the email to me if it is not included in the outline. Please feel free to put any disclaimers on the outlines if you feel the need to do so.

Thank you to everyone who sent me outlines last semester! I know they were a great help to everyone :)

[SAALS board member]

This e-mail soliciting outlines from all courses underscored the nature of academic support within panethnic organizations. Law students mentioned the availability of outlines and the benefit of studying from them as a major factor shaping their decision to join panethnic organizations. In the words of Sara Espinol, a first-year, Colombian American law student, "They'll [SLLS] just give you outlines, and if you have questions about professors or classes, they'll all help you!" In this way, student organizations help forward the academic success of their members.

Panethnic student organizations also provide review sessions where advanced students share their trials and tribulations with specific courses and professors. SAALS and SLLS at both schools, but primarily Private

Metropolitan, hold comprehensive exam review sessions toward the end of each semester. These review sessions are led by students who have excelled in certain subjects or served as teaching assistants (TAs) for a particular professor of a specific course. These review sessions are all-day affairs complete with lunch and intermission. An example review session agenda that I made by merging one from Private Metropolitan's SAALS and one from SLLS looks like this:

Saturday, April 23rd
CONTRACTS: 1:30–3:30 P.M.
Professor Johnson—Room 30 (led by two former TAs)
Professor Meng—Room 16 (led by one former TA)
Professor Mendez's Contracts review will be held Thursday, April 21, at 4:30–6:15 in Room 11

Sunday, April 24th
CIVIL PROCEDURE: 10:00 A.M.–12:00 P.M.
Professors Ellis and Baldwin—Room 11 (led by one former TA)
Professor Taylor—Room 16 (led by one former TA)
Professor Granger—Room 33 (led by one former TA)
Lunch: 12:00–1:30 P.M., Room 30
PROPERTY: 1:30–3:30 P.M.
Professor Lariety—Room 11 (led by one former TA)
Professor Lowenstein—Room 16 (led by two former TAs)
Professors Pool and Harrison—Room 33 (led by one former TA)

Advanced and first-year students must coordinate to put on review sessions. Advanced students spend considerable time consulting the academic calendar, finding appropriate students to lead the review sessions, ordering food, and reserving classroom space.

Panethnic organizations also attract students of other racialized groups because of these academic services. Outline banks and study sessions permit members to prepare for the successful completion of exams. As Rose Fong, a third-year, Chinese American student at Private Metropolitan, exclaimed, "[SAALS]'s great! They have really good reviews and a lot of good support. They're very open to offering their services to, also, non-Asian students. There are a few Caucasian people who are active members of SAALS [giving] academic advice around the 1L reviews."

Another service provided by these panethnic organizations is the circulation of course materials. Because law books are expensive, SAALS and SLLS at both schools operate two distinct programs to help their members acquire books: book exchanges and organization libraries. Book exchanges allow students to swap books with each other, thus avoiding the cost of purchasing new books. So if student A took criminal law with Professor James during fall semester and student B will take criminal law with the same professor, or with a different professor who is using the same books, during winter semester, student B can borrow the books from student A. At the end of winter semester, student B returns the books to student A. In other instances, students may sell their books instead of lending them to peers.

The panethnic organizations also operate libraries that function a little differently than book exchanges. Current and former law students donate books they no longer need to a depository—this could be a locked locker in the law school (to which members know the code) or a bookshelf in an organization office. The organizations encourage students to borrow books on an honor system from the libraries so long as they return them. Book exchanges and libraries alleviate some of the financial stress of law school.

Asian American and Latino law students also join panethnic organizations to socialize with other law students. Organizational leaders create opportunities for members to unwind from reading, note taking, and examinations. Planned social events include happy hours, karaoke, and soccer games. Sometimes social activities are combined with other organizations. For example, the Private Metropolitan SAALS and SLLS sponsor joint happy hours where members can interact and spend time together away from the confines of the law school.

While the SAALS and the SLLS at both law schools provide opportunities for socializing, the types of activities vary somewhat. The most obvious example is the annual retreats hosted by the organizations at Western Elite (Private Metropolitan did not host retreats). Retreat planning happens at the beginning of each school year and is carried out by a planning committee led by advanced students. Consider this e-mail, edited to preserve anonymity, from the Western Elite SAALS planning committee to its membership following spring break:

> Welcome back, we hope everyone had a fabulous break!! The ~Annual [SAALS] Retreat~ is in [a recreational area] this year and we have lodging all ready to go for the weekend of March 4–6. There will be indoor and outdoor activities, bbq, socializing, and even karaoke! Those of you who choose not to take part in outdoor activities will have plenty to do at the house, so plan for a weekend of fun.

An SLLS e-mail about their retreat included not only an agenda but also pictures:

> Tentative Agenda
> Friday:

> Vans and cars leave at different times. Arrival at destination and
> room setup. Dinner followed by Karaoke/Poker/other activities.
> Saturday:
> Vans and cars leave for outdoor recreation. Breakfast, lunch and din-
> ner provided.
> Evening entertainment
> Sunday:
> Clean up and depart.
> Let me know if you have any questions, otherwise get ready for
> the . . . fun, FUN, FUN!!!

These social activities, especially retreats where students can temporarily forget about law school responsibilities, allow members to further bond with one another as law students and as copanethnics. Fred Ngo, a Chinese-Vietnamese American whom we met in Chapter 1, noted how being a member of Western Elite's SAALS is a social experience that allows him to feel that he is a part of a community: "I think as most people understand it, [SAALS] is almost exclusively a social organization. And to the extent that socializing with your peers and your friends and building a sense of community at your law school is important, I think, yeah. Korean barbecue is important, right?" Fred might be right that many students' impetus to join panethnic organizations may be social. As we have seen here, SAALS and SLLS members at Western Elite also benefit from professional networking and academic support. This Western Elite experience contrasts with that of students at Private Metropolitan, where students relate that they joined panethnic organizations for professional development reasons.

Reflecting the broader culture of the lower-tiered law school, Private Metropolitan students focus on learning how to become attorneys (Mertz 2007). In law school they are inundated with messages about the importance of networking and establishing professional relationships with future colleagues. Unlike respondents from Western Elite, members of SAALS and SLLS at Private Metropolitan join panethnic organizations primarily for academic and professional reasons, not social reasons. For example, within Private Metropolitan, the SAALS is well known for their exam review workshops. As discussed previously, the Private Metropolitan SAALS leadership meticulously plans review sessions for each group of first-year members. My field notes from a September 8, 2010, SAALS meeting capture the dedication of this organization to panethnic student success:

> Jillian shares that her role (and that of the other three academic di-
> rectors) is to guide the 1Ls on what they should be doing. SAALS
> will provide a workshop on how to outline later in the semester.
> They also help students prepare for exams by providing substantive

reviews before midterms and finals. She knows that the 1L midterms are scheduled for [mid-October], so [SAALS] is sponsoring review sessions [in early October]. The review sessions are tailored to each professor's class and their class outlines. During their reviews, they teach in the professor's style and provide review topics for the students. They have sample questions from old practice exams (that are available online), and they provide multiple-choice questions that are similar to each professor's actual exams. The reviews give students a full picture of which topics to focus on before the exam. Also, [SAALS] brings in, as teachers, students who had the professors (receiving highest honors in the class) or had been the professors' TAs. Jillian continues to share that [SAALS] has put together a 1L survival crash course this year, which will take place on 9/14 from 12–1. The focus is to get students on the right track so that they are thinking about what they should be doing to prepare for the rest of their first year. Current students will be there to answer questions about necessary supplements for classes, study groups, etc.

Private Metropolitan's SAALS highlights its academic services, evidenced by the presence of four academic advisors who serve in the organization's leadership.[7] In addition to the outlines and exam reviews, the organization offers a crash course for first-year students to assist their transition to being law students. Rose Fong, the Chinese American student mentioned earlier, explained how she has benefited professionally as an SAALS member: "I think in a way, there is a connection because [SAALS] is very proactive in Asian community events. [The organization is] sort of linking up not only alumni from [Private Metropolitan] but Asian lawyers in the [area to serve] as mentors to [Private Metropolitan SAALS] students."

Although law students join panethnic organizations for professional and academic reasons, they also give back to panethnic communities in tangible ways—whether by volunteering at food banks, staffing particular cultural centers' events, or tutoring low-income youth, to name just a few options. I was struck by the enormous amount of time these students managed to devote to community service. One particular example is the commitment of Private Metropolitan SAALS members who regularly tutor low-income Chinese children residing in an ethnic enclave. Some of the law student volunteers are of Chinese ancestry, but many are not. They are Filipino, Japanese, Korean, and South Asian. In ways such as this, copanethnic activism and the conflation of ethnicities further binds members of racialized umbrella groups.

We have now seen how panethnic student organizations at both law schools are more than just social clubs. While these groups do promote social events, such as Korean barbeque dinners or soccer games, they also provide academic guidance and opportunities to network with copanethnic attorneys, in addition to participating in community service. In this way, these organizations become an intrinsic part of Asian American and Latino law students' socialization into the profession. Aside from professional, academic, and social support, panethnic student organizations also serve another purpose: they provide a safe space. Whether during meetings, in organization offices, or during social events, these organizations offer shelter for Asian American and Latino law students to discuss their experiences as racial minorities in law school.

A Home Away from Home: Panethnic Organizations as Safe Spaces

Attending law school can be an isolating experience, prompting students to look for on-campus support. As previously explained, many Asian American and Latino law students consider their respective panethnic organizations to be their second families. And like a familial support system, members of SAALS and SLLS turn to one another for help and guidance when confronting adversity. When these students feel marginalized by interactions with other law students or law professors or in course discussions, as mentioned in Chapter 4, they seek out their SAALS and SLLS friends to vent and blow off steam. This opportunity arises when members of the organizations use the informal portion of meeting times to discuss their discontents and frustrations.

As an example, the Western Elite SLLS held a final meeting before the end of the 2009 fall semester and, because it was the final meeting, the co-chairs did not provide a set agenda. Students were scattered in groups of three to five in a large lecture hall, eating, laughing, and talking about law school and non–law school topics. While I was observing this low-key and friendly socializing, I noticed Raquel Cortez, a first-year student, storm through the lecture hall doors, scan the room, and quickly walk to and sit down among a group of first- and second-year students (who happened to be seated two rows in front of me). Raquel looked very unhappy. I strained to listen to the conversation and heard snippets that included, "white guy," "race is a predictor of success," and "ridiculous." The others looked at her sympathetically, shaking their heads. Marco, the only man in the group, counseled her to not let the incident bother her so much and that it was not worth her time or energy to dwell on it.

Raquel's entrance into the meeting reminded me of the numerous times when I would fling open the front door, storm into my childhood home, and complain to my mother about something, such as a squabble with a friend at school or a teacher giving me a lower grade than I felt I deserved. While my mom often turned the blame on me (i.e., I should not have provoked the fight, I should have worked harder on the assignment), Raquel's friends in

SLLS were sympathetic but also tempered in their responses. Marco suggested that these types of incidents happen all the time in law school and that Raquel should just learn to let it go. Perhaps what was most striking about the interaction, however, was seeing that Raquel felt comfortable enough to complain to her friends at an SLLS meeting in the same way that I did in my childhood home. Raquel's behavior underscores how panethnic organizations create a space where students feel comfortable sharing their frustrations.

Three months later I interviewed Raquel and asked her to talk about the incident she shared with her peers that day. She sighed, rolled her eyes, and told me the following: She was in torts class, and the professor presented a hypothetical case involving a child who was disabled and could not work for the rest of her life. The professor then explained that the court reached its damages calculation by assessing the probable future employment earnings based on the employment statistics of the child's neighborhood. Raquel did not agree with this method and told the professor and class that she found the ruling to be unethical because people's eventual careers may not necessarily reflect the environments in which they were raised. In particular, Raquel was thinking about the many Latinos in law school who, after graduation, will be earning four or more times the amount their parents made. She suggested that the court's unfair ruling would be more ethical if everyone received damages based on a set formula that did not differentiate on the basis of class or residence. In reply, a white student commented that the odds were against some people breaking out of the environment where they grew up. To Raquel, this student's comment implicitly suggested that not all people are of equal worth and that it is acceptable to form judgments based on an individual's income or background.

Raquel is of mixed Salvadoran and white ancestry and identifies as Latina. She grew up in a lower-middle-class neighborhood, but her frustration stretches beyond her personal experience: many of her peers (especially peers of color) are the first in their families to graduate from college. Raquel felt personally attacked by the white student's remark. That comment, coupled with her background, led her to view her classroom as a hostile place. After speaking with her friends from SLLS, Raquel reported that she now understood comments like these to be par for the course for students of color in law school and acknowledged that she needs to learn how to brush them off in order to survive and succeed.

Raquel's story is one of many in which white students' or professors' comments and attitudes made the nonwhite students feel like outsiders in law school. Thus, they sought shelter among copanethnics, and many also retooled how they may use their law degrees (a topic I discuss in Chapters 6 and 7). The presence of panethnic organizations helps temper some of the negative interactions in law school hallways and classrooms.

SLLS provides a safe space for members like Raquel to voice their frustrations about being rendered outsiders. James E. Blackwell argues that black professionals are "outsiders" in their respective fields because there were so few of them before the more tolerant educational admissions policies of the 1960s and 1970s. Becoming "mainstream[ed]" as "outsiders" can be a considerably trying process, as each individual must balance her or his cultural history, racial position in society, and budding professional identities (Blackwell 1987). To have the support of what feels like a second family during this tumultuous time lightens the burden.

Being part of a law school "family" provides not only a safe space to decompress about negative interactions but also financial assistance—once again, not unlike the relations within families. During interviews with Asian American students at Western Elite, several of them said they were involved in SAALS because they needed a "law school family" and the organization served that purpose. Many students pointed to one particular incident to illustrate how organization members are, in fact, like a family: An SAALS member's car was broken into shortly after the start of the 2010 spring semester, and the student's law books and laptop were stolen. When SAALS members heard about this incident, within days they pooled together enough money to buy a new laptop for the unfortunate student. Yuan Zhang, a third-year law student who joined SAALS only because a friend recruited him, described SAALS as a community and used this particular incident to illustrate his point. He said, "One girl had her car broken into and had her laptop stolen and all her books. Then, we bought her a new laptop. . . . I mean a bunch of us in [SAALS]. You know, it's an extreme example, but . . . without the [SAALS] structure that would not have happened."

This emotional and financial support allows members to feel as if they are a part of a true family. Their peers are more than willing to pool time, energy, and resources to ensure, in this case, that a member does not lack the essential laptop. Panethnic student organizations further resemble family through their dedication to their members. Collegiality and familiarity thus support a sense of panethnic cohesiveness.

A Special Place for Mixed-Race Panethnics

Among my respondents were eight mixed-race law students. Their experiences should not be dismissed. They are Asian and white or Latino and white; one person is of Latino and Asian ancestry. All but one of them identified with their nonwhite lineage. These mixed-race respondents were referred to me through peers or expressed interest in this project when I made announcements during student organization or class meetings. They joined panethnic organizations because they felt a sense of connection to their nonwhite culture and wanted to be among other law students who understood their background. Take, for example, Kurt Waters, a third-year student at Western Elite. Kurt is Taiwanese and white. The majority of his friends in law school are Asian American, likely because he joined SAALS. He says, "Joining [SAALS], I made a lot of friends who were Asian [American]. . . . [Y]ou also have that shared cultural background sometimes with Asian [American] friends as opposed to white friends or Hispanic friends. So that's another layer to bond and share experiences."

Similarly, Jocelyn Brady, a second-year law student at Western Elite, half Korean and half white, describes both cultural and social advantages of belonging to a panethnic student organization: "There are a lot of social advantages. But there are of course cultural advantages. So when we get together and we go have dinner, where do we go? We go to a Korean barbecue restaurant, right? As opposed to whatever. So you have cultural experiences, shared cultural experiences, that you get to share with other people." Both Jocelyn and Kurt used their nonwhite ethnic affiliation to facilitate entrance into SAALS. They made friends through panethnic kinship and cultural knowledge.

Interestingly, however, while mixed-race law students at Western Elite involve themselves in panethnic organizations for cultural reasons, mixed-race law students at Private Metropolitan do not. Mixed-race students at Western Elite primarily view SAALS and SLLS as entities for socializing and making friends, while mixed-race students from Private Metropolitan focus on professional development. Take, for example, Brandon Shi, a second-year student of Chinese and white heritage who is active in SAALS:

> I joined because a friend of mine said, "Hey, you should join this." But I stayed in and stayed active because they are a well-run organization that suited my needs and my interests very well. I have no care at all about that they're the Asian group. I don't care. They're the best run, they're the best organized, they put together the best events. And because they provide a lot to me, I want to provide a lot to them. So that's how I got in and why I stayed active.

Unlike Jocelyn and Kurt, Brandon does not mention culture, familiarity, or friendships (although he does identify as Asian American and volunteered to be interviewed for this project). His involvement in SAALS is strategic and he was active in the organization because he felt that he must reciprocate for the help that the organization had provided him. It should be noted, however, that while Jocelyn and Kurt are second-generation immigrants through their nonwhite parents, Brandon is third-generation and thus may exercise his Chinese ethnicity in a more symbolic manner. Jocelyn and Kurt grew up surrounded by their respective ethnic languages and eating ethnic foods, whereas Brandon did not. Being surrounded by ethnic language and foods may heighten some mixed-race individuals' sense of ethnic allegiance.

Mixed-race law students like Brandon appear to exercise a more arm's-length attachment to their nonwhite ethnicities while involved in panethnic student organizations. Scholars of immigrant assimilation refer to this as symbolic ethnicity, as discussed in the Introduction (Alba 1985, 2005; Gans 1979; Waters 1990). The belief that intermarriage would lead to successful assimilation is predicated on European Americans' experiences. Over time, ethnic allegiances become symbolic or optional. Mary Waters defines contemporary European identities among white Americans as

> something that does not affect much in everyday life. It does not, for the most part, limit choice of marriage partner (except almost in all cases to exclude non-whites). It does not determine where you will live, who your friends will be, what job you will have, or whether you will be subject to discrimination. It matters only in voluntary ways—in celebrating holidays with a special twist, cooking a special ethnic meal (or at least calling a meal by a special ethnic name), remembering a special phrase or two in a foreign language. (1990, 147)

White Americans can choose to assert their ethnicities to honor ancestry or demonstrate cultural knowledge. Recent scholarship on the assimilation trajectories of new immigrants has suggested that the white racial boundary is expanding yet again—this time to include Asian Americans and Latinos (Lee and Bean 2010). Given increases in interracial white-Asian and white-Latino marriages and social mobility among Asian and Latino immigrants, some scholars argue that a twenty-first-century color line now separates nonblack Americans from those who are black (Lee and Bean 2004, 2007).

But if ethnicity no longer matters for Asian Americans and Latinos and mixed-race Asian Americans and Latinos are becoming white, then mixed-race respondents would still likely join panethnic student organizations for purely symbolic reasons. And indeed, the reasons themselves for joining might change over time. Symbolism might provide the initial motivation for mixed-race individuals to become a part of these organizations, but students' eventual panethnic allegiance suggests that there may be more to the story. It appears that mixed-race Asian American–white and Latino-white law students are *racialized* and tracked, through formal and informal channels, into panethnic organizations. The context of law school, as a historically white institution, may propel these students to identify, if only for the moment, with their nonwhite ancestry. While this identification may not necessarily organize mixed-race students' lives, at a minimum they are cognizant of their underrepresentation as individuals of color in the legal profession.

Backstage Racialization

As we have seen, panethnic student organizations provide academic support, professional resources, and a safe haven from racial marginalization in law school. The overwhelming majority of Asian American and Latino respondents were not involved in affinity groups while in college, but law school changed that. Most Asian American and Latino students described being recruited to join panethnic organizations during law school orientation weekend or before even stepping foot on campus. Maisy Sandoval, a second-year, Chicana student at Western Elite, along with several other women law students of color, phoned every single woman of color accepted to the 2013 graduating class.[8] Maisy believes it important to bolster the presence of women of color at her law school, and she helps do so by volunteering her time and extending a friendly welcome.

While this friendly gesture may be perceived as a mere recruitment tactic, many Asian American and Latino students express commitment to promoting their panethnic group's presence at their law schools. SAALS and SLLS members take time out of their busy schedules to personally welcome newly accepted students. Consider this announcement sent through the Western Elite's SAALS e-mail list before the law school's admissions weekend:

> There are around 80 [Asian American] admits that we would personally like to reach out to in order to answer questions and provide general information on life [at Western Elite]. It's a very rewarding process and is a great way of building relationships with the incoming 1Ls before school starts up again. Please email me back if you can help by this Friday; you would have to call no more than 5 people between now and the week we get back from Spring Break.

Normally, e-mails sent through the list seeking volunteers for events are followed by several reminder e-mails. This e-mail had no reminders, which suggests SAALS members readily stepped up to call new admits.

In addition to reaching out to Asian Americans and Latinos accepted to Western Elite by calling them personally, current students also house prospective students. Current SAALS and SLLS members recalled staying with advanced law students when they visited the law school and reported that the experience instilled an immediate and welcome sense of familiarity. For example, during candidate speeches in elections for the following year's SLLS recruitment coordinators, Tia, a first-year student, spoke about her own recruitment weekend and how it was instrumental to her decision to attend Western Elite. Tia described being sick during recruitment weekend, and her two hosts from SLLS brought her tea and made sure she was comfortable in their home. Moreover, since Tia was going to be moving from the East Coast to attend Western Elite, she was apprehensive about leaving behind her family. But her hosts' considerate actions during recruitment weekend helped her make that leap by making her feel as if she had already found a second family. After that, Tia herself hosted students during recruitment weekend and expressed a desire to reach out to the Latino undergraduate population to encourage them to consider Western Elite for law school. Stories such as Tia's were shared by a number of students of color at both Private Metropolitan and Western Elite.

It is important to note that Western Elite students appear to have access to, and a vested interest in, the recruitment of panethnic students. The student organizations at Private Metropolitan do not recruit as heavily after admissions, perhaps because they are a lower-ranked law school and do not have comparable incentives to offer those who are admitted. For example, they do not phone prospective students, and they do not host recruitment weekends. Even so, student leaders at Private Metropolitan rally the troops at the beginning of the semester and diligently recruit through word of mouth or at schoolwide organization events to expand their law school families.

The "law school family" exists because of panethnic identification but serves as a racializing tool. By the third year of law school, most students are no longer actively involved in SAALS or SLLS, but they do remain on e-mail lists, and the majority serve as mentors for incoming first-year students in addition to attending special meetings or events. Most law students, regardless of race, become less involved by their third year as they look toward the bar exam and their budding careers.[9] Margaret Cha, a third-year, Korean American law student from Private Metropolitan, explained that she was an active member of SAALS during her first two years of law school because the organization hosted the best review sessions and maintained an informative outline bank. Margaret said, "I haven't really been involved [this year]. I did some stuff first year and second year, but I don't really go anymore. . . . I'm just studying now and keeping my head in the books." Not unlike other third-year law students, Margaret's focus shifted to preparing for the bar exam.

Asian American and Latino law students appear to have cultivated intertwined racial and professional identities by their third year in law school. Involvement in panethnic organizations instills and reinforces a racialized professional identity for these law students on the backstage. Beyond professional affinity groups such as the National Asian Pacific American Bar Association or the Hispanic National Bar Association, the law students who elect to work for large firms are provided opportunities to network with other attorneys of color.[10] What began in law school as seeking a refuge from a color-blind agenda and in unknown terrains of law, legalese, and white, upper-middle-class legal culture seems to shift over time to become an important aspect of a racialized professional identity.[11]

Panethnic organizations do not exist with the intent to racialize law students of color. SAALS and SLLS mission statements at both schools highlight that the organizations exist to provide academic and social support for law students. Recruitment and retention are key concerns for these student groups, and racialization emerges as an unanticipated outcome. As Mario Small demonstrates in his study on mothers who enroll their children in child-care centers, the social networks, friendships, and resources gleaned by the mothers are "unanticipated gains." Small writes, "A network or group is a source of support for an individual because the group feels solidarity or because informal norms encourage everyone to give to others. . . . Through either mechanism, the social capital to which an actor has access is said to result from informal dynamics" (2009, 117). In a similar way, the increasing racial or panethnic identification (or acknowledgment) is an unanticipated gain for Asian American and Latino law students who join identity groups to seek refuge, make friends, and reap the benefits of professional networks and academic resources.

This chapter explores the mechanisms of backstage racialization in law school through the medium of panethnic student organizations. On the front stage, Asian American and Latino law students are socialized by professors and through coursework to become emotionally neutral (i.e., exhibiting emotions that follow white, masculine feeling rules) attorneys; at the same time, they find themselves continually reminded of their race and immigrant background (see Chapter 4). They often find classrooms to be hostile spaces that disregard analysis of race and gender. To escape this environment and find refuge, they turn to their peers in panethnic student organizations. SAALS and SLLS provide social, academic, and professional support for students who belong to the respective racialized groups. Consequently, Asian American and Latino students' social networks in and out of law school elevate the value and significance of their respective racialized identities. In this way, the holistic experience of law school unintentionally cultivates a *racialized* professional identity for Asian American and Latino law students. The next chapter explores how that racialized identity works for students who aspire to a race-neutral career track: the law firm.

6

BETWEEN "MARTYR" AND "SELLOUT"

*Managing Professional and
(Pan)Ethnic Identities*

On a sunny spring afternoon, I met Susan de Castro, a third-year law student at Western Elite. We talked about her experiences in law school while sipping iced teas in a campus courtyard. Susan was finishing her last year of law school and appeared thrilled at the prospect of working at the immigration court in San Juan, Puerto Rico. She speaks fluent Spanish and spent a few years before law school working with Latino communities in Washington, D.C. Susan thought her new job in Puerto Rico would be ideal because she could employ her linguistic and legal expertise. Even more, it satisfied her desire to contribute to what she calls her "community." Yet Susan, a Filipina, also reflected on the pros and cons of students of color not placing themselves in more mainstream positions, in particular law firms:

> I think sometimes when you're a person of color in law school, you get a little pigeonholed. Because people are like, "Oh, you probably want to do the people-of-color thing. You probably want to do social justice work. Oh, your parents are immigrants? You probably want to do immigrant-related stuff. I think I'm doing [immigration] because it's meaningful to me. But I think it's easy to feel like I have to do that. I have to stand up for my community because I'm the only one here like that. And in some ways, I think that it perpetuates the white male dominant culture because you're putting yourself into working for your communities rather than trying to go work at a

big law firm. Or try to go work for, like, the antitrust division. You know, I just feel like, for students of color, they feel like they have to do public interest things because they feel like they have to be the martyrs or something.

Susan went on to speak about the standard legal culture that focuses on professional identity assimilation:

> This corporate culture of law school—I mean, come on! [The on-campus interview program] happens like the second week of school, so as a 1L, the first thing you're introduced to is law firm recruiting. Everyone's getting suited up and playing this sort of networking game; obviously, most of the lawyers who come talk to you that have some kind of power in the firms are white males. I think you just kind of have to learn how to play in this culture. I think I know how to play into that culture; I think I learned that from [working on Capitol] Hill; I think I learned that from going to a school like [my elite private college]. I think that I learned how to act white, and I think I know how to not be threatening to people as a person of color who is attuned to person-of-color issues. But I think you have to play that. I think you have to act white a little bit in order to get by.

What does it mean to "act white?" Who are these students who feel pressure to be "martyrs"? Susan described a sense of in-betweenness, of knowing how to play the game, but also not wanting to become a martyr. She feels that she put in her time in corporate America before law school, and she decided to become an attorney precisely to work on immigration issues. No one can accuse her of acting white, because she will be working on immigration concerns in Puerto Rico.

How do Latino and Asian American law students simultaneously demonstrate their commitment to becoming attorneys *and* their devotion to their (pan)ethnic communities? These students learn how to properly assume the role of attorneys and contend with co(pan)ethnic allegiance by virtue of being nonwhite. While the previous chapter showed how panethnic student organizations are significant for law school socialization, this chapter finds students negotiating dueling roles. I build on the previous chapter by examining how identities matter alongside professional socialization. In what follows, I introduce a repertoire of strategies used by students to manage their professional and (pan)ethnic identities. Through this endeavor, we learn that while some students are marginally committed to a (pan)ethnic identity, others conceptualize their careers in altruistic and instrumental ways.

Becoming a Lawyer of Color

In the classic 1973 film *The Paper Chase*, John Houseman's character, Professor Kingsfield, announces to his students on the first day of class that he performs brain surgery, teaching them to think like lawyers. Movies such as this convey the gradual transformation of doe-eyed law students into attorneys-in-training. Scholars have written about this transformation for decades. Most students, regardless of their aspirations before entering law school, will choose the career path of least resistance—namely, a position in a law firm. These jobs often require the least legwork to obtain, are the industry norm, and are seen by many as an indication of one's intellectual abilities as a lawyer.

Numerous studies have shown the effects of corporate legal training, whereby students trade in their altruistic ideals in favor of being reasonably responsible professionals (Schleef 2005).[1] A law student's professional identity no longer includes being socially responsible but instead relies on pro bono opportunities to give back to the community to which the student has the most affinity or allegiance. One could then describe these students as focusing their energies on cultivating acceptable professional identities. Yet respondents at Western Elite and Private Metropolitan reveal complex negotiations as they talk about commitments, whether to respective panethnic student organizations or the panethnic groups that these organizations represent. Araceli Baez, a second-year, Mexican American law student, was actively involved in the Society of Latino Law Students (SLLS) and the *Journal for Latino Law Students*, where she served as the editor for a year. Her interest is in real estate and land use law, and she expressed frustration with how this choice was sometimes perceived by other Latino law students:

> I think it [fellow Latino students' assumptions about my practice choice] happens in our group [Latinos] because there's so many people in our community that need help. How could you not help? No, wait, I can, just in a different way.... [I]n law school ... I spoke with some undergrads, and it was a little comment like, "Why are you working for a private company? Aren't you going to do immigration?" "No, I'm not. Let me tell you why not." So I go on a long spiel about how there are different ways of helping the community. I think now I'm very much more like the defender of it [alternative ways of helping the community]. Because it's like, don't dismiss my passion and my background just because I have an interest [in a different area]. Like, it's still legitimate! And I feel very much involved [in Latino issues]. Sometimes more so than the people that are talking. So that's why I take a little offense to [their attitude].

Students without traditionally defined public interest career plans, such as Araceli, give calculated reasons for electing to work in private industry as opposed to more altruistic options. And they cultivate creative strategies to ensure that they continue to contribute to their panethnic communities. In Araceli's case, her contributions come through involvement in the Latino student organization and Latino law journal:

> I feel like here at [Western Elite], I had to make comments to people who would make comments like, "Oh, so-and-so is selling out because you're going into private company or whatever." And I feel like if your heart is in helping but just in a different way, that doesn't mean it should be dismissed. . . . If you can get a Latino student to be a [law] clerk of some sort, everybody would be very excited. But the steps that lead up to it—"Oh, you're in [the school's] law review"— you might get some flack for it. And I don't think that's right, because the whole point is getting people in positions that could help others.

As Araceli explained above, Latino students who decide to pursue corporate law are afraid of being seen as sellouts. Becoming a sellout also includes acting white, such as taking a position on the school's law review journal to bolster one's résumé.[2] Copanethnic peers scorn as sellouts those with no intention of pursuing a public interest career. Latino and Asian American law students achieve the normative ambition when they embark on a law firm trajectory. But their peers assume that they do so by prioritizing their careers, or professional identities, at the expense of panethnic allegiances.

What does it mean to be a sellout? Jonathan Song fits that profile. As a second-generation, Korean American immigrant, Jonathan majored in psychology and was active with Asian American organizations while in college. At the time of our conversation, he had just signed on with a well-known, large law firm and was set to become a junior associate at graduation. Yet it was only with minor enthusiasm that he shared the news:

> I worked at a firm this past summer, and I'll be going back. I did get an offer—I'll be in their real estate transactions practice group, so that's what I'll be doing most. Kind of didn't have an interest in it at all, so kind of unsure what it entails. But I really love the people in the group.

Jonathan began law school with an interest in intellectual property but was unable to secure an internship and so accepted the offer he got. Neither real estate transactions nor intellectual property law relate (directly or obviously) to panethnic causes or concerns, but as the editor in chief of a panethnic journal at Western Elite, Jonathan keeps one foot anchored in issues that do affect co(pan)ethnics.

Like Jonathan, many Latino and Asian American law students intend to take the path of least resistance. Scholarship on legal education describes the mechanisms of legal socialization but does not provide an in-depth understanding on how students of color extract and apply meaning to their experiences. Law students begin their career trajectories focused on getting high-quality training and hope to secure creative and meaningful work—goals that can be met by initially following a firm trajectory (Stover 1988). Some scholars hint that white women and nonwhite students benefit least from a language and culture characterized by elitism, masculinity, and white Anglo-Saxon Protestant normativity.[3] Little scholarship, however, examines the gap often felt by students of color between their subjective identities and their experiences with law school socialization.

What is the impact of race and ethnicity for these students' experiences? Up until this point, the profession has embraced and reproduced the status quo of "bleached out" attorneys (Wilkins 1998). Diversification of the profession is both necessary and inevitable. But effectively integrating diverse people, experiences, and perspectives will require concerted reflexivity and commitment to change on the part of the legal profession (Sommerlad 2007).

Intersections in Law

Some sociolegal scholarship addresses Hilary Sommerlad's (2007) challenge for the profession to critically evaluate its socialization process. Several theorists reject treating race as a variable because, they argue, doing so denies understanding the actual experiences of racialized individuals—their conditions, histories, and sociocultural identities—and conceals a history of domination and hegemony (Delgado and Stefancic 2001; Haney López 2006). Since *Brown v. Board of Education* (1954) and the civil rights movement, the law and, indeed, American society in general have focused on how to best incorporate racialized individuals into mainstream America.

Education, acceptance into an elite profession, and earnings are often used as measures of successful integration into mainstream America. Theories of integration, however, often overlook distinct cultural differences within nonwhite communities. By these measures, Asian Americans are a success story because they are highly educated and, on average, Asian American men earn more than white men (Hirschman and Wong 1986; Kim and Sakamoto 2010). Latinos too, have made compelling strides toward mainstream inclusion. Household names such as Sonia Sotomayor and Alberto Gonzalez attest to this success. Nonetheless, the socialization process remains a mystery. In Pawan Dhingra's (2007) study, Asian American professionals speak about managing identities as panethnics and professionals.

Similarly, Maria Chávez's Latino lawyers describe a marginalization, wherein they are often "mistaken as 'court clerks, bailiffs, or interpreters' rather than as the representing counsel . . . [and] receive belittling treatment from their colleagues" (2011, 159).

Research in both the United States and in the United Kingdom has examined the unbleached ways that attorneys of color experience the profession. Scholars on both sides of the Atlantic contend that the legal profession reinforces a white, male cultural norm (Garth and Sterling 2009; Sommerlad and Sanderson 1998; Sommerlad et al. 2010). But how exactly is the profession masculine and white? Most scholars assume that to overcome racism (in law and in society at large), one must first overcome race. The sociolegal scholarship on race thus offers only a limited understanding of race as social, political, and individual experience.

Some work on gender in law underscores the presence of a dominant male culture to which women are expected to adapt (Epstein 1993; Pierce 1995). The professional discrepancies between men and women at law firms illustrate gender stratification in the profession. Men possess (or are seen to possess) masculine traits as "Rambo litigators," while women are feminized as "mothering paralegals" (Pierce 1995, 50, 83). According to Jennifer L. Pierce (1995), men perform a masculinized form of labor as litigators who dominate in the courtroom and exert control over others. Women, on the other hand, are deferential, subservient, and overrepresented as paralegals. Cynthia Fuchs Epstein (1992) describes how the policing of gender boundaries transcends all types of work. With regard to law in particular, she notes, "The few women attorneys who managed to receive law degrees were clustered in a limited number of specialties and types of practice, such as domestic relations, child custody, voluntary legal defense of the poor, and government work. More from the coercion of limited opportunity rather than free choice they devoted themselves to doing good" (1992, 244). Further, male litigators exercise their human capital by "being in with the lads," while women litigators may at best hope to be "honorary men." But that honorary status is short-lived because "the sexual objectification of women must serve ultimately to further undermine the professional status and authority of the female lawyer and to reaffirm stereotyped gender identities and hence relations of domination" (Sommerlad and Sanderson 1998, 181).

Parallels can be drawn between the experiences of white women attorneys and attorneys of color who seem to benefit from the profession's tolerance and openness to diversity yet continue to face professional obstacles (Garth and Sterling 2009; Wilkins 2000; Wilkins and Gulati 1996). Some of these obstacles include lack of mentorship, stereotypes about ability, and failure to receive promotion. As David B. Wilkins notes, black attorneys and other traditional outsiders will "inevitably be seen as being less than 'real' lawyers, whose racial or ethnic backgrounds are presumed to be irrelevant to the performance of their professional role" (1998, 145).

Although the racial and gender status quo appear to favor white men, some scholars suggest that black women in predominantly white professions can succeed if they take advantage of their unique positions. Black women working in predominantly white professions are not seen as potential career threats or sexual distractions, thus they are protected by colleague support and respect (Epstein 1973). Yet despite some progress, black professionals continue to experience marginalization, as described in Chapter 4.

Current research findings speak to the racial inequalities in mainstream professions and education, including law. In general, attorneys of color (black, Latino, Asian American, and Native American) experience some discrimination at work and yearn for more mentorship and training from senior colleagues (Wilder 2008).[4] While variation exists among pan-ethnic groups, the fact remains that nonwhite lawyers, while not exactly separate, are not exactly equal either. Susan, Araceli, and Jonathan, introduced earlier, provide a glimpse of how being a martyr or sellout affects individual experiences in law school. For Latino and Asian American law students, managing one's identity is an ongoing and sometimes exhausting process. These students bring compelling histories with them to law school at Western Elite. On the surface, most appear privileged. They attended prestigious undergraduate institutions. Many have professional parents. Why, then, are they conflicted? And why do they struggle between selling out and being martyrs? I turn to two law student experiences to illustrate these tensions.

Daniel Rincón we met in Chapter 5. He is the first in his family to attend college. Both of his parents completed only the sixth grade in Mexico, so neither could provide academic guidance to Daniel. As a result, he had to look beyond his family to find opportunities and explore academic options. Daniel reflected:

> My family lived in kind of a bad area of [a midwestern city]. So I definitely did not want to stay in that community. The fact that I was able to go to private school, which was, like, an hour commute for me, was totally worth it because I was able to get out of that community, out of that mentality, and go to a more diverse school that focused on academics and students working in groups. So that was very important.

Generous alumni from his private high school provided Daniel with a scholarship that nurtured him academically and enabled him to attend a private university in his hometown. Daniel is grateful to his sponsors for the educational opportunity, and he hopes to excel as a lawyer. He explained that becoming a successful lawyer means earning a positive reputation among colleagues:

> When I did my first summer [internship], they kept telling me that the partner was kind of like my client. Like, I had to make sure that he was happy with my work. And after that, I kind of noticed that people that did a good job, partners and associates kept going back to the same person. To . . . help them out. To me, being successful would be someone that is desired. Someone that people want to work with. Their ability to work with others and basically get the job done.

Daniel thinks about success in terms of recognition from other lawyers. But he also expressed conflict. A private secondary education earned him a ticket out of his impoverished community, yet he remains tethered to that community because his parents reside there. Moreover, his brother gave up on education and thus serves as a constant reminder to Daniel of the high dropout rates in the Latino community.[5]

While Daniel Rincón comes from humble beginnings, Diego Sanshes has a different story. Both of Diego's parents have doctorates, and both worked as community activists. Diego grew up in relative financial comfort. Unlike Daniel, Diego attended a public high school, albeit in a desirable neighborhood. He graduated college with an Ivy League education. When he reflected on his educational history and the socioeconomic background that led him to law school, Diego said:

> My parents have been very generous in putting me through law school, and so I don't have any loans. And it certainly frees me up in the options that I can seriously consider professionally. I think my parents have always encouraged me and supported me and wanted me to succeed. And I don't think I would have got into a hard-to-get-into college and a hard-to-get-into law school if it hadn't been for that drive. And I think they had taught me the transformative value of getting an education that really changed their lives and took them from poverty to relative comfort, and has allowed them professionally and personally to play a role in shaping their lives in their community.

Diego was influenced from a young age to succeed in school but also to not forget his parents' humble beginnings. Nevertheless, his immediate goals for success as an attorney are tempered by his understanding of the realities of the profession:

I'd want to feel first that my work product is good—that would be measured by the feedback I get from clients, maybe feedback that I would get from other attorneys. I would want to feel as though my contributions within my profession are respected, and that might also come from other attorneys, [or] it might come from clients. I'd want to feel as though I have a good balance between my professional life and my personal life, that I could do good work but also have a personal life separate from my work. And I'd want to be representing clients whose interest I genuinely believed in. And nice house, picket fence, dog.

Diego's career aspirations are not unusual among his peers. The desire to excel in law and maintain a thriving personal life, including a "nice house, picket fence, [and] dog," reflects the standard American dream. Yet Diego's parents' immigrant histories and climb to academic success and financial stability serve as reminders that education should not be taken for granted. For Diego, these reminders spur him to represent clients with interests in which he "genuinely believe[s]." The combination of a recent immigrant history and lower socioeconomic background contributes to different understandings of what it means to be successful.

How Law Students Learn to Sell Out

As we saw with Daniel's and Diego's stories, becoming lawyers means assimilating and taking on a professional persona. But why is that so important? A vital component of professional socialization hinges on one's persona. According to data collected by the American Bar Association (ABA), approximately 65 percent of Western Elite's 2012 graduates went on to work for law firms.[6] Of that population, approximately 65 percent joined firms with over five hundred employees (also known as big law), which are also usually international law firms. Law students from Western Elite learn that success equals securing initial employment with a prestigious firm. The story is different for students from Private Metropolitan. Approximately 41 percent of Private Metropolitan's 2012 graduates went on to work at law firms, with 70 percent of that group working in small outfits of two to ten employees. The next most popular types of employment are business and industry (19 percent), public interest (17 percent), and government (15 percent).[7] Graduates from Western Elite and Private Metropolitan are funneled into different types of firms. These discrepancies demonstrate status inequality and a reproduction of the elite. Large, national firms offer much higher starting salaries and typically recruit from highly ranked institutions compared to smaller firms that cannot offer similar compensation.[8] Nevertheless, at both institutions, the norm is to sell out and turn one's back, at least partially, on (pan)ethnic communities.

Take, for example, Adam Rhee, a Western Elite, Korean American student who grew up in the American Southwest with parents who earned medical degrees in Korea. While Adam's mother became a stay-at-home mom in the United States, his father practiced as a physician. Adam was the only respondent involved in both the SLLS and the Society of Asian American Law Students (SAALS). As a child growing up in the Southwest, Adam had many Latino friends and cultivated an affinity with Latino culture and language. He is committed to immigration issues and spends the majority of his free time as a board member on the *Journal of Latino Law Students*. Nevertheless, Adam said the following about being a successful lawyer:

> A lot of times, people talk about reputation, and part of the reputation you want to cultivate is a reputation of competence, intelligence.... [I've] certainly overheard conversations about others where people [imply] that they're not very bright or haven't done the work or they're not competent. I've also heard conversations where [they say], "Oh, that person's really intimidating." So similarly in the law field, because I think so much is about reputation.

Adam continued to speak about his initial career plans: "A [job with a] firm, because it pays. And so I'll use that money to pay off my education. And it looks impressive or prestigious to do something like that. So I will hopefully use that to leverage better opportunities down the line." In short, Adam intends to work for a firm to signal his competence and aptitude. Although working at a firm will not guarantee a direct, immediate contribution to Latino or Asian American communities, he assures himself that he will use his early career to create future opportunities.

The Latino and Asian American law students from Private Metropolitan differ dramatically from their Western Elite counterparts, reflecting the clear stratification within the legal academy of how students imagine and talk about success. For Private Metropolitan students, professional success is intertwined with personal success. To help illustrate these different ways of defining success, I turn to Margaret and Kevin.

Margaret Cha's parents have been in the dry cleaning business ever since they arrived from Korea; the business served a white client base in a racially homogeneous community. Although Margaret appreciates that her parents moved to that community for the better public schools, she grew up mainly among whites and very few co(pan)ethnics. This experience colors what she perceives as success. Now a third-year student at Private Metropolitan, Margaret described a successful attorney as

> someone that's effective in their practice, in what they are trying to achieve [and] provides effective representation of clients.... I think

that as an attorney, you should always do as much as you can. That's what they teach you, but I really do believe that! Not just out of convenience, I don't think you should ever cut corners with your clients. You should treat each of your clients as if they're your only client. If you can't, I don't think you should take them on. And I know that's very hard work [when working] for firms that require you to take on certain clients. So I think being able to treat each one like they're the most important client to you is a sign of a very successful attorney.

For Margaret, then, interpersonal dynamics with clients dominates her thinking about what constitutes a successful attorney. Though she believes that being a good attorney means maintaining a positive attitude while nurturing clients, she also made a backhanded comment directed at firms that expect their attorneys to take on clients with whom they may not necessarily be able to cultivate meaningful relationships. Despite her negative remark about law firm attorneys, Margaret expressed awareness that her law school's reputation will limit her job opportunities:

> [Private Metropolitan] was the only school I got into. I was waitlisted at [a slightly higher-ranked law school], but I ended up not going there. I mean not getting in. It was definitely my fault. . . . I didn't take advantage of everything that was [at my prestigious public undergraduate institution] and that's my biggest regret, because then I would have [had] more options than [Private Metropolitan], you know?

Margaret understands how rebelling in college inadvertently tracked her into Private Metropolitan. Although she thinks she is receiving a good legal education, she is considering getting an LLM (master of laws) in tax law to broaden her career prospects, given Private Metropolitan's low ranking.

Kevin Gu's story is similar to Margaret's, as he too worries about his career prospects. His parents, small-business owners who migrated to the United States from Hong Kong, met in the United States while attending the same undergraduate institution. Like Margaret, Kevin's parents also emphasized education. As described in Chapter 1, his older sister earned a master's degree, and Kevin's parents expected him to also pursue graduate school after graduation from his prestigious college. But, Kevin openly admitted, "I spent most of my college days drunk all the time. So I didn't do well in college." Although he managed to graduate in four years, Kevin's impressive LSAT score could not offset his poor GPA, and he was admitted to only tier-four law schools, eventually settling on Private Metropolitan.

Kevin, like Margaret, believes that a lawyer should be a good listener who is genuinely interested in representing clients. Majoring in the humanities in college taught Kevin compassion. He explained his understanding of what it means to be a good lawyer:

> You'll spend the time to talk to your clients about the case and not just ask for the facts for your argument. Obviously if [the client is] about to lose [her] house, [she] is going to be worried about losing [her] house and not about just the specific facts this lawyer needs to formulate an argument. So hopefully a good lawyer will explain what the judge is looking for so they can work together: "This is how you can help me help you," that sort of thing. I think a good lawyer should help the community.

For Kevin, *community* is broadly defined and encompasses all individuals without regard to race or ethnicity. Successful lawyers must dissect the facts of cases and connect with all clients on a personal level.

This is not to say that students from Western Elite do not value community or getting to know their clients. Rather, for them, success is contingent on their reputation in the legal community. As mentioned in Chapter 1, most of the students represented in this book are from the West Coast, the location of the two law schools examined. Latinos and Asian Americans are concentrated primarily in California (Portes and Rumbaut 2006). Proximity to co(pan)ethnics and exposure to relevant community issues affect law students' impressions about their chosen careers.

Strategies to Avoid Selling Out

Latino and Asian American law students who intend to pursue the law firm trajectory use three strategies to manage professional and (pan)ethnic identities or, to put it bluntly, to avoid being seen as sellouts. Some students anticipate engaging with panethnic issues when their schedules permit, while others insist that being responsible panethnics requires dedicating time and effort to aiding panethnic communities. Still others resort to working within ethnic communities in part because of few alternative career prospects. Latino and Asian American students' techniques to manage identities represent three distinct strategies, which I describe as marginal panethnicity, tempered altruism, and instrumental ethnicity. I discuss these in turn, along with factors that influence how students enact these strategies.

Panethnicity—if Time Permits: Marginal Panethnicity

Matt Yoon is a second-generation, Korean American student at Western Elite. In his second year of law school, he is a board member of the SAALS and is described by a peer as a "skywalker" (a very smart law student—one who walks the sky with ease). Matt grew up in the American South and was never involved in affinity groups until law school. He attended a magnet high school with mostly black and white students and only a sprinkling of Asian Americans and then graduated from an Ivy League undergraduate institution. He recalls being "kind of nerdy" in high school and says he "grew up feeling pretty white." So why, in law school, is he on the board of SAALS? "To meet girls," was his first response. He then laughed and went on to explain:

> I don't know, it's random. I really wasn't intent on it, you know? But my sister actually played a role. She actually was in [SAALS] when she was in law school, and she liked it—they have chapters everywhere, right? And so I went, and it was pretty fun. In college, I never participated in like the Korean Association or whatever associations.

Since joining SAALS at Western Elite, Matt finds himself regularly providing legal services to co(pan)ethnics through the Asian immigration clinic.

Marginal panethnics, like Matt, manifest peripheral interest in panethnic issues as a part of their legal training. They did not participate in identity groups while in college and typically grew up in communities lacking coethnics or nonwhite individuals. In law school, these students join respective panethnic organizations for what they claim to be serendipitous reasons—they attended diversity recruitment events when they visited the schools or went to activity fairs on campus and established immediate acquaintances with panethnic organizations. Araceli, who earlier expressed her frustration with charges of selling out, recounted visiting the SLLS booth at an orientation fair: "I think, coming in, I was, like, [SLLS] is going to be where I'm going to meet people that have my experience. So that's how I started going to stuff. And then I met friends there, and that kind of kept me going." New students like Araceli maneuver the first few days of law school among familiar faces and naturally begin to spend more time with them.

These students' experiences mirror that of Robert Park's (1996) "marginal man." Park describes the twentieth-century American immigrant as "a cultural hybrid, a man living and sharing intimately in the cultural life and traditions of two distinct peoples; never quite willing to break, even if he were permitted to do so, with his past and his traditions, and not quite accepted, because of racial prejudice, in the new society in which he now sought to find a place" (1996, 165). Park's concept of the marginal man captures the experiences of Latino and Asian American marginal panethnics. These students migrate from the comforts and familiarity of college or work into the unknown terrain of law school. Joshua Vera Cruz is a modern-day example of a marginal man. A Filipino American, second-year law student, Joshua is from the American Northeast and aspires to become a litigator at a midsized firm. When I asked whether he plans to incorporate Asian American issues into his role as an attorney, he responded:

> What I'm trying to do through [SAALS] now is to connect our alumni to undergrads, so we have a stream of community, so that people feel connected. So undergrads feel encouraged to apply to law school. So they can understand better what the profession is and what they can or can't get out of a law degree, and [I want] to encourage them as much as possible and to be out there. And just because [Asian Americans] are underrepresented in law school and in the legal community, it shouldn't stop them from wanting to do it; it should cause them to want to apply to law school even more.

Law students like Matt and Joshua represent a subsample of students who use marginal panethnicity as a strategy to connect with panethnic communities. They volunteer at clinics or sit on panels to recruit more Latino or Asian American law students, although they do not necessarily foresee providing direct service to their respective communities unless such opportunities are presented to them. These students align primarily with their professional identities yet remain cognizant of the dearth of minority representation in the legal profession.[9]

On the whole, they anticipate connecting with co(pan)ethnics by providing pro bono services or through mentorship. Their career trajectories are not amenable to working directly with copanethnics. Diego, introduced earlier, further explained his position: "I [would] like to think that I'll get out there and find plenty of time to do pro bono work for all sorts of wonderful people. I don't know if that will be the case. We'll see." Similarly, Arely Zapata, a Puerto Rican first-year student, said, "I'd absolutely love to work, if I'm at a firm, pro bono with the Latin community because I feel like they could relate to me. I could understand their issues, and with that understanding maybe I could be able to provide them with guidance or legal advice." Born and raised in Puerto Rico, Arely pursued higher education in the continental United States. She became aware of issues affecting Latino communities while in college and, although she looks phenotypically white, feels an affinity with American copanethnics.

Marginal panethnics can act as interested panethnics when opportunities arise. The ability to peripherally invest in panethnic issues is, for these students, similar to the way that European ethnics are able to choose and assert their ethnicities (Waters 1990). Most of the law students who adopt marginal panethnicity moved to a different part of the country to attend law school and thus feel minimal connection to the (pan)ethnic communities near their law schools. Law students at both Western Elite and Private

Metropolitan adopt this strategy but in different ways because there are fewer local students at Western Elite than at Private Metropolitan.

Where one grew up, then, dictates how marginal panethnics identify panethnically, since their panethnic affinity does not necessarily extend beyond law school or the legal profession. These students are marginally interested in (pan)ethnic issues through hypothetical pro bono cases or student mentorship.

Panethnicity for the Greater Good: Tempered Altruism

Unlike marginal panethnics, other law students use direct services to fulfill their sense of altruism and obligation to panethnic communities. Manuel Casas is a second-generation, Mexican American law student at Western Elite who grew up in the American Southwest. His parents completed high school in Mexico but did not continue on to college. Manuel attended a local state college and remained close to Latino communities in his hometown. Manuel's family is solidly middle class—his dad owns a business and his mom stays home.

Ostensibly, Manuel's family—homeowner parents and college-educated or college-aspirant siblings—does not seem that unique. But then Manuel described one of his first memories, living in a trailer park. His family had hard financial times when his father worked as a gofer for a businessman while supporting a family of five. Eventually, the tide turned, and Manuel's father started his own business:

> And now he has a successful business. And now we're definitely in the middle class, maybe even upper middle class. But I'll never forget the struggles my parents went through. The fact that we were poor at one time. I definitely lived through that, and I just can't forget about that. . . . So I definitely want to reach back and help the individuals. It's just the right thing to do. And the community has given so much to me. It's the least I could do.

Manuel is not alone. Many Latino and Asian American law students desire to engage directly with their respective (pan)ethnic communities for the greater good. Like Manuel, they talk about it being the "right thing to do" since these communities gave them "so much." Black professionals do the right thing by helping family members and engaging in community-specific projects. Successful black lawyers do well by doing good and strategically apply themselves to the betterment of their communities.[10] Although my respondents did not explicitly speak of strategically "doing good," it is possible that they intend to build their reputations through public service. In other words, altruism may not be the only motivator shaping copanethnic decisions.

The Latino and Asian American students who enact tempered altruism for the greater good emphasize professional development along with service in disenfranchised communities. They see themselves assisting co(pan)ethnics beyond law school. The temporality of their obligation intertwines law school with a legal career. These law students negotiate professional socialization by remaining committed to transformative work. In doing so, their actions and attitudes resonate with those observed among other professionals of color. Debra E. Meyerson and Maureen A. Scully's "tempered radicals" identify with, and are committed to, their nonactivist employment but are also passionately dedicated to causes, communities, or ideologies that do not resonate with their work culture. Tempered radicals are "individuals [who] must struggle continuously to handle the tension between personal and professional identities at odds with one another. This struggle may be invisible, but it is by no means rare" (1995, 586). Likewise, Cheryl Townsend Gilkes's (1982) black "rebellious professionals" maintain commitment to causes that positively connect to black communities. Latino and Asian American law students reflect Gilkes's "rebellious professionals" as they negotiate becoming a part of an elite mainstream profession while giving back to (pan)ethnic communities.

I further parse tempered altruism into two subcategories, organic and cultivated. Those who adhere to the organic form of tempered altruism were raised in or near immigrant communities and feel a sense of urgency to contribute, first, to their respective communities and, second, to disenfranchised populations in general. For instance, Luis Pérez, a second-year law student of Salvadoran and Mexican descent, grew up in an impoverished neighborhood on the West Coast. He credits his community and his family's unconditional support as motivating him to graduate from college and enroll in law school. He intends to work for a law firm because he is interested in intellectual property litigation. Luis explained:

> I grew up in a mostly poor, predominantly Latino neighborhood, and I'm very proud of where I've come from. A part of being a successful attorney to me would be to work with communities like this. Really in any way that I can, whether it be mentoring high school or college kids, or providing free legal services to these types of groups, or participating in legal clinics, or taking on some pro bono work. Whatever it may be.

For Luis, becoming a successful attorney means being an active participant in his community. Unlike Matt, Joshua, Diego, or any of the marginal panethnic students we met earlier, Luis intends to actively identify opportunities to help the Latino community.

Similarly, Angela Kim, a second-year, Korean American law student, describes the urgent need for children of immigrants to assist their communities. Angela's parents immigrated to the United States in the early 1980s and started a family in a metropolitan city. Angela emphasized the unspoken obligation she feels to immigrant communities, especially those in the blue-collar, working class:

> If my parents didn't have me or my brother, they would just be lost with everything. And I just feel that without someone that has some sort of background information or education, they wouldn't know who to turn to. I feel it's very important that they know what their rights are and where they can go seek help. But they're all blue-collar workers. They're all in the service industry and things like that. It's mainly their children, like myself or within the community, if they have a professional career, that's who they're going to turn to, to ask questions. But there aren't that many people that are in those professional communities, yet.

Angela's sense of organic duty is obvious from her description of blue-collar immigrant communities. This obligation, whether personal or expected from the community, is emotionally laden, and she is passionate about providing services to them.

Other respondents who subscribe to tempered altruism focus on relevant concerns beyond their respective (pan)ethnic communities. I describe *cultivated tempered altruism* as a connection to (pan)ethnic and disenfranchised communities through education or political activism. Unlike Luis or Angela, students who align with cultivated tempered altruism did not necessarily grow up in immigrant communities but feel tethered to particular causes and issues that shape their own life experiences. Beatriz Mendoza is one such example. A third-year law student of Salvadoran descent, she is married to an Irish immigrant and plans to focus on employment law at a small law firm. With both parents born in El Salvador, Beatriz feels an intimate connection to the country but also proudly asserts that she is an American. She plans to balance her "day job" with volunteer work for immigrant communities:

> I'd have a day job, Monday through Friday. And then if I could somehow do extra hours during the week or maybe on weekends, I wouldn't mind doing that. I wouldn't mind lending myself to that at all. Yeah, especially with the whole immigration thing I see

happening now. My husband was an illegal immigrant. It's not just
Mexicans or Latino people who come here illegally; there's also Europeans. And when we got married, he was still deportable. You can
get deported even if you're married to a United States citizen. . . . And
it took us like ten months for him to eventually get his green card. So
it's kind of scary when you think about it, that your loved one could
be sent far away.

Although Beatriz did not grow up in an ethnic enclave, the issue of immigration is near and dear to her heart. Immigration reform is often framed
as targeting Latinos, a community of which she is a part; her husband was
an undocumented immigrant from Ireland. The combined political framing of the issue and her personal experiences propel her to remain committed to immigration, even if her "day job" makes this difficult. Beatriz's
commitment to working on behalf of immigration concerns on the weekends or during nonwork hours reflects Debra E. Meyerson and Maureen A.
Scully's "small wins" approach. Small wins do not distract from daily work
responsibilities, yet "because it involves continuous pushing, a small wins
approach sustains the tension between what it means to be an insider and
what it means to dissent" (Meyerson and Scully 1995, 598). Although Beatriz
has other career interests, she intends to focus her energy on making small
strides in immigration concerns.

Jonathan Song, the Korean American, third-year law student we met
earlier who was lukewarm about venturing into real estate law, did not grow
up among copanethnics and, unlike Beatriz, he is not married to an undocumented immigrant. Yet Jonathan is also dedicated to a professional repertoire that includes panethnic causes because of his experiences in college:

I definitely fell into a lot of those Asian American studies courses in
college, and I would say they were pretty transformative. I really was
into them! So I've always been interested, and I think it's something
that I feel like I could have had when I was [living] in [the major metropolitan area on the West Coast where I was born], but I lost that
because my parents moved to [a state in the South]. . . . No matter
what career I'm in . . . I feel like it's part of my community.

Jonathan's interest in Asian American issues stems from visceral pining for
the type of community in which he imagines being raised had his family
not moved. He chose to take Asian American studies courses while in college and cultivated a connection to the panethnic community through that
experience. He now identifies as part of the Asian American community.
His understanding of what it means to be a successful attorney thus includes
serving co(pan)ethnics.

The Latino and Asian American law students who adopt tempered altruism may not necessarily dedicate their careers to public interest work, but they are committed to serving underserved populations in addition to their paid jobs. Individuals with an organic interest grew up in the same region where they attend law school, are familiar with their communities, and thus feel an urgent need to provide assistance. Like Luis's and Angela's commitment, their commitment stems from a sense of duty as upwardly mobile individuals who benefited, in one way or another, from their co(pan)ethnic communities. Those who lean toward cultivated tempered altruism were not necessarily raised in the same region where they attend law school, but they feel connected to disenfranchised communities through their education or political leanings. Both types of tempered altruism link students' professional identities with their altruist obligations, thus differing from students who exercise marginal panethnicity. A third strategy, instrumental ethnicity, prioritizes cultural brokerage between professional and ethnic communities.

Panethnicity because One Can and Must: Instrumental Ethnicity

Logan Camacho is a Mexican American and Native American, first-year law student at Private Metropolitan who grew up among coethnics. He attended a public high school and graduated from a state school where he was an active member of the campus community. Logan studied abroad in Mexico during college, which boosted his Spanish-language abilities. He proudly informs me that he now possesses a more intimate understanding of Mexican culture and Mexican American issues. He desires to use his linguistic and cultural abilities to work on behalf of the West Coast Mexican American population. Logan noted that it is not just a personal benefit to know Spanish but something that will serve him well professionally too. He candidly explained, "I speak Spanish, which is a real plus in the legal field. Every legal organization in [my metropolitan city] has to deal with a large amount of people who speak only Spanish." He also feels his best career chance is to capitalize on his heritage: "because of my background, because of my ethnicity, and because of the gifts I received when I went to Mexico: one, learning Spanish, [and] two, really honing my cultural communication skills . . . and getting a sense of Mexican culture too." For Logan, enacting his ethnicity makes the most professional sense. He has an intimate understanding of Mexican culture, and the legal market in and near his metropolitan city demands proficiency, if not fluency, in Spanish. In this way, ethnic allegiance can be used in a strategic manner.

Instrumental ethnicity refers to the strategic use of legal skills as a resource to serve coethnic communities. Unlike marginal panethnicity or tempered altruism, instrumental ethnicity features insider cultural knowledge and proficiency, if not fluency, in the languages spoken in the students' respective *ethnic* communities, not panethnic ones. Law students who lean toward instrumental ethnicity act as "cultural brokers"; they want not only to deliver services to their ethnic-specific communities but also to act as a bridge between mainstream America and their respective immigrant groups. Social scientists have examined cultural brokerage in the strategic hiring of black employees in Jewish- and Korean-owned businesses in predominantly black neighborhoods (J. Lee 2002); in urban classrooms where teachers' aides serve as a bridge between middle-class teachers and the impoverished students and families they serve (Weiss 1994); or in the case of "cultural straddlers," a term coined to describe high-achieving black high school students (Carter 2005, 13). I extend this concept of cultural brokerage to law students who can and must use ethnicity in their professional repertoire.

As Logan's vignette demonstrates, law students who adhere to instrumental ethnicity seek to become a bridge for coethnics who are neither fluent English speakers nor proficient with American culture. As neophytes, these students see an untapped community to which most mainstream attorneys do not extend their services. For example, Evelyn Villarosa, a Filipina American, third-year law student who eventually plans to become a solo practitioner, noted:

> I think there's an untapped clientele I could reach in the Asian American community because most of the clientele that my boss takes care of are white people. And I know a lot of people in the Filipino community that don't have wills and don't have an estate planned. And I could reach out to them.

Evelyn was working at a small firm downtown in a metropolitan city when she and I spoke. She enjoys working at small outfits and plans to remain at one until she can build a sizable client base. That client base, she hopes, will be mostly Asian Americans and, in particular, Filipinos. She plans to link ethnic networks and cultural knowledge with her newly acquired professional skills.

Evelyn's instrumental strategy speaks to the dearth of attorneys who directly serve the Filipino community. She intends to fill a niche while also securing a foothold in the Filipino legal market. Immigrants often serve coethnics out of necessity, becoming known in the process as "middleman minorities." Developed by Edna Bonacich in the 1970s, this theory examines the importance of coethnic businesses for immigrant communities. Discrimination often forces poor immigrants to turn to ethnic-specific businesses and entrepreneurs who are "middleman minorities." More often than not, they climb the ladders of social and economic mobility at the expense of integration within mainstream America. Bonacich explains, "They keep themselves apart from the societies in which they dwell, engage in liquidable occupations, are thrifty and organized economically. Hence, they come into conflict with the surrounding society, yet are bound to it by economic success" (1973, 593).[11] The Latino and Asian American law students from lower-tier Private Metropolitan find themselves in a similar predicament but one that is characterized by a professional lacuna coupled with a personal desire to assist copanethnics. Consider what Andersen Lee, a Korean American, third-year law student, had to say about using his legal knowledge to work in his ethnic community:

> I want to be a bridge for the Korean American community to be able to utilize the American legal system because they have these barriers: one, for language, and two, cultural difference. I actually have spoken with some Korean business owners who have been sued, and . . . they want to stay away from the whole legal system, period. . . . My sense was they are really afraid of the whole legal process. So I want to be able to be a bridge because of my language ability. Because I feel like I need to help them understand what's going on instead of living in their own little world. So the Korean community can grow and be a part of America.

Andréa Rodriguez, a second-year law student of Guatemalan and Mexican heritage, expressed similar sentiments:

> I feel like it's very important. If you speak the language, why shouldn't you be out there helping people? My parents always taught me that if you see someone on the street who's struggling, trying to speak English, you should help them. It was just something I was brought up with. The same with this [profession].

As these quotations reveal, Andersen wants to work within the Korean American community and provide a bridge between them and mainstream America. Andréa shares that same obligation because she can speak Spanish and thus can help coethnic clients who are not proficient English speakers. Other bilingual law students, especially those at lower-ranked Private Metropolitan with limited career options, have a sense of instrumental duty to share their skills with ethnic communities.

Language fluency aside, law students who align with instrumental ethnicity negotiate the tension between being seen as a martyr or a sellout. They intend to give back to co(pan)ethnics but rely on diverse strategies. This sense of obligation, then, partially resonates with Jody Agius Vallejo and Jennifer Lee's (2009) findings that while middle-class Mexican Americans give back to their ethnic communities, their approaches vary depending on their socioeconomic upbringing. Individuals from the working class are more likely and willing to assist their family members financially than those from the middle class, who subscribe to individual meritocratic rewards. The Latino and Asian American law students featured in this chapter, however, intend to give back to their communities, not necessarily through monetary assistance to family or extended kin, but by becoming mentors in order to increase the numbers and presence of Latino and Asian American attorneys, by being connected to their respective communities, and by providing direct legal services. Their motivations do not vary by socioeconomic background, and thus, they differ in this respect from Vallejo and Lee's respondents. Factors that influence (pan)ethnic-professional identity management include region, community from which these students hail, issues that resonate with the students, and the ability to speak an ethnic tongue (Table 6.1).

As seen in Table 6.1, students who adopt marginal panethnicity were not raised in the same region as the law school they attend, and they also did not grow up in or near ethnic enclaves. Recall Matt Yoon, who grew up in the American South, or Joshua Vera Cruz from the Northeast. Law students like Matt or Joshua were introduced to particular concerns that affect co(pan)-ethnics in law school and were unfamiliar with pertinent issues within their ethnic enclaves or were unaware of regional concerns that are important to these groups. Notably, marginal panethnics lack fluency or proficiency in an ethnic language and thus feel less qualified to be of genuine assistance

TABLE 6.1: FACTORS INFLUENCING (PAN)ETHNIC PROFESSIONAL IDENTITY STRATEGIES

Strategy	Region	Community	Issues	Language
Marginal panethnicity	Not from the same region as the law school	Did not grow up in/near ethnic enclave	Introduced to issues that affect copan-ethnics in law school	Not fluent/ proficient in an ethnic language
Tempered altruism	*Mixed:* some from region of law school and some from out-side region	*Cultivated:* did not grow up in/near ethnic enclave *Organic:* grew up in/near ethnic enclave	*Cultivated:* intro-duced to issues that affect copanethnics through college or work *Organic:* familiar with issues because grew up in/near communities	*Mixed:* some are proficient/ fluent in an ethnic language
Instrumental ethnicity	From the same region as the law school	Grew up in/near ethnic enclave	Very familiar with issues because grew up in/near communities	Proficient/ fluent in an ethnic language

to co(pan)ethnic communities. In comparison, law students who exercise tempered altruism are a mixed bunch, hailing from either the same region as the law school or elsewhere. Those who display cultivated tempered altruism (e.g., Jonathan or Beatriz) were not raised in or near ethnic enclaves and were introduced to issues that affect co(pan)ethnics only during college or while working. In contrast, Latino and Asian American law students with organic interests (e.g., Angela or Luis) were raised in or near ethnic enclaves and experienced firsthand the issues pertinent to (pan)ethnic communities. Tempered altruism transcends language boundaries since students who may or may not be proficient in an ethnic language adopt this strategy.

Lastly, students who subscribe to instrumental ethnicity are generally from the same region as the law school and are intimately familiar with the issues affecting particular ethnic communities. These students are at least proficient, if not fluent, in an ethnic language and cultivate their identities as attorneys while simultaneously securing a legal niche in the communities with which they are familiar. Language proficiency and cultural knowledge frames how Evelyn, Andersen, and Logan think about managing their identities. Notably, only students from Private Metropolitan adopted this strategy. The institution effect could be a function of fewer job prospects for graduates from lower-tiered schools, necessitating a retreat to ethnic communities.

This chapter examines how Latino and Asian American law students who intend to work for law firms negotiate dueling professional and (pan)ethnic identities. They contend with these identities as a result of their experiences with racialization in law school. While it appears that some students are selling out their communities by not aspiring to a career in public interest, a career that would make them martyrs, the Latino and Asian American students presented in these pages actually pursue nuanced approaches vis-à-vis their racial or ethnic identities and their professional aspirations. Although the students vary by socioeconomic background, particular racialized identities, and law school rank, all nevertheless think about giving back to their respective (pan)ethnic communities by using a repertoire of strategies.

As demonstrated throughout this chapter, the panethnic group to which students belong was not significant in the strategies they used. Rather, geography mattered most, as relationships with co(pan)ethnics dictate the extent to which respondents envision working with (or on behalf of) respective communities. Similarly, socioeconomic background did not cause variations either, at least not for students at Western Elite. Significantly, only students from Private Metropolitan, who are typically from lower socioeconomic backgrounds, adopt instrumental ethnicity. Geography and socioeconomic statuses thus appear to be the most salient for law-firm-bound students managing their dueling identities.

This chapter also explores how some law students understand their roles at the juncture of sellout and martyr. Race, ethnicity, socioeconomic background, and geography influence these students' lives. If these often nonvisible factors (i.e., socioeconomic status and geographic background) are significant to how Latino and Asian American law students manage their identities, what about overt signifiers? Chapter 7 explores the multiple expectations of women law students and how these expectations shape the way Latinas and Asian American women think about their roles in the legal profession and their future career plans.

7

TYPECASTING IN LAW SCHOOL

The Intersection of Race, Gender,
and Immigrant Background

met Elina Reyes at her apartment several miles from Western Elite. It was mid-April, and Elina had just returned from a brief trip home to visit her visually impaired mother, who often relies on Elina for day-to-day assistance. On this occasion, Elina had gone to help transition her mother into an assisted living home located three hundred miles from Western Elite. Despite this end-of-semester disruption, Elina was thrilled to be finishing law school. She is a first-generation college student, and although she did not have a job lined up postgraduation at the time of our meeting, she was clearly proud to be earning her JD degree. Her achievements have been in spite of tremendous self-doubt, however, as Elina frankly shared with me:

> I can't think fast enough to say it properly with the right vocabulary so I'll be taken seriously, because already they look at me as a woman of color . . . so anything I say out of my mouth needs to be top notch, I guess, in the way that I am saying it and portraying it because that is going to be additional fire. An additional reason for them to say, "You see? They're not good enough to be here."

Gendered expectations are a normal part of professional socialization, but the combination of gender *and* race heightens anxiety for particular law students.

While the previous chapter explored how some Asian American and Latino law students manage dueling identities, this chapter adds gender into the mix and includes the expectations that Latina and Asian American women confront. I begin by introducing how white women speak about their gendered expectations, thus providing a base for comparing the experiences of women of color. I then explain how law encourages women to "become gentlemen" and define the ways that the nonwhite women represented in this book are typecast as a part of their socialization. The women's stories reveal the multiple, often conflicting societal, professional, and personal roles that they are expected to fill.

Elina's fear of being "not good enough" is common among Latina and Asian American women law students. Most of these women express trepidation regarding their role as minority minorities—a term used by some students to capture the double burden of women of color. They contend simultaneously with the expectations placed on women *and* people of color in the legal profession. As we see in the following pages, the Latina and Asian American women represented in this book describe these expectations in different ways, and though they sometimes resist the expectations, they nevertheless subscribe to them. And not unlike the typecasting of film actors and actresses of color, these students undergo professional socialization that typecasts them as well. The mental energy Elina spends ensuring that anything she says is "top notch" and thus positively represents Chicanas speaks to the toll of gendered and raced expectations.

Social science scholarship finds that professional women are frustrated with their gendered experiences, despite the numerical increase of women in traditionally masculine fields.[1] As discussed briefly in the previous chapter, women must assimilate masculine professional norms while still meeting society's gendered expectations (Epstein 1992). Although women attorneys are becoming more prominent in American society, the culture of law remains stubbornly masculine.

Becoming Gentlemen

As we have seen thus far, the field of law is culturally white and masculine. Women are taught, both implicitly and explicitly, to behave like gentlemen. Learning to think like a lawyer means learning to behave and act like a man. Lani Guinier and her colleagues document the comments made by one male professor to a first-year class of women law students: "To be a good lawyer, behave like a gentleman" (Guinier, Fine, and Balin 1997, 29). This process, however, of becoming a gentleman is far from easy—particularly for women. Cynthia Fuchs Epstein (1992) calls women attorneys political tokens in the work environment. As tokens, women attorneys must fit within gendered boundaries at work such that "women who were (and are) tough faced the disapproval of both men and women colleagues and even of feminist attorneys, who faulted them for assuming a 'male model' of behavior (or for wearing clothing regarded as 'masculine' in style) and otherwise deviating from sex-role-appropriate attitudes" (Epstein 1992, 245). And even when women attorneys are not explicitly made tokens, their inability to assimilate into the profession remains stark. Gendered segmentation reflects a larger structural understanding that expects women attorneys to bring to the profession better camaraderie and sense of communication (i.e., feminine characteristics). Simultaneously, the women must endure skepticism about their commitment to the profession resulting from stereotyped family and child-rearing responsibilities.[2]

The women featured in this chapter reflect the aforementioned gendered patterns and expectations. Like their male peers, they too aspire to challenging and fulfilling careers. But the prospect of getting married or having children weighs heavily on their minds as they look toward their future in the profession—a future that for many will begin in corporate America. Candice Jacobs, a second-year, white woman at Western Elite, slated to work at a large firm explained:

> You know, I sort of worry about my career at the firm as a woman, but that was definitely one of the factors of why I selected [this firm] when I was looking at firms. You know, how much ability [do I have] to start a family? Do I stay on partner track, or do I not stay on partner track? But at least you can stay at the firm, so that part of being a woman has definitely come into play.

Like Candice, most women expressed concerns about balancing work and family. This sentiment came up only a handful of times with men. Further, the masculine culture of law left a lasting impression. Clara Tierney, a white woman in her final year of study at Western Elite, met with me at a coffee shop on a weekday, between classes. Despite my arriving ten minutes early, I found her waiting for me at a table with coffee and her BlackBerry in hand. With her greeting and her firm handshake, Clara immediately conveyed an impression of confidence. She rejected the idea that being a woman would pose an obstacle to her education and drew heavily on a narrative of meritocracy. But when we spoke about being a woman lawyer, she surprised me:

> I used to not [think that being a woman would matter], then over the summer [internship] I realized that it might. I had a training at my firm, an all-day training in negotiations, and it was like mock training. You practice doing negotiations with the fellow summer [associates], most of whom are women. Out of eight summer [associates] at the . . . office, there were four women. The [other] office, there were four of them [total], two of whom were women. So when we did the training, 75 percent of us were women. So we did mock negotiations all day. And at the end of the day, they got two partners to come in

and show us how it was done. And both partners were men. And all day, the people who were observing us, giving us feedback, were all men. And it was like I had this epiphany, because as I was watching these two partners play it out, and they had told us that one of the keys to being a good negotiator is you want to definitely develop a persona in the room. But you want that persona to be consistent with your personality. So you don't want to fake something that's not you. So as I was watching these guys, I realized there was no way in hell I could ever comport myself like that because it was so masculine— just this swagger—that if a woman acted like that, it wouldn't be charming. . . . It would be weird, and it would just make people feel uncomfortable. So as I was watching this, I was like, "Oh shit! This is what we're supposed to do." Yeah, I can see how being a woman might pose problems.

I was surprised by Clara's comment in part because, until that point in our conversation, she seemed so sure of herself. She knew exactly what she wanted to do with her law degree. Yet as demonstrated, the masculine culture of law, or one could say the masculine standards of law, made even this otherwise self-assured individual doubt her ability to fit in.

What is the solution? Becoming a gentleman is not a genuine strategy for women but rather creates precisely the kind of fake persona students are simultaneously told to avoid. Being a good negotiator requires presenting a confident persona. But as Clara recognized, the "swagger" associated with confidence is coded as masculine, such that "if a woman acted like that, it wouldn't be charming." Gendered boundaries regarding appropriate demeanor and presentation thus limit professional women's acceptance as colleagues. Women who embrace and assert stereotypical masculine attributes are often seen as intimidating and unbecoming. As Cynthia Fuchs Epstein points out, women who cross professional boundaries by practicing fields of law traditionally characterized as male or by wearing masculine attire are deemed tough—but not in a good way.

Women law students interact with male peers and subscribe to the masculine professional culture. For example, Hollie Jackson, a first-year, white woman at Private Metropolitan said:

There are a decent number of guys in my classes who I know think less of women, and you can see that just by the way they react to women who speak in class versus men, how they even talk to the teachers, the professors, and it's annoying. I know that law has a lot of older-generation attorneys who are in charge of a lot of things. And a lot of them—not even a lot of them, but some of them think less of women, just from a generational perspective.

Gendered interactions are not a surprising phenomenon. Sherryl Kleinman's (1996) work on gender and identity exposes how calculated emotions benefit men and women differently. Men gain status when they show their emotions, while it is thought inappropriate for a woman to do so. Symbolic interactions thus reinforce gender boundaries and interactions. Interactions in law school are also symbolic and bounded by gendered scripts. Women students recognize a pattern of unequal treatment, based on gender, by professors that privileges one gender over another. Hollie went on to describe how male students engage with women professors. Their subtle mannerisms and language are semiotics that speak to a gender hierarchy in law:

HOLLIE: Yeah. I mean, it's not like they said, "You're a woman; I'm not listening to you." For example, our torts professor is African American, and she's a woman. She's really smart. She went to Princeton [for undergrad], taught at Stanford. She's probably—if you look at those types of qualifications—probably more qualified than some of our other professors who are male. But one time in class, this guy asked a question, and it was just a regular question about some regular subject, nothing special. And she answered him and gave him a good answer. And he kind of sat back in his chair, crossed his arms, put his feet up on the chair next to him, and just—I can't remember exactly what he said, just a rude comment. And all his body language was just disrespectful. His response to her was disrespectful. He just kind of talked to her like she was dumb and [like] she was wrong. Even though she's a professor! But this guy, he asks questions in all of our other classes that are all taught by men, and when they didn't even understand the question and gave wrong answers or whatever, he's never responded to anybody else like that.

ME: Did any other students follow up after that, after his comment?

HOLLIE: It was at the end of the class, so it was just over. He wasn't the only one who's done that to her. It could be because she's a woman; it could also be because she's African American. But then, we have a male professor who's African American, and no one's ever disrespectful to him.

Hollie's example illustrates how body language can convey and reinforce gender hierarchies. Notably, in her retelling, Hollie downplayed the significance of race in favor of gender, emphasizing the incident as an example of gender-based inequality in the classroom—even though she did not volunteer any stories of male students disrespecting other women professors.[3] I did not speak with the black woman professor whom she referred to, but if the students taught me anything, it is that the intersection of race *and* gender warrants critical attention.

Typecast Socialization at the Intersections

The fifty-one Latina and Asian American women law students in this study described undergoing "typecast socialization" through their indoctrination into the profession. Erving Goffman's (1959) theory of impression management speaks to this process. Individuals manage impressions depending on the actors present and the regions, or stages, they use. For Latina and Asian American women law students, the actors consist of their peers, professors, families, and friends. These law students perform on stages, otherwise known as classrooms, family gatherings, professional mixers, and social events among friends. Goffman's dramaturgical perspective aptly illuminates the simultaneous performances in which Latina and Asian American women law students must engage in while learning to become attorneys. Like their white and male peers, Latina and Asian American women become fluent in the language of law and worry about securing jobs. Yet unlike their male and white peers, these women must also confront stereotypes and assumptions about their politics and career devotion.

As we have seen in the stories up to this point, law is undoubtedly masculine. Women are, in some respects, expected to adopt a male persona as they learn to become attorneys. What does it take to become masculine? Logical thinking and appropriate professional demeanor are the general standards. Take, for example, Jyoti Kaur's response when asked what she anticipates for her career:

> What makes me successful is the ability to take sides, question, answer fast, answer effectively. And I think part of a lawyer's job is to tease out the underlying questions with his [or her] clients or the company. So when clients come to you, their real legal problem is something. But as a lawyer, you have to ask the right questions, and you often realize their problem is actually something else. An effective lawyer can do that in minutes.

Jyoti is a third-year, Indian American woman. She and I met on a sunny afternoon and sat on a low wall of the student café at Western Elite for well over an hour talking about her family, law school peers, and potential employers. Surrounded by fellow law students, Jyoti at first provided calculated responses but opened up during the course of our conversation. She candidly expressed disdain for the profession and disappointment in her peers. Jyoti's initial answers echoed the typical responses that most law students would provide when asked about their chosen career, especially those at highly ranked institutions. Similarly, Sara Espinol, a first-year, Colombian American student at Western Elite did not miss a beat describing her aspirations: "Winning cases. . . . Having respect among your colleagues. Yeah, that's about it, and just respect and the clients are happy with your work. That might go hand in hand with winning cases. . . . I guess just that [clients] see you in the capacity that you're a good lawyer. If someone were to ask them about you, they would recommend you."

At first blush, these responses seem similar to those in Chapter 6—professionally appropriate, mundane, and perhaps not interesting. Further, these attributes of success mimic those cited by men and white students. But Jyoti and Sara, and their Latina and Asian American women counterparts, further anticipate their career in raced and gendered terms. In the following pages, I investigate how and why that anticipation matters.

Future Mommies and Filial Daughters

Most women, and especially Latina and Asian American women, are typecast in the future-mommy role. That is, peers and employers alike expect these women to opt out of their careers at some point to bear children and become primary caregivers. Recall Jyoti, who thinks about being a lawyer in a neutral, no-nonsense way: "Take sides, question, answer fast, answer effectively." She went on to relate an experience that added to her trepidation about the profession—an awkward interaction during an interview for a summer internship at a law firm:

> I went to one interview where the [interviewer] said straight out, "We're not cosmopolitan." Translation: we're not diverse. And then he starts talking about how all the women left to do the mommy thing. So I sat there, knowing he sees me as a South Asian female. And I've had that experience at least once or twice more. Where it was that direct.

This interaction led Jyoti to question, and eventually internalize, how to be an effective woman attorney of color. The interviewer assumed that women will leave the firm to become primary caregivers for their children and, furthermore, suggested his disdain for this choice through the condescending language of the "mommy thing." This assumption creates expectations that are held by women law students. Further, Jyoti understood the comment as deriving from stereotypes of subservience among South Asian American women in particular. Latina and Asian American women then internalize these expectations as a family devotion schema—one they are both pressured to fulfill by one group of peers and looked down on for consider-ing by another.

Mary Blair-Loy (2003) describes two devotion schemas for profession-als: family and work. Men are mostly assigned to the work devotion schema because it requires one to devote time, commitment, and emotional alle-giance to one's career. This schema emerged from capitalism but is now a semiautonomous and normative force. More than income, devotion to work brings a sense of competence, identity, belonging, and meaning. In contrast, women are mostly assigned to the family devotion schema, which allows them to reap the rewards of financial security and livelihood in exchange for taking care of husbands and children. As a cultural schema, family devo-tion describes intensive mothering, is emotionally absorbing, and centers on rearing children. In other words, women are expected to become mommies and devote their lives to their families, while men devote their lives to their paid work.

Of the sixty-three total women respondents, three had children at the time of interviews, and another woman was entering her last trimester of pregnancy. The other fifty-nine women were childless. Yet having children, or rather the expectation that they would, came up repeatedly during our conversations. Women do not live in a bubble. They interact with and be-come aware of the assumptions made of them as women—specifically, to balance work and family. Professional women clock in for the "second shift" as soon as their workdays end, while most of their male counterparts do not (Hochschild 2003).[4]

For most of my respondents, these gender expectations are compounded by familial demands and their peers' race-based expectations (as discussed in Chapters 4–6). The masculine professional culture affects these women students to such an extent that they report stress just thinking about their future careers. June Taveras, a third-year, Dominican American student, who was engaged to be married at the time of our meeting, explained this anticipatory stress:

> It's really hard to be a working mom when you have billable hours and clients calling you all night and stuff. So that's one of the things that worries me the most. And actually, I just basically decided with my fiancé that I would probably only want to have one child because I don't think I could handle two and working full-time. Basically, just the idea of having—I get stressed out! Even the idea of having two children, even though it's not going to happen for a little while, was, like, stressing me out! Because I just, I don't think I can do it. . . .
> I think that when you go into the working world and you realize, if you look at the boards of directors of corporations and stuff, there's no women, top CEOs—no women.

June becomes anxious when she thinks about how to be an attorney mother, at the same time that Jyoti comments on the prevalent expectation that women will (and should) become mothers. What these women express are professional and societal norms and expectations. That women are expected to opt out of their careers and "do the mommy thing" conveys to female law students the less serious, only temporary place they are accorded within the industry. Concomitantly, the lack of role models—no or few women as top directors of corporations, CEOs, or senior partners at prestigious law firms—elevates gender disparities in the profession and induces stress as these students imagine their career trajectories.

Moreover, familial obligations extend beyond childbearing and child-rearing. These mostly second-generation immigrant women also mentioned the need to take care of parents, siblings, and other family members. Here, socioeconomic class colors how they further conceptualize familial obligations. Arely Zapata, a first-year, Puerto Rican law student expressed her worries about being a woman lawyer:

> It seems like there's a certain amount of hours you have to put in every week, and when you're single and young, you can absolutely do that. But when you're married and you start having children, it starts becoming more and more demanding. I know women are able to balance it, but there's a lot of sacrifice involved there.

Growing up in a financially comfortable home in Puerto Rico, Arely arrived in the United States to attend a prestigious private university. Her parents are financing her legal education, something she appreciates deeply: "I think I'm very, very fortunate that I have parents that are so supportive and that are financing this. And I owe them the world!" But her sense of financial security is not that of the majority of her Latina peers. Whereas Arely and June express apprehension about being women attorneys who intend to start their own nuclear families, others feel the need to take care of other family members, beyond themselves.

Marta Ortiz is a second-year, Mexican American law student who migrated to the United States at age eight. She is the first in her family to attend college. Her mother, a stay-at-home parent, completed only sixth grade. Her father, a cook, completed only second grade. When asked about her parents' reactions to her attending law school, Marta remembered that her father was concerned about her ability to finance her education:

> I think money for me is a big issue. It's a big issue to know how to pay for law school. And afterward, know how to pay off my loans. . . . I think about it on a daily basis. I think that plays a part in the pressure of getting good grades and trying to get a good job.

Marta specifically addressed the pressures of being a neophyte Latina attorney:

> One of the biggest problems is, how do I deal with having a family
> and, at the same time, being a lawyer? A good lawyer. Because it
> seems like you do, in some ways, have to give up so much of your
> time to your career that it seems a little bit impossible to do both.
> And I'm sure there are women that manage it and do a really good
> job at it. It's just not what we hear about, during career panels and
> stuff. A lot of women complain about that aspect of law.

But family, for students like Marta, means more than a future partner and
children. It conjures parents, siblings, and others.

Marta also talked about the financial burden of needing to care for her
parents and the simultaneous pressure of wanting to serve as a role model
for her four younger siblings. She has already started to plan their futures for
them: "My sister, I told her she should go into business. Stuff like that. My
little sister, I told her she could do nutrition or something kind of doctory.
And my brother, I was like, you should be an engineer." Her eyes lit up when
she talked about her younger brother and the future she envisions for him:

> I just think he's really good at math, and it would be a shame for him
> to transfer to something else. So I just tell him, get all your required
> units done. And get As and Bs. If you don't want to go to a four-year
> [university], go to a [junior college]. It's not the end of the world, but
> you need to go to college. You need to. It's not an option for you. You
> need to. I was like, "I will give you a car if you go to college."

As a first-generation college student, Marta shoulders tremendous responsibility to guide her siblings' educational paths. Although male law students
mentioned their siblings during the interviews, only two spoke of feeling
responsible for their education.

Angela Kim, whom we met in Chapter 6, chose to attend Private Metropolitan in order to remain near her parents. Thinking about how they were
disadvantaged by a lack of familiarity with the law informed her own interest in a career as an attorney:

> I think that throughout their life in [their metropolitan city], just off
> the top of my head, they owned businesses and restaurants and Laun-
> dromats, and now they own a dry cleaner. But they [were] kicked
> out of their leases. And at the time I was still too young to even un-
> derstand what was going on. But in hindsight, they had rights with
> those leasing agreements. And [with my parents being] tenants, the

landlords definitely took advantage of my parents. I think because they were immigrants, and they did not know.

Although Angela's parents scraped together enough money to buy a building for their dry cleaning business, Angela still feels the pressure to take care of her parents in their old age; as she put it, "I'm the one that kind of helps them call the bank or call the credit card companies. Any kind of question that they have, legal or nonlegal, I'm always the one that's helping them." Unlike Angela, her two older brothers did not follow a conventional college trajectory—instead, one joined the military and completed an online bachelor's degree, while the other dropped out of a local state university. Taking care of family, then, for Angela means more than balancing work and family with a child. She candidly explains, "They kind of, in a way, motivate me to do well in school. Not just for myself but for my parents as well. I want them to have a better life. I want them to retire. They are one of the reasons why I push myself here."

Arely, June, Marta, and Angela are all Latina and Asian American women who anticipate a demanding career while taking care of their families. They each differ, however, in how they conceptualize family. For Latina and Asian American women from middle- and upper-middle-class backgrounds like Arely and June, it is defined as taking care of children. For others, like Marta and Angela, balancing work with family requires more than considering their nuclear families. Angela lives with her parents and frequently staffs the dry cleaning business they own, poring over her law books the whole time. Marta often makes the six-hundred-plus-mile round trip between her law school and her family. While becoming future mommies characterizes how their peers and colleagues may perceive them, as we see here, the women of color from lower- and working-class backgrounds also contend with being dutiful daughters.

Angry and Submissive Women of Color

When the Latina and Asian American women law students describe their classroom experiences, many refer to the "angry woman of color" image often ascribed to nonwhite women who are openly critical of race or gender issues (Guinier, Fine, and Balin 1997). Many women respondents are passionate about issues that concern disenfranchised communities and voice these opinions in classrooms when their peers are silent. But they also fear that doing so risks delegitimizing their position among peers and instructors who perceive them as angry. To remediate this image, many work hard to manage such perceptions and resist such stereotypes.

Felicia Álvarez, a first-year Chicana student with scholar-activist parents, remembers being in tow with her parents at demonstrations and organization meetings. She believes it is in her blood to be an advocate for underprivileged communities and describes herself as an activist in grassroots movements. She is also keenly aware that classmates often misconstrue her comments. Felicia told me:

> I don't want to offend people and I also don't want to be the "angry woman of color." . . . People characterize other women or peers that speak on these topics [of race and gender] as angry, frustrated. They can't empathize with them. I think people have grown up in such segregated societies, and especially at this caliber of a school [Western Elite] and in graduate education, period. It's a pretty heteronormative, white student body. . . . So I'm pretty rational, pretty articulate, fact-based. I'm not talking with passion. But still, these issues are issues that I think my classmates and America in general are uncomfortable with. So with that discomfort comes stereotypes, and I think the "angry woman of color" [image] is definitely alive.

Felicia obtained a master's degree in public policy at another prestigious institution. She remembers being typecast as angry when she spoke about issues that affect communities of color. With those memories fresh in her mind, Felicia attempts to tamp down her passions to avoid being associated with these characteristics. Despite this effort in all of her first-year courses, she believes the label has already been applied:

> My first semester, [I felt I] was pretty quiet. I took [classes in] torts, property, civil procedure, and the legal writing class and really didn't speak up except in property, which is a small class. And I heard people saying that I was the "critical race theory" person when I felt like I really hadn't even begun to touch on what I could. So again, I've been very conscious about not speaking up about these issues. And yet with that, [the label is] already translated [to me].

Although she makes an effort to curtail her comments, Felicia cannot shake the typecasting as an "angry woman of color."

Bryn Singh, a second-year, Indian American law student, echoed Felicia's sentiments. Unlike Felicia, Bryn grew up with working-class parents who worked several jobs to make ends meet. Bryn became the surrogate parent to her two younger siblings, helping them with homework and feeding, bathing, and putting them to bed each night. This experience taught Bryn to not take anything for granted and to appreciate the struggles of other working-class families. She became impassioned about working for social justice and aspires to a career in public interest. It is thus difficult for her to keep her comments to herself in classes, yet like Felicia, she tries not to ruffle feathers:

> I don't think anyone wants to feel like they have to speak for their race or political position or that they have to out themselves that way. There's a real fear that your viewpoint will not be considered seriously if you are "the angry black woman," or the "angry person of color," or the "crazy radical." And there's a real fear in the first couple of months of being stereotyped that way because we're colleagues for life.

Bryn's words illustrate how Latina and Asian American women manage their impressions in such a way as to build rapport with their peers. Yet despite their efforts, many still feel stereotyped as angry the moment they open their mouths to speak about a gendered or raced topic, such as domestic violence or undocumented immigration. This fear of being typecast as angry haunts the students at Western Elite in particular. The women at lower-tiered Private Metropolitan do not share this dilemma.

Although the women from Private Metropolitan feel pressure to conform to certain stereotypes, they did not express the same level of frustration. Estelle Ngan, a second-year, Chinese-Vietnamese American law student, described the expectations for Asian American women:

> There are two extremes, in my mind, that people think when they first look at someone who's Asian and is getting her law degree. . . . You have the one aspect [that] is "Oh, she must be really smart and really have an extremely high GPA, because all she does is probably study. That's the way she grew up, in terms of having really strict parents who are like, 'You better go to school! You better go get this degree and that degree! You become a doctor, or you become a lawyer!'" That type of thing. And then, the other extreme is "Oh, she must be a complete and utter bitch. You know, she's one of those. She must be a complete utter bitch, because [of] who she is, trying to rage against the stereotypical subservient generalization about Asian women." So I feel like, yeah, you have that.

Estelle's emotions here were raw—likely because of a recent a negative experience in which she believed a student thought her to be a bitch and treated her poorly because of that. Research on race and gender speak to the common stereotypes ascribed to Asian American women and femininity (S. Lee 1996; Wong et al. 1998). Asian Americans are expected to be model minorities, a stereotype that depicts Asian Americans as academic superstars.

Stacey J. Lee describes the stereotype: "Asian Americans are successful in school because they work hard and come from cultures that believe in the value of education" (1996, 52). Even so, note how this image still conjures Asian Americans as essentially foreign because of their unusual accomplishments and, thus, not truly a part of American society.

For Farrah Khan, a second-year, ethnically mixed Pakistani and Indian student, race and gender matter in the classroom. Farrah often finds herself wondering why her professors treat her differently from her white, and especially male, peers. She does not cite race as explaining her situation but rather seems baffled by the divergent treatment. Farrah described one particularly irksome classroom experience:

> There was an assignment. We had to do the same kind of statements. I went up [to the front of the classroom] and did mine, and, I don't know, it felt like everything I did was really wrong [according to the professor]. And a white male went up [to the front of the classroom] after me. And I swear he did it worse than I did. But everything he did was "so great" and "Oh my god, you did this right, and you did this right, and everything you did was so perfect!" And I was just like, "What?!" I was like, "Okay, maybe it's just in my head. Or maybe I just suck and he's great."

Farrah continues to describe how this incident reminded her that Asian American women are often stereotyped as quiet and submissive.[5] And perhaps because Asian American women are expected to be quiet and speak with softer tones that project less confidence, the professor felt the need to give Farrah more feedback. The stereotypes for women of color, for Asian American women in particular, become more complex depending on the law school they attend. In this case, the students from Private Metropolitan mentioned that they were thought to be passive and subservient, while those from Western Elite were assumed to be angry.

Latina and Asian American women law students contend with two presentations of self as they undergo professional socialization. Like their male peers, these particular students attempt to embody the standard definition of successful attorney—winning cases, developing a healthy client base, cultivating a reputation, and so on. They also make an effort to avoid being seen as angry or passive in the classroom for fear of being cast in the stereotype often ascribed to women of color. Yet despite their efforts to conform to that traditional masculine set of goals characterizing the profession, they are typecast as budding attorneys who are passionate about particular social issues and are therefore angry or bitchy in the context of Western Elite or passive and demure at Private Metropolitan.

Becoming "Too Intimidating"

Although Latina and Asian American women may be perceived as angry or submissive in the halls of law school, their parents do not think of them this way. The women I interviewed generally described their parents as being proud of them and cheering on their educational success. Yet negative parental pressures also affect these women's thoughts about their careers. Many of these women make their parents proud through their educational achievements, but they also anticipate offering concessions regarding their eventual careers and gender role expectations. For example, one student's mother could not fathom why her daughter would want to pursue a law degree. Growing up in an impoverished neighborhood, Elina Reyes, introduced earlier, feels fortunate that a teacher noticed her potential and nurtured her academically, encouraging her to attend college and, eventually, graduate school. Elina's mother, however, would rather she just marry and have kids. As Elina explained, "I know that my mom doesn't understand. She doesn't get it. She still believes I'm going to eventually marry and have kids, and she doesn't get why I'm [going to law school]. She doesn't even understand the concept of college." Although Elina's mother did not actively discourage her from pursuing a law degree (or higher education all together), she expects her daughter to fulfill her duty to marry and have children.

But overall, the women law students, irrespective of race, talk about excited parents who are proud of their daughters. Brittany Adams, a third-year, white law student from the Midwest, described her parents' reactions when she announced that she was going to law school:

> Oh, they were really happy about it. My dad especially. I think he's proud of it. My dad thinks it's great! Maybe I'll make a lot of money; I'll get some prestige, whatever it might be. I think he's . . . happy about me and proud for that reason. My mom, I think she's also proud but for a little bit different reasons. She just says she's more, like, impressed. She's like, "I know I couldn't do law school, blah, blah, blah." I try to tell her, no actually, anyone can do law school, it's really not a big deal.

Brittany's father is proud that his daughter will be an attorney and will, they all hope, draw a large salary. As a real estate appraiser who went back to school as an older adult, he is content that his child is setting off on the right course. Brittany's mother, an elementary school teacher, is impressed that her daughter is seeking a career in law. This being "impressed" came up several times in interviews but only with women law students. Take, as another example, white, third-year student, Cindy Cooper, a former engineer, and her analysis of her father's reaction to her attending law school: "My dad was more proud I had the chutzpah, as he said, to go and do something with my career. He more admired the ambition side of it." These students are appreciative of their parents' emotional support. Nonetheless, they sometimes struggle with the factors shaping that support and pride. Julia Mirren, a third-year, white student, attempted to explain why her mother is proud: "She's from . . . that money type: that type of person that likes to wear really nice things so that everybody's impressed. So she gets a boosted stature from this. Her status goes up because of this. So it's good for her status." Julia, Cindy, and Brittany all have supportive parents who are proud of their achievements. Their parents are impressed that *as women*, they have the "chutzpah" to embark on a prestigious profession. And the parents also reap some personal gains from their daughters' achievements, holding their heads up higher or earning bragging rights.

Being proud of one's children's achievements transcends race. But non-white parents have further expectations of their daughters. Aside from pride, Latina and Asian American women also talked about parental expectations that derive from culturally specific and immigrant-related norms. These additional expectations did not surface in conversations with white women or white men law students. For example, Andréa Rodriguez is an aspiring entertainment lawyer. Her parents are Mexican and Guatemalan, respectively, and she is the first in her family to attend college. She told me that her parents "were super excited. They were all about it!" But in the same breath, she continued:

> My dad's always very, very critical about everything. So when I first switched over from poli[tical] sci[ence] to global studies [in college], he was like, "What is that? You can't even say that in Spanish." And then going to law school, he was like, "What kind of law are you doing? Are you doing immigration law?" It was one of those things where he automatically assumed that's what I was doing. And then when I told him that I was doing entertainment law, he was like, "You're wasting your time going to law school then."

Andréa's story demonstrates how parental support can be conditional among second-generation-immigrant women law students. Another example comes from Jillian Wong, a third-year, Chinese American student:

> I think my dad is somewhat confused about why I want to go into entertainment [law]. He doesn't really believe the entertainment industry needs attorneys. So he doesn't think there are many opportunities. He always wants me to get back and use my science background. He was like, "You know, there was a reason you went

to [an elite private university] for college. There's a reason you have a degree. Use it."

Jillian's and Andréa's fathers freely voice their opinions on the types of careers their daughters should pursue. It is not uncommon for immigrant parents to assert control in the lives of their children, especially daughters. Scores of studies on intergenerational relationships speak of parental expectations and how they vary according to the sex of their children.[6] This is one other layer of pressure with which these students must contend.

Aside from career options, Latina and Asian American women's parents also meddle in their children's personal affairs, such as offering their assumptions about the purpose of professional training. For example, Lydia Kang is a second-year, Chinese American student whose mother quit her corporate job to stay home with her two children. Lydia stated:

I think for both of [my parents], it's always been emphasized to have a family. So, for me, it's never been to think [of achieving the status of] partner or think [of making] x amount of money. My parents want me to be happy, have a family. [For] my brother, it has always been, "You should support your wife," and for me, it's kind of less of a professional aspect. Like, my mom is afraid I'm going to get too intimidat[ing] now.

Although not overtly discouraging, Lydia's mother seemingly encourages a career as a marginal interest; she prioritizes Lydia finding a husband and being a good mother. Further, her mother fears that with a JD, Lydia may become "too intimidating" as a marriage prospect. Lydia's degree is thus less consequential when compared with her brother's career aspirations.

Elina, Andréa, Lydia, and Jillian all have supportive parents who are thrilled that their daughters are pursuing law. However, these parents also expect their daughters to conform to parental and societal expectations. Andréa's father wants her to pursue immigration law, Elina's mother does not understand why she will not just marry, Lydia's mother fears she will be too intimidating for marriage prospects, and Jillian's father seems skeptical of the market for entertainment law. These women must grapple with parental expectations that discourage their efforts while simultaneously learning how to become good attorneys in an environment that provides them with few role models. They carry with them an emotional burden, fearing that they will disappoint their parents. In many respects, these women embody Denise Segura's (1992) assertion that gender and race for Chicanas not only intersect but interact. Facing cultural pressure, Chicanas in white-collar professions negotiate expectations as primary caregivers to their children. Their

Chicano peers, however, do not need to entertain the same expectation, as Segura explains:

> While women usually enjoy their jobs, work is not so much "liberatory" as intensifying their accomplishment of gender both in the tasks they do at work as well as the sex-typed tasks they continue to do at home. Moreover, their attachment to family is linked ideologically to the survival of the culture, rendering their accomplishment of gender an overt act of racial-ethnic and cultural politics. (1992, 178)

Chicanas "do gender" at work and in their families. They are also tethered to the politics of ensuring cultural survival. Pursuing a professional goal then becomes fraught with racial-ethnic or cultural politics. In the office, the conjoined ethnic-gender negotiations leave Chicanas feeling as if they have a more difficult time securing work or advancing when compared with male or white women counterparts. They must prove themselves more at work and at home, simultaneously performing the role of a Chicana professional and mother.

As this section demonstrates, many Latina and Asian American women law students negotiate professional, societal, and familial expectations based on their race and gender. They recognize how white peers perceive them and also know that Latino and Asian American men experience less pressure to appease their parents. Parental demands become a part of Latina and Asian American women's socialization into the legal world. These students perform for their families and also for their peers, professors, and future colleagues. Further, they resign themselves to balancing professional expectations and familial demands that will no doubt influence their long-term career goals. They must "become gentlemen" yet are also assumed to be angry women of color. Moreover, their families demand that they get married and have children or pursue career paths in which they have little interest. In general, these women foresee working long hours in the initial stages of their careers and plan to adjust their career plans in five to ten years, when they anticipate starting families. At that point, they intend to decrease their work hours or devise other means to juggle work and family. These simultaneous professional and familial concerns appear to affect Latina and Asian American women as they progress in their legal education.

Tiered Optimism

As my mother always cautions, one should not use a bamboo pole to tip over a canoe full of people. Or as the more common English expression goes, painting with a broad brush may overlook individual variations. In this case, the Latina and Asian American women's career outlooks are significantly tied to their law school ranks: those from Private Metropolitan appear to be more positive about their professional futures. Recall Farrah, the Indian-Pakistani American student frustrated by the way her professors treat nonwhite women students. Moments after her initial complaint, above, Farrah rationalized:

> It's good that you get the criticism because you can use the criticism and you can try to make yourself better. Whereas if they're [white men who are] told everything they're doing is right, . . . [they are] just going to think that they're right. And they're just going to suck forever. So I try to put a positive spin on it in that way.

This learning experience resonates with the students at Private Metropolitan, as another law student's comment illuminates:

> I'm rarely called on, which I find surprising. Before coming to law school, it was like [you learn that] the Socratic method [means] you get called on, you get cold-called on very often. But . . . in some classes, I'm never called on, especially in bigger classes. . . . I'm not sure if that has anything to do with me being Asian, though.

This was Leah Xie, a third-year Chinese Canadian student, from British Columbia. She speculated during our conversation that, aside from difficulty pronouncing Asian surnames, some professors harbor assumptions about Asian students—namely, that they are reluctant to participate in class. But she also expressed uncertainty as to whether her being Asian affects the way professors treat her.

Why do these particular Latina and Asian American women express more relative optimism? For one, these women attend Private Metropolitan. As a lower-ranked law school, Private Metropolitan focuses on teaching students how to *become* lawyers. Robert Granfield (1992) asserts that students at Northeastern University Law School, a lower-tiered institution, learn the practical tools needed to become attorneys as opposed to experiencing the intellectual exercise of law at Harvard Law School. Martha Kimes's (2007) memoir, *Ivy Briefs*, corroborates Granfield's assertion. A graduate of Columbia Law, Kimes reflects on associating, for the first time, with other law graduates who attended lower-ranked law schools in New York State—Hofstra, Pace, and Brooklyn, among others—and how meeting them made her recognize the differences in legal education:

> As it turned out, while I had been busy at my fancy school cite-checking lofty journal footnotes and taking negotiation seminars

and studying European Community Law and blowing off Spanish for the Legal Profession and having my mind filled with legal
theory, those people from the "lesser schools" had been learning actual, practical, useful, bar exam–relevant law. They had been taking
classes in Wills and Trusts and New York Procedure. While I had
been learning how to think like a lawyer, they had been learning
how to *be* lawyers. And that put them in far better shape than me.
(Kimes 2007, 256)

Kimes's "lesser schools" describes a place like Private Metropolitan, which
attracts law students who do not fit the tier-one law school prototype described in Chapter 3. Most law students at Private Metropolitan entered with
lower LSAT scores and lower GPAs compared with their Western Elite counterparts. Many are returning to law school for a second career. The Latina
and Asian American women law students at Private Metropolitan focus on
cultivating a professional demeanor and emphasize the importance of not
only learning the law but also how to practice it effectively.

When asked how race or gender affected their law school experiences,
these women often mused that their minority-minority status would likely
benefit them professionally. For example, Jenna Ito, whose voice is heard a
few times in this book, expanded on the positive rewards of being a minority minority:

There's always that feeling when you walk into a room full of students—you do notice that you are the minority. And that's an interesting feeling. It's not necessarily bad per se, but it can make you feel
a little bit uncomfortable by virtue of being the "other" in the room.
Being a woman of color, it's interesting because I've heard it go both
ways. I've heard people say that's great because that's an advantage for
you, because you're like a *minority* minority. You're not just a person
of color, you're a *woman* of color. But at the same time, I'm sure there
are still employers out there who might have difficulty with that.

Jenna surmised that being a woman of color could benefit her career when
she searches for work, but she also recognizes that being a nonwhite woman
may engender difficulties with some employers. But she chooses to be positive, as does Beatriz Mendoza, the third-year Salvadoran American student
with the undocumented Irish husband:

I think speaking Spanish and being Latino is a good thing, but I
could see how it might be a negative, especially if . . . you end up
working somewhere where there's absolutely no diversity. It's kind
of like a little bit of an isolating experience. And I felt that during

law school, especially like my first year. So I would imagine it might be a continuation of that same feeling. . . . I guess the way I see it is, I know my own personal worth and if others feel uncomfortable about it or have issues with it, that's their problem. I'm going to move forward and this [career of being a lawyer] is something I've always wanted my whole life. So I'm not going to just step aside and give it up because other people don't like it.

Although these women law students from Private Metropolitan contend with professional expectations, and raced *and* gendered ones, they are fairly optimistic about their career outlook. These sentiments corroborate Judith Fischer's (1996) finding that women students at lower-ranked institutions are generally happier and experience less stress. Students from lower-ranked institutions interact with professors who support them, experience more diversity, have more available role models, and are more confident.[7] Thus, they appear to be more optimistic about how race and gender may affect their careers.

What's Age Got to Do with It? Performing Gender, Managing Race

Age also factors into Latina and Asian American women students' optimism at Private Metropolitan. As mentioned earlier, lower-tiered law schools tend to enroll older-than-average students. In Table 7.1, the average age of Latina and Asian American women respondents from Western Elite is twenty-five, while the average age of respondents from Private Metropolitan is twenty-eight. Disaggregating the sample, we see that while the average age of first-year students is the same (twenty-four) for both institutions, the real differences are in years two and three. Second-year Latina and Asian American women from Private Metropolitan are, on average, twenty-six, while third-year women are, on average, thirty-one. This is two and four years older, respectively, than their Western Elite peers. Some of the respondents from Private Metropolitan have already experienced gender and racial inequality in the real world and draw on those experiences as they prepare for a legal career.

TABLE 7.1: AVERAGE AGE OF LATINA AND ASIAN AMERICAN WOMEN LAW STUDENTS IN SAMPLE

Average age	Western Elite	Private Metropolitan
1L	24	24
2L	24	26
3L	27	31
Combined	*25*	*28*

Students at both law schools interact with agents of socialization that affect how they prepare to enter the legal profession. Messages from alumni and the unspoken understanding of legal culture gleaned from films, books, and word of mouth, combined with parental and cultural expectations, build the initial framework of these students' socialization. But the students at Private Metropolitan cite a third agent that contributes to their socialization: real-world expertise. Thus, Cynthia Fuchs Epstein's observation that, "for women going into the legal profession, law school was the first place where they would learn what it meant to be a minority in an inhospitable work world" (1993, 61) does not quite represent the Latina and Asian American law students from Private Metropolitan. These students know that the legal culture is not necessarily hospitable for women or law students of color, but they hear about alumni or their own professors who seemingly manage it all. Take, for example, Andréa's comment about one of her role models: "My art and law professor herself is a woman of color, not exactly sure what her origin is, but she seems to be doing fine. So I figure it can't be that bad for me." Consider, also, Anjali Chatterjee, a second-year, Indian American student who is a single parent, working part-time at a tech start-up company while attending law school full time. When asked about gender and law, Anjali said:

> I think over half the legal department [where I work] at this point [are women]. There are a lot of women. All the companies and firms I've seen, there are a lot of women. I think a lot of women end up contracting when they have kids. But I don't see that as a negative. I'd love to do that at some point.

The option to contract[8] after having kids is desirable. From their role models, women at Private Metropolitan learn about alternatives for their chosen profession; they can, if they want to, transition into less demanding forms of employment, such as contracting.

The Latina and Asian American law students from Private Metropolitan also look to seasoned attorneys who have already learned how to balance work and family. They conceptualize success differently than their peers at Western Elite do and recognize it as something they can attain. Compared with students from Western Elite, these women have a more positive outlook for their careers and career options in part because they have access to women professors, alumni, or other attorneys who seemingly balance work and family successfully. Jenna, the third-year, Japanese and white student who spoke positively about being a minority minority, met several women mentors through her involvement in off-campus organizations or unpaid internships. During a mixer where she interned, she met an inspiring woman:

And the woman, who is the cofounder of the [small nonprofit] organization, she's an attorney, and she went to Harvard Law. She's
extremely smart—has her master's in criminology and all this kind
of stuff. It's just amazing! I feel like I'm so lucky to have worked
there kind of on a whim. . . . I feel like I was incredibly lucky to have
met her.

For Jenna, being able to meet an inspirational woman professional gave her
hope that it is possible to find happiness and balance as an attorney. This experience also introduced her to a mentor who has helped guide her through
the challenges of completing law school and securing a job. The future appears hopeful for Jenna.

Like their Private Metropolitan counterparts, women from Western
Elite also turn to attorney role models. Unlike their Private Metropolitan
peers, however, those from Western Elite, for the most part, look up to corporate attorneys who must meet extreme billable-hour demands that include
regularly working over sixty hours per week. In these law students' minds,
their role models are under constant pressure to keep their jobs. Although
women at Western Elite, regardless of race, overwhelmingly expressed concerns with this pressure, it should be noted that Latina and Asian American
women contend with this fear in addition to the other expectations described
in this chapter. For instance, Marie Chiang, a first-year, Taiwanese American
student from Western Elite, shared her trepidation:

For a single man, success may be, and for a lot of people probably is,
being at the top of their fields, being at the most prestigious firm or
agency, and being involved at the most cutting-edge field of law that
you practice. But for a woman who is married and is thinking about
starting a family, that cannot define her success as a lawyer, because
that is most likely impossible; there are not that many opportunities
for women who want to have children to be on the partner track at
a very large firm or to be the right-hand star at a large government
agency or a nonprofit agency, because there is an immense amount
of time and energy to sacrificing other parts of your life in order to
achieve that position.

Compare Marie's comments with those of Leah, the Chinese Canadian student at Private Metropolitan:

I know a lot of female attorneys—they do have to balance the work-
life schedule. One good thing, well, not a good thing—one thing is
that, again, with our school ranking, it's difficult for us to get into
a big, big firm. But that isn't necessarily bad because the hours are

crazy and it may not be as family oriented as mixed firms or small firms. . . . I do also want to maintain a healthy work-family balance.

Students like Leah have realistic expectations for their careers. Earning their law degrees from a lower-ranked institution restricts their job options (as we saw in Chapter 6). Yet these women relish having the flexibility to maintain "a healthy work-family balance." Women students at Private Metropolitan not only have positive role models who seemingly handle work-life balance well but also know their place in the law school and legal-market hierarchy. The lower rank of their law school works to their benefit as they consider and plan their careers.

The Real World

The Latina and Asian American women at Private Metropolitan spoke of real-world experience, meaning having worked either before or during law school, as an asset. Many of these respondents returned to school after a hiatus working in the real world, and many continue to work while attending law school. Having already experienced raced or gendered inequalities in work environments, these women see themselves as veterans of inequality. For example, Helen Trieu, a third-year, Chinese-Vietnamese American law student who was a scientist at a biotech company before returning to law school, reflected on gender disparities in the natural sciences versus law: "There's just not a lot of females in science, in that field of science. I think there's more women in law, actually, than there are in science." Helen was pregnant with her third child at the time of our interview and did not appear too concerned with balancing work and family.[9] So when I asked whether she felt apprehension about entering a male-dominated field of law, she answered, "No, because I'm already accustomed to that. That breakdown. And I'm actually quite comfortable with it." While Helen anticipates gendered discrepancies in law similar to what she witnessed in biotechnology, she maintains that her real-world experience prepared her well to face any obstacles she may encounter in law. And as she stressed, she is "already accustomed to that."

This chapter examines the multiple professional and personal agents that socialize Latina and Asian American women into the legal profession. These women are expected not only to conform to a family devotion role but also to fulfill their obligations as dutiful daughters and siblings. These are matters of insignificance among the men in this study, irrespective of race. Thus, we see Latina and Asian American women experiencing typecast socialization. Typecasting agents of socialization shape the ways that Latina and Asian American women think about their future careers. Taken together, legal culture, law school, alumni, and the real world act as agents of socialization (see

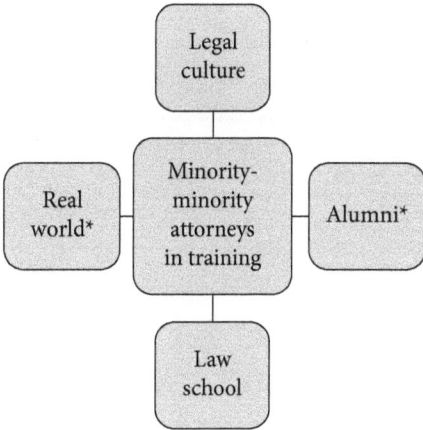

Figure 7.1 Agents of typecast socialization
* Agents affecting optimistic outlook at Private Metropolitan

Figure 7.1). As we see with the women's stories in this chapter, parental expectations also contribute to these women's notions of success. Some parents cannot comprehend why their daughters would pursue higher education. Others fear that a law degree will render their daughters "too intimidating." Parental stressors thus contribute to the multitude of expectations that create anxiety as Latina and Asian American women imagine their career trajectories. And all too often, these anticipatory anxieties transform into realities as the women finish their law school tenures and begin working. In the Conclusion, I tie together these multiple processes of assimilation and examine how racialization happens incidentally, alongside professional socialization. I also describe, in the "Epilogue" section, how race continues to matter for these former law students as they embark on their careers.

CONCLUSION

Learning to Become a Successful Racialized Lawyer

first conceived of this project because I spent considerable time on a law school campus. I was a doctorate-seeking student at the University of California, Irvine, and used to study at the UCLA Law School, sitting in the Lu Valle Commons—the law school café—each Friday, reading for my graduate seminars while my husband attended his first-year law classes. My sociological readings were punctuated with unfamiliar overheard words, like "torts" and "OCIP," and familiar words such as "outline" used in unfamiliar ways. My curiosity piqued, I found myself eavesdropping. I learned that in law school an outline is a comprehensive amalgamation of lecture and reading notes compiled by students throughout the semester in preparation for their final exams. I learned that course grades almost always derive solely from this single final exam. I also learned that OCIP stands for On-Campus Interview Program, something regarded as singularly important to the career trajectory of many law students. During OCIP, attorneys from law firms, typically large corporate outfits, descend on campus to interview prospective interns. I quickly found that the suit-clad students nervously milling around in Lu Valle Commons were between OCIP interviews. And while I learned that torts is not a delicious dessert, I must admit I never quite learned more than that.

During my trips to UCLA, I became fascinated with law students and how they were socialized into this elite profession. I recall one visually striking memory of a woman walking out of Lu Valle Commons in a tank top, jeans, and flip-flops; returning a short while later in a black skirt suit, white blouse, and black pumps; and then disappearing again only to return in her original outfit. Wandering the halls of the law school, I saw advertisements for student organizations: the Black Law Students Association, the Asian Pacific American Law Students Association, and La Raza, among others. Why did these organizations exist? As far as I knew, UC Irvine did not offer an Asian American sociology graduate student organization or any other type of panethnic graduate student organization for that matter. I thought panethnic organizations were left behind in college.

From my perspective as an outsider, law school seemed a fascinating place. On the one hand, the presence of lockers reminded me of the more carefree days of high school, even if the purpose was to store heavy law books. On the other hand, the flyers announcing panethnic organizations reminded me of college—yet this was a professional school, so why the apparent popularity of so many clubs and associations? This strange congruence of a school offering professional socialization paired with a focus on extracurricular activities that reminded me of college, even high school, led me to wonder about what actually happened in the three years of law school. What did it mean to be a neophyte in this profession and through what processes was one indoctrinated into the profession? What role did these panethnic organizations play in this transition, and did the experience look the same for everyone? My original project sought to understand the purpose of these organizations for those in the racial middle—Asian Americans and Latinos. I initially thought that these panethnic clubs existed for social purposes only—that is, for the students to hang out together and perhaps celebrate (pan)ethnic holidays. But that idea quickly shifted about two months into my formal fieldwork at Western Elite and Private Metropolitan, when I realized that the organizations actually serve three purposes: social, academic, and professional. I also realized that understanding the organizations' role afforded me a window into these students' experiences.

Legal socialization is intense. Without regard to race, law students share similar socialization experiences. They attend the same classes, they join law journals, and generally each aspires to prestige and success. But students' experiences also differ. Asian American and Latino law students, the foci of this book, experience this socialization in conjunction with racialization. This racialization happens on the front stage, while attending classes and interacting with professors and peers, but it also happens on the backstage, through participation in panethnic organizations.

Asian Americans and Latinos in Liminal Space

As mentioned in the Introduction, I do not intend to dismiss the differences between these two panethnic groups by using them as the combined unit of measure. The distinct experiences characterizing Asian Americans and Latinos as groups begin with their place in the American imaginary.

Asian Americans are seen as model minorities, while Latinos are presumed to be undereducated. Numbers from the Bureau of Labor Statistics support this perception: approximately 59 percent of Asian Americans hold bachelor's degrees or higher, compared with 18 percent of Latinos (trailing black Americans' 27 percent and white Americans' 37 percent) (U.S. Bureau of Labor Statistics 2014). Latinos earn a median of $578 per week, and Asian Americans' median is $942. These figures suggest an almost opposite relationship, and indeed, superficially, it appears difficult to find any similarities between the two groups.

Yet demographic measures notwithstanding, there *are* similar experiences between Asian Americans and Latinos in and out of law school. Historical processes of racialization and citizenship frame Asian Americans and Latinos as "others," ill captured by a narrow black-white binary. As shown in Chapter 2, members of both groups fought for their rights to legal, cultural, and social citizenship. Court cases established how members of these two groups were a part of nonwhite and nonblack "races," pushing the boundaries of a narrowly conceived color line. The new color line recognized the varied ways immigration racialized members of these two groups as (permanent) foreign outsiders. Being seen as a foreigner transcends history and follows Asian American and Latino students into the halls of law school, ensuring that they are always seen, as one student put it, in the "skin of a foreigner."

Law school enrollment represents another similarity between members of these panethnic groups. Many white law students were encouraged by the diversity they experienced in law school and found themselves benefiting from it. As Chapter 3 demonstrates, white law students evoke *paternalistic exoticism* and harbor convoluted emotions about the role of diversity in law. Without regard to the law school, Asian American and Latino law students saw the numbers of their copanethnics decrease from high school to college to law school, and they also witnessed a decrease in the number of other nonwhite students. Chapter 4 presents students from both panethnic groups describing law school as being white and using the example of law student racial demographics to support this claim. Asian American and Latino students experience similar racialized lessons in law school through the omission of race in the classroom, interactions with peers and professors, and accusations that they have been admitted thanks to affirmative action and not thanks to their own merits. Through this process, these students become keenly aware of their racial otherness.

Law students joined panethnic organizations for similar reasons: to be among copanethnics and for cultural familiarity. As Chapter 5 describes, panethnic student organizations provide professional, academic, and social services. Members study, network, and socialize with their copanethnics. This was the case for both the Society of Asian American Law Students and the Society of Latino Law Students. Luis Pérez described it best when he called the conjoined mentor and friendship facet of these organizations "one of the[ir] beauties." Members support one another in countless ways and learn to rely on their law school second families.

This support continues as students plan their career trajectory. Asian American and Latino students hoping to work at firms share similar strategies regarding their relations with their panethnic communities. The three strategies Chapter 6 discusses—marginal panethnicity, tempered altruism, and instrumental ethnicity—offer different routes through which law-firm-track Asian American and Latino law students can become lawyers while managing their relations with their respective communities. The strategies vary according to their particular sense of proximity and connection to their panethnic group: those who grew up in predominantly white communities were more likely to assert marginal panethnicity, whereas those who grew up in or near panethnic communities who were more likely to subscribe to tempered altruism or instrumental ethnicity. Far from being mutually exclusive, however, these strategies often intersect, particularly in the case of women of color.

As Chapter 7 discusses, Asian American and Latina women described a similar need to juggle intersecting professional, immigrant, and gendered identities. Already concerned with how to most effectively achieve work-life balance, women law students—even at this precareer stage—worried about how to best support their families. Marta Ortiz is already planning the careers of her younger siblings, while Lydia Kang's mother fears that a law degree has made her daughter "too intimidating" to find a prospective spouse.

Although Asian Americans and Latinos may be seen differently in the American imaginary, their experiences are quite similar, especially in law school. The sense of racial awareness they develop, combined with their experience of recognizing law schools' lack of diversity, heightens their sense of racial otherness. As immigrants and racialized nonwhite Americans in and out of law school, they occupy a liminal space between the polarities of black and white America. They are in the middle. It would be wrong to say there were not differences between these groups of students—there were, but more than anything else, these differences were school based.

Western Elite versus Private Metropolitan

Why study law students at differently ranked law schools? The answers are simple: to examine similarities in legal education, writ large, and to enunciate different life chances based on rank of law school. In other words, to understand how career trajectories differ for students at different law schools. I anticipated differences between Western Elite and Private Metropolitan, but what I discovered was not what I had expected.

On the basis of previous research, I assumed there would be a stark socioeconomic difference between students at the two schools: students from
Western Elite would probably hail from upper-middle-class, highly educated families, and those from Private Metropolitan would likely be from
working-class, less educated families. But this was not reflected in my findings. Instead, a bifurcated socioeconomic background characterized the
students from Western Elite, with about half the sample hailing from upper-
middle-class, highly educated families and the other half from the working
class with parents who had a high school diploma or less. Meanwhile, most
respondents from Private Metropolitan were solidly middle class and from
college-educated families with a few whose parents earned advanced degrees
or completed only high school.

Despite socioeconomic differences, the respondents also shared similarities. Students from both law schools took the same first-year courses, used
the same legalese, and belonged to similar student organizations (although
there were fewer journal options at Private Metropolitan compared with
Western Elite). The students described similar reasons for going to law
school and even dressed in similar outfits. At Western Elite, this could be
seen during OCIP interviews in particular, when law-firm-aspiring students
sought to dress the part. Students at Private Metropolitan did not have the
opportunity to participate in an OCIP, as firms target only highly ranked
schools, but this did not prevent students here from usually wearing business casual attire. But in this case I suspect this was because many of them
worked (paid and unpaid) and needed to present themselves professionally.
Thus, one apparent similarity between contexts—a particular presentation
of self—actually revealed a difference, specifically, the reasons *why* students
wore business casual clothing.

We also see in Chapter 6 that those from Western Elite aspired to work
at large firms, whereas those from Private Metropolitan spoke of working for
smaller firms. The instrumental nature of activating one's ethnicity speaks
to this—working for smaller firms focusing on tax, real estate, or elder law
and finding these opportunities in ethnic niches. Law students from Private
Metropolitan network for future work and business opportunities, and this
begins in law school, where they join panethnic organizations for practical
purposes. Unlike the students from Western Elite who appear to be immersed
in panethnic organizations as a part of their law school experience, those
from Private Metropolitan joined for reasons related more to professional
development. But similar to their Western Elite peers, they stayed and became involved in panethnic causes at the community level. Recall the striking example from Chapter 5 of the group of multiethnic Asian American law
students from Private Metropolitan who tutor youth in a Chinese enclave.

How Asian American and Latino students from two differently ranked
law schools activate their panethnic allegiance has important theoretical

implications. In both law schools, most Asian American and Latino law students had not been involved in panethnic organizations in college. Law school changed that. Yet their reasons to join panethnic organizations differed by school: those from Western Elite cited cultural familiarity, while students from Private Metropolitan cited academic support. Because many respondents from Private Metropolitan were second-career students or engaged in paid and unpaid work while also attending law school, they had more limited time to socialize and were thus more strategic about their decision to join panethnic student organizations.

Like their peers from Western Elite, those from Private Metropolitan recognized the omission of race in classrooms or the visible presence of only a few faculty of color. Some experienced what they felt to be prejudice in the classroom but made excuses for their professors. Remember Farrah Khan from Chapter 7, who felt that her professor favored her white male peers but rationalized how she could still benefit from the situation by saying, "It's good that you get the criticism because you can use the criticism and you can try to make yourself better. Whereas if they're [white men who are] told everything they're doing is right, . . . [they are] just going to think that they're right. And they're just going to suck forever. So I try to put a positive spin on it in that way." In contrast, respondents from Western Elite unapologetically discussed their experiences with race in the classroom. For example, in Chapter 4, Esperanza Macias openly shares her annoyance at her professor's inability to pronounce her name correctly. Instead of providing an excuse for him, Esperanza fumed with anger at his insensitivity.

In *Managing Elites* (2005), Debra Schleef argues that elite business and law students have a blasé attitude about their schooling and future careers. Although the students from Western Elite did not always vocalize a blasé attitude, they did appear jaded. Perhaps because of this, the students of color at Western Elite needed something to invest in, something out of the ordinary but also an intricate part of law school. This something was provided by panethnic student organizations. Western Elite Asian American and Latino students' commitment to such organizations reflects their process of assimilation to their law school. In contrast, Asian American and Latino law students at Private Metropolitan hustled to get through law school, constructing various possible explanations for their professors' behaviors. Because Private Metropolitan is a lower-ranked law school, the students are aware that they must perform well in classes and on the bar exam, and they thus tend to not divert their energies elsewhere, such as panethnic concerns. In the end, it appears that students at Western Elite have the luxury to think more about how race matters for their schooling and profession, compared to the students at Private Metropolitan.

Regardless, the legal profession (including law school) still lacks racial diversity. In spite of increases in Asian American and Latino law students and lawyers, law schools perpetuate Wendy Leo Moore's (2008) institutional white space. Even the white students whose voices we heard in Chapter 3 recognized that "law school is white." These students spoke about the need for professors of color to mentor nonwhite law students and the importance of having a student body that reflected the population of their school's city. These sentiments were expressed at both schools, and both white and nonwhite law students advocated a more diverse profession.

Incidental Racialization through Performative Assimilation

At its core, this book describes the incidental racialization of Asian American and Latino law students. I identify two types of assimilation that panethnic students experience at law school: (1) elite professionalization, through which students are integrated into mainstream America as members of a prestigious profession, and (2) legal socialization, through which students are integrated via law school into the legal profession. Through racialization, present in both processes, students learn to identify and be identified in terms of their panethnic identity on the front stage and backstage. Law students simultaneously absorb expectations as a part of professional socialization and racialization and also perform them. They may be less vocal on the front stage of a classroom to depress racialized expectations (e.g., the "angry person of color") but will voice their concerns on the backstage while among peers in panethnic organizations. Their decisions in doing so demonstrate their own agency as a part of this dual process of assimilation and racialization.

Racialization and assimilation are not just prescribed by a hegemonic society. In the early 1900s, Antonio Gramsci wrote in his *Prison Notebooks* that hegemony exists and survives through a process of coercion and consent. Stuart Hall elaborates on Gramsci's theory: "There is no pure case of coercion/consent—only different combinations of the two dimensions. Hegemony is not exercised in the economic and administrative fields alone, but encompasses the critical domains of cultural, moral, ethnic, and intellectual leadership" (1996, 426). If we were to view racialization as hegemony, then Asian American and Latino experiences in law school support this endeavor, even if not intentionally.

More globally, this book examines a microcosm of society—law school—to understand the experiences of second-generation racialized immigrants. But these lessons, while context specific, speak more broadly to race relations and continued racialization within American society in general. In the course of professional socialization, law students are taught, through covert and overt language and action, the proper decorum for attorneys—how to speak, how to dress, and how to argue. When these students are nonwhite, they are also taught, through less formal interactions, that they are racial "others" in this environment and that they belong to particular umbrella affinity groups. They learn in the classroom that they should avoid raising issues related to race and that their best chance of success involves finding academic, professional, and social support among copanethnics in affinity groups.

Between sips of coffee, while sitting in cafés, law school libraries, parks, and living rooms, I listened as students shared their stories. Classrooms can be hostile, and peers can speak hurtful words. Front-stage interactions in the classroom with professors and peers introduce Asian American and Latino law students to the unfamiliar world of law school—its curriculum, culture, and language. At the same time, students find comfort by seeking out the familiar among copanethnics in student organizations, soon to become their law school families. The panethnic nature of these organizations anchors each outing, study session, or networking event. Through their participation in these groups, students undergo backstage racialization.

Performing on these stages becomes a valuable lesson in immigrant assimilation and racialization, more generally. On the societal level, immigrant adaptation varies by history, politics, and culture—both for the host and the immigrant. Broadly speaking, contemporary U.S. culture embraces Asian Americans and Latinos, and institutions, such as law, extend a welcoming hand. Members of these two panethnic groups enter the legal profession, but not without keen awareness of their own histories, politics, and culture. In law school, Asian American and Latino students assimilate to legal professional norms but also come to recognize how they as nonwhite "others" also, inevitably, deviate from the standard. They recognize that neither their communities nor their histories align with those of the modal student. Furthermore, they learn these lessons in classrooms where they are numerically and culturally outnumbered and where they experience marginalization. This sense of deviation from the norm heightens their panethnic or racial awareness, and then mingling with copanethnics further fosters this awareness. Their experiences with racialization then affect how they position themselves as racialized attorneys. Specifically, as Chapter 6 documents, Asian American and Latino law students who aspire to a law firm trajectory intend to strategically carve out a meaningful personal and professional space in their careers.

But fostering an environment where panethnicity becomes salient is not intentional on the part of panethnic student organizations. The intent, rather, is to provide academic, professional, and social support. It is for this reason that I saw Asian American and Latino law students incidentally assimilate to panethnic student organizations while surrounded by copanethnic causes, peers, and networking opportunities. The presence of racial otherness or racial familiarity results in incidental racialization. Joining panethnic organizations is a deliberate decision, but the effect of that decision is incidental.

Asian American and Latino law students not only learn to identify with copanethnics but also advocate on behalf of their respective communities through volunteer work and plans for their future careers.

Why is this important? Because the demographics of the legal profession are changing and so is our country. The United States is projected to be a minority-majority nation by 2050, and Asian American and Latino demographic growth are responsible for much of this change. The findings from this study have far-reaching implications that speak to larger processes of race, marginalization, and immigrant adaptation. The immigrant experience is diverse, and one formula does not capture the differences among cultures, languages, and histories.

I propose that while immigrant assimilation happens in broader society, it also happens elsewhere—schools, organizations, and broader panethnic communities, to name just a few. These diverse venues and routes of assimilation constitute a malleable racial order. As Eileen O'Brien puts it:

> The future of race may be thus not in academic theories and racial terminology, but in the everyday experiences of the racial middle themselves, as they do the work of carving out a space that they can call their own. This space values bilingualism, even multilingualism, languages "of the world," whether or not they seem to correspond to one's particular ethnicity. This space values cultural traditions that do not emanate from the dominant culture, and welcomes the opportunity to celebrate multiple traditions simultaneously. (2008, 217)

Asian American and Latino law students exist in this space that values cultural traditions and languages "of the world." This space also conjures multiple facets of racialization and assimilation. In this space, professional socialization is neither innocuous nor "bleached out." It is nuanced, processual, and perpetually reinforces mainstream norms and frameworks.

Epilogue

In December 2012, shortly after I started my position at Brooklyn College and about a year after I completed my fieldwork, I received an e-mail from one of the respondents. This respondent and I had not spoken in about three years, but he remembered my study and had touched base to tell me that he was leaving the legal profession. He provided me with anecdotes about his friends' professional trajectories and dissatisfaction with their jobs. Originally, I had not planned to follow up with respondents for a few more years, hoping their real-world experiences would help me understand the racialization that continues after law school. But when I heard from this respondent, I was motivated to jumpstart the process and extend the current study.

I began to contact and interview former respondents. The data collection is still ongoing, but this epilogue provides a sneak peek into the results of my new effort, a look into socialization on the job and continued racialization. With the help of a doctoral student at the City University of New York Graduate Center, I located 85 of the original 101 respondents (5 more were added in 2013). Through public searches and professional biographies (such as on LinkedIn), I now have a better picture of these respondents' career trajectories, where they reside in the country (and the world), and the types of professional organizations in which they are involved. The information gleaned from locating the 85 respondents and reinterviewing 20 underscores that race continues to matter for these practicing attorneys. But it now matters in different ways and for different people. That is to say, depending on the career track, one may assert one's race or contend with racialization. The remainder of the epilogue discusses the emerging patterns.

Where Did They Go?

Where did the respondents go two to three years after earning their juris doctor degrees? Unsurprisingly, over 50 percent of the Latino and Asian American respondents now work at firms (roughly 31 percent at large firms, and roughly 21 percent at medium and small firms). About one-quarter of them are employed in state or local government, while about 11 percent work in the nonprofit world. The remaining roughly 20 percent are spread among business, education, self-employment, and outside the field of law. What does this tell us? In the aggregate, these figures closely track the expected career trajectories of law students as reported in other research, such as the After the JD project supported by the American Bar Foundation.[1] But when disaggregated on the basis of race and law school, some interesting patterns and telltale signs of stratification emerge.

First, the visible measures of success. Unsurprisingly, which law school respondents attended bears a strong influence on career trajectories. Although over 50 percent of the respondents currently work in law firms, a clear relationship exists between rank of law school and firm size. The majority of Latino and Asian American respondents who attended Western Elite work for large corporate firms, while their peers from Private Metropolitan work for medium to small outfits. The data become even more interesting when looking at the career trajectory for those not working at law firms. Asian American respondents who attended Private Metropolitan tend to be concentrated in local government, with a few employed by business or nonprofit organizations. Asian American respondents who attended Western Elite are also concentrated in business and nonprofit organizations, although they are less likely to work in government. There appear to be differences among the Latino respondents too. In addition to working for law firms,

Latino respondents are either working in the nonprofit world or in government. This is the case for Latino respondents from both law schools and requires further investigation.

What is more, preliminary analysis of completed interviews reveals that race matters differently for attorneys depending on their jobs. Respondents employed by large firms report feelings of being one of a few Latinos or Asian Americans in their offices. While those who work for government or nonprofit organizations may encounter more copanethnics, they experience alienation and discrimination within the profession at large. The respondents convey related reasons for their involvement in professional panethnic organizations: for networking if they intend to leave their current jobs, for finding a job, and for socializing.

Some of these new conversations were face to face and some were over the phone. I reestablished rapport with respondents and began each conversation by saying I was "catching up." People told me about taking the bar exam, their current work environment, and their significant others. I told them about finishing my dissertation, my move to New York City, and my students. Importantly, and most significant to this book, we talked about their career trajectories. I learned that they are still forging their identities as attorneys, as Latinos and Asian Americans, and in most cases, as attorneys of color. Four primary themes emerged from these conversations: (1) the legal world is even more white than law school, (2) race-based stereotypes are experienced at work, (3) panethnic camaraderie and obligations to one's community remain important issues, and (4) respondents grapple with the pros and cons of current or future involvement in panethnic organizations. I now discuss each of these themes in turn and underscore how they matter for the career trajectories of Asian American and Latino lawyers.

Law Is (Still) White

As now practicing attorneys, these respondents still experience law as a white space. Racialization in law school prepared them for such demographics, but they did not realize this until they began working. Indeed, they feel this institutional whiteness even more strongly than when they were law students. A feeling of alienation was especially profound among those who now work at law firms and find themselves trying desperately to assimilate to the dominant culture. Margaret Cha, a Korean American respondent from Private Metropolitan and now a tax attorney at a large firm on the East Coast, described the cultural and professional pressure to fit in:

> And now we're working for these Fortune 500 companies, and the next minute, I'm in the room with the VP of tax of these huge companies. And I just suddenly feel like I need to act a certain way, which

is not to let my unruly immigrant side out. I have to act eloquent and polished like I grew up in a country club. It's like this act that I feel I need to put on . . . [and] I'm trying to mimic everyone else's behavior. . . . I already feel like my Asianness is highlighted. And I need to adjust it so I can kind of assimilate better in that meeting environment—not stand out like a sore thumb or not to misrepresent the company.

A sense of imposter syndrome, particularly as an "unruly immigrant," appears to haunt many respondents even after law school. Margaret attempts to adjust her demeanor when in meetings with white clients but is acutely aware that she is unlike everyone else in those rooms. While law school heightened racial awareness, the lack of people of color in the work environment further signals to the respondents that they are still and always outsiders—both as immigrants and as nonwhites.

A similar story unfolds for respondents who work in the nonprofit world, which is presumed to be filled with attorneys of color. Many would-be attorneys expect that, here, they will experience fewer instances of alienation or unfamiliarity. Yet these organizations can also be predominantly white. Esperanza Macias, the Mexican American respondent who graduated from Western Elite, now works for a nonprofit organization that provides immigration services. She said, "A lot of my colleagues, even outside of [my place of work] that do immigration work, are not primarily Latino." Similarly, Jenna Ito, the mixed-race (Japanese and white) attorney who graduated from Private Metropolitan, put the racial composition of the legal profession into perspective:

I think when you're in the nonprofit legal world you're going to encounter more minorities. . . . I don't know if it's the nature of the work that draws them to it. It's also [that,] in a lot of nonprofits, they're looking for people with language skills other than English. And so that's when you tend to see more Asian [American] and Latino attorneys. . . . [W]hen I have gone to other things, like whether it was continuing legal education things or whatever, it's pretty evident that people of color are still a minority in the field.

When asked whether she still felt this way now that she lives in Hawaii, where Asian Americans (including many people who identify as mixed race) are over half the population, Jenna elaborated on assumptions made about numerical representation:

Hawaii is largely Asian [American]. So . . . there are more people in this field who look like me. But there is still, I think, yeah, there's

still something about, even if you're Asian—especially if you're local, right? . . . I was born and raised here. So I know what I've noticed for myself and for a lot of my colleagues who are the same. You
know, they're mixed race, they're local, they're born and raised here.
We . . . have to overcompensate a lot around that. I went to a networking thing recently, and so a lot of the more prominent sort of legal
figures in the room were white, older white men. Which is an interesting dynamic for Hawaii because, again, Hawaii is largely Asian.

Although there are more Asian American attorneys in Hawaii, Jenna was
struck by the overrepresentation of older white men among prominent lawyers. This type of encounter reinforces for these respondents once again that
they fall outside the modal representation. While one could argue that the
demographics of law are changing and that there will be more prominent
Asian American attorneys in ten, twenty, or thirty years, the fact remains
that respondents *currently* feel marginalized in the profession.

Bryn Singh, an Indian American respondent from Western Elite, talked
about her experience working in the nonprofit legal world:

You have the inherent, I call it kind of a fratty, culture. Like, lawyers
are a little fratty—I don't know what other ways to describe it. It has
a very dude kind of culture associated with middle-to-high-income
straight white guys. And that was what it was like at the law school
as well, but I guess a little less intensely so . . . but for the most part,
straight white men are the lion's share of attorneys.

The legal profession and the culture surrounding it remain predominantly
white, even in the nonprofit world. In law school, at least there were a readily available population of copanethnics and easy access to organizations
to turn to for support. Yet these opportunities are less available in the profession itself. That these respondents notice racial underrepresentation and
continue to feel like "others" demonstrates the insidious culture of whiteness
in law. In this sense, my preliminary follow-up findings corroborate those of
the *Washington Post* article (Rhode 2015) cited in Chapter 3—that law sorely
lacks diversity. It is perhaps no surprise then that Latino and Asian American respondents have either joined or are considering joining panethnic bar
associations.

Race Is Not a Problem, I Think

In line with Eileen O'Brien's argument, those in the racial middle characterize their experiences in the United States as "inclusion, acceptance, and

unfettered access to the American dream" (2008, 124). For the most part, respondents are grateful for their jobs and acceptance into the fold of main-stream America. At the same time, they are also unequivocal products of an American society that stubbornly defines racism as solely a black experience. Thus, although Latino and Asian American respondents appear to downplay race, it is largely because they lack acceptable vocabulary to articulate how their outsider treatment and experiences are race based, despite not being black.

The majority of the respondents work in environments where there are few copanethnics. Kurt Waters is mixed-race (Taiwanese and white), gradu-ated from Western Elite, and now works for an international firm in a met-ropolitan city. When asked whether his panethnicity matters to him at work, he replied:

> It's funny, because our office is trying to revitalize the mentorship program, so they asked us to try to select partner mentors. And I'm gravitating toward the [only] Asian American male partner. When I contacted him, I was kind of thinking, "It's either because he's Asian American or he's just a really nice guy and I get along with him. . . ." I think it's part of it—I think his [pan]ethnicity does play a part. And it's subconscious. You can kind of assume, I guess, a shared background and experience.

At no particular point in his response did Kurt explicitly state that he thinks about being Asian American while at work, except to identify this potential mentor. When I asked what he meant by "shared background and experi-ence," Kurt replied, "Just because he was an Asian American associate before he became a partner. In a predominantly white firm." Even though Kurt lives in a racially cosmopolitan urban center, he seeks mentorship from the sole Asian American partner at his firm for a sense of familiarity and also to gather survival tips on being an Asian American associate. That Kurt feels it necessary to seek out an Asian American mentor signals his sense of racial alienation in his predominantly white firm.

The awareness of being a racial minority is quite stark for these practic-ing attorneys. Susan de Castro, a graduate of Western Elite, now lives in a racially diverse, major city on the East Coast, working for a small law firm. When asked about her current experiences as an Asian American attorney, she said:

> Here in [my city], I'm definitely aware [that, out] of maybe thirty people [in my office], I'm the only Asian person. There was another young Asian [American] attorney but she left earlier this year. . . .

I don't know how to describe it. I've definitely been aware of being an Asian [American] person. But I don't know if it's affected me, if that makes sense.

Susan shares Kurt's reluctance to affirmatively analyze how being Asian American has affected her at work. This sense of uncertainty, again, could arise from insufficient vocabulary to describe how race matters for those in the racial middle.

It is not necessarily always negative to be aware of one's racial otherness. Latino respondents, especially those who speak Spanish, noted how being Latino can benefit their career; Natalia Melendez, who graduated from Western Elite, explained:

There are so few of us, especially in [this large city on the East Coast]. . . . [T]here's actually five hundred attorneys in our office. And I think there's maybe three or four Latinos. . . . And so they knew I spoke Spanish, and they knew that a new attorney was starting who did speak Spanish. Me! I have felt like my skills are in high demand, which has been nice and gives me sort of job security in a way. I know some of my friends [who don't speak Spanish] also started when I did, [and] they've been feeling a little bit of pressure when there's not a lot of work and layoffs [loom,] and [they are] nervous about how secure their position is.

Although Latinos may be underrepresented in particular legal sectors, some respondents feel that their Spanish skills trump that awareness of otherness. They feel valued and appear to be more confident in their job security.

Panethnic Camaraderie and Obligations

Some respondents feel a sense of obligation to their panethnic communities on both a personal and societal level. As they did in law school, these respondents learn about community needs, only now they actually have the tools to assist. Some respondents were supported by copanethnics in their budding careers and noted the value of being involved in their communities. Lucia Gutierrez, a Mexican American graduate from Western Elite, credited established Latino attorneys for helping her secure a job:

There was one Latina who worked for a Latino organization along with four other Latinos who really had my back. They were like, "Hey, there's a job opening up. . . . We will try to advocate for you to get that position." So I think that was also something I hadn't really realized. You draw on relationships, and . . . I do hold working on

reproductive health and health policy, when it comes to affecting Latinas, close to my heart. . . . But I think that [this Latino] organization
really highlighted and identified that. They really have been a great
help in this process.

Because there were so few Latinos in the health policy field, Lucia realized
that camaraderie among copanethnics was crucial for her career growth.

Respondents also noted how they feel a sense of duty to adequately represent their communities, especially now that they have the requisite skills
to do so. Jessica Laus graduated from Western Elite and now works for a city
government on the West Coast. She described her sense of obligation as a
Filipina to represent her ethnic community:

Filipino Americans . . . were just this past election able to vote some-
body into the legislature, assembly member Bonta [of California].
First time in a hundred years that a Filipino has been in the state legislature, assembly or senate. And then our numbers [in law schools]
have stayed the same. . . . I definitely think we need more political representation or legal representation. And I do feel this kind of
sense of responsibility for that. . . . Sometimes people will ask me,
"Oh, have you ever considered running?" If I was the most qualified candidate and I was ready for the position, I would do it. And it
would be because there hasn't been anybody else.

For Jessica, political representation is crucial. And now that she is an attorney, she is better credentialed to take on a political role if she so desires (and
feels ready). This sense of obligation to the community goes beyond generous
donations, pro bono services, or networking. It appears to be a conjoined
camaraderie and obligation to represent one's community and support its
endeavors and those of the people in it. These respondents then also recognize the value of panethnic bar associations.

Who Is in, Who Is out of Panethnic Bar Associations

Natalia Melendez, with whom we reconnected earlier, found it difficult to
secure a job immediately following graduation. She joined the Hispanic National Bar Association to gain access to job postings. After she finally found
a job and started work at her current firm, a fellow Latina associate suggested
that she remain involved in the association. Natalia recalled, "She recom-
mended that I come to one of the meetings, and so I did. And this is a good
networking opportunity—seeing a lot of different people with similar backgrounds in different areas of law. . . . I think it's good to keep up with these
people and see what else, what other interesting work, people are doing. And

[it's good for] not just work [but because of] just being so involved with your work and not keeping up with other people and making friends and all that." Natalia initially joined the panethnic association for practical reasons but ended up making friends there. The other respondents who joined panethnic bar associations reported similar motivations, such as joining to find jobs or to network for future job opportunities. They also mentioned the general desire to be involved in a professional bar association. Joining the panethnic one just seemed to make sense because of shared background, or as Kurt Waters said about joining the Asian American Bar Association, "It just felt like the natural thing to join."

The respondents who were not yet a part of panethnic bar associations all plan to join one in the future. When I spoke to Lucia Gutierrez, she was completing a fellowship in a major city on the East Coast and in the midst of packing to move back to a Western state. She had struggled with acclimating to the world of work:

> Everything is so much work! It's hard to think of doing anything else outside of my job. It was maybe a greater challenge to keep a life-work balance this past year than even my last two years of law school. . . . I think that once I'm a little more financially stable then I'll have the opportunity to actually financially support organizations that work [for Latinos] and maybe have a little more time for that life-work balance.

Lucia's comment about the struggle to balance work and life was common for the respondents who found themselves too overwhelmed with adjusting to a new job, trying to secure a job, or learning how to navigate a new city. They have not yet found time for panethnic associations. Like Lucia, who plans to be involved in such organizations once her life stabilizes, Jenna will join the Asian American Bar Association. After moving back to Hawaii from a Western state and starting a new job, Jenna is acclimating to her work and life surroundings. When asked whether she was a part of the Asian American Bar Association, Jenna responded no:

> I've had a conversation about this with somebody else recently, because they were kind of like, "What's the point of joining AABA [Asian American Bar Association]? Because everyone is Asian here [in Hawaii]." But I think, for me, it's just because of my experience in [that Western state] and understanding that there is still this huge underrepresentation of Asians in the legal field. Still pretty important to me.

Jenna mentioned her negative experiences in the Western state as motivating her to join AABA to support its mission of providing professional support to

Asian American attorneys. She also mentioned the underrepresentation of Asian Americans in the legal profession as another motivator. Other respondents articulated the same concerns—that the legal profession lacks people who look like them, and joining a panethnic association will allow them to network with respective panethnic attorneys. Unfortunately, however, those who were interested in joining bar associations also noted logistical constraints: they were just too busy with work to attend panethnic functions. Unlike panethnic student organizations that are housed at law schools, it is far more difficult for practicing attorneys to become and remain committed to such organizations. Lack of access to copanethnics could further isolate these new attorneys.

Moving Forward

So far, the follow-up interviews provide some insight into the lives of these practicing attorneys. But the picture is not yet complete, and the interviews have led to more questions. Most of the follow-up respondents are women; men were also contacted to speak with me, and many initially responded enthusiastically but then ceased communication while coordinating interview logistics. There could be a host of reasons for this gender imbalance, ranging from the amicable relationship I cultivated with the women respondents to the women's desires to speak about their experiences, to perhaps more flexibility in these women's jobs as opposed to the men's. These are future questions to explore and perhaps ask respondents about directly during follow-up interviews.

As I discovered in the interviews, respondents still think about race and diversity. But the work world differs from law school in that it lacks a readily available support group. While there may be a few copanethnics in one's firm or nonprofit organization, the number pales in comparison to the multifaceted panethnic student organizations in law school. This leads to the questions: How will panethnicity matter (or not) without such ready access to the backstage process of racialization? And do panethnic bar associations provide support similar to that of the law student organizations?

These questions anchor my inquiries as I continue interviews. I seek to understand whether respondents continue to experience racialization and how they adapt to this larger process of assimilation as a part of an elite profession. I also continue to examine divergences in career trajectories between the respondents who went to the two differently ranked law schools. Prior research has found stratification in the bar according to law school rank, but to what extent does this matter and shape the lives of Latino and Asian American attorneys?

Although there are still more questions to ask, my preliminary findings indicate the importance of race at both institutional and personal levels.

Thus, racialization continues into the job and could affect respondents' career trajectories. Research on nonwhite attorneys finds that many are concentrated in ethnic niches or nonprofit organizations (Wilkins and Gulati 1996; Wilkins 2004). Some believe that a sense of affinity or altruism leads them there, but it also seems likely that nonwhite attorneys are driven to these outlets because they experience alienation in mainstream jobs (Levin 2009). This theoretical conjecture speaks to larger processes of covert discrimination within a society that normalizes and prioritizes a white racial framework. For Latino and Asian American lawyers, becoming a part of mainstream America is to experience long periods—if not an entire career's worth—of incidental racialization.

APPENDIX

Respondent Characteristics

Name	Law school	Year in law school	Race or ethnicity	Immigrant generation	Region
Aaron Thompson	Private Metropolitan	1L	Japanese-white	2nd (mom)	West
Abby Valenzuela	Western Elite	1L	Mexican-white	2nd (dad)	Northeast
Adam Rhee	Western Elite	1L	Korean	2nd	West
Ahn Tran	Western Elite	2L	Chinese-Vietnamese	2nd	West
Andersen Lee	Private Metropolitan	3L	Korean	1.5	West
Andréa Rodriguez	Private Metropolitan	2L	Guatemalan-Mexican	2nd	West
Angela Kim	Private Metropolitan	2L	Korean	2nd	West
Anjali Chatterjee	Private Metropolitan	2L	Indian	2nd	West
Araceli Baez	Western Elite	2L	Mexican	2nd	West
Arely Zapata	Western Elite	1L	Puerto Rican	1st	U.S. territory
Asha Patel	Private Metropolitan	3L	Indian	1.5	International
Beatriz Mendoza	Private Metropolitan	3L	Salvadoran	2nd	West
Ben Brightmore	Private Metropolitan	3L	White	3rd+	West
Binh Nguyen	Private Metropolitan	2L	Vietnamese	2nd	West
Blanca Vasquez	Private Metropolitan	1L	Chicana	3rd+	West
Brandon Shi	Private Metropolitan	2L	Chinese-white	3rd+	Midwest
Brett Larkin	Western Elite	3L	White	3rd+	South

(continued)

Name	Law school	Year in law school	Race or ethnicity	Immigrant generation	Region
Brittany Adams	Private Metropolitan	3L	White	3rd+	South
Bryn Singh	Western Elite	2L	Indian	2nd	West
Candice Jacobs	Western Elite	2L	White	3rd+	Midwest
Christopher Gonzalez	Western Elite	1L	Mexican	2nd	West
Cindy Cooper	Western Elite	3L	White	3rd+	Midwest
Clara Tierney	Western Elite	3L	White	2nd (dad)	West
Corey Mott	Private Metropolitan	3L	Ecuadoran-white	2nd (mom)	West
Cyrus Dulay	Private Metropolitan	3L	Filipino-Chinese	2nd	West
Daniel Rincón	Western Elite	3L	Mexican	2nd	Midwest
Dean Tam	Private Metropolitan	3L	Chinese	3rd+	South
Debbie Kwan	Western Elite	2L	Chinese	1.5	West
Diego Sanshes	Western Elite	2L	Mexican	2nd	West
Eddie Ma	Private Metropolitan	3L	Taiwanese	2nd	South
Edmund Huang	Western Elite	3L	Chinese	2nd	West
Elena Chaidez	Private Metropolitan	3L	Mexican	3rd+	West
Elina Reyes	Western Elite	3L	Chicana	2nd	West
Elise Brown	Private Metropolitan	1L	White	3rd+	West
Ernesto Chavez	Private Metropolitan	3L	Mexican	2nd	West
Esperanza Macias	Western Elite	2L	Mexican	2nd	West
Estelle Ngan	Private Metropolitan	2L	Chinese-Vietnamese	2nd	West
Evellia Moreno	Western Elite	1L	Mexican	1.5	West

Name	Law school	Year in law school	Race or ethnicity	Immigrant generation	Region
Evelyn Villarosa	Private Metropolitan	3L	Filipina	2nd	West
Farrah Khan	Private Metropolitan	2L	Indian-Pakistani	2nd	West
Felicia Álvarez	Western Elite	1L	Chicana	3rd+	West
Fred Ngo	Western Elite	2L	Chinese-Vietnamese	2nd	West
Gregory Watts	Western Elite	2L	White	3rd+	South
Helen Trieu	Private Metropolitan	3L	Chinese-Vietnamese	2nd	West
Hollie Jackson	Private Metropolitan	1L	White	3rd+	Midwest
Itzel Lopez	Private Metropolitan	3L	Mexican	3rd+	West
Jenna Ito	Private Metropolitan	3L	Japanese-white	3rd+	West
Jessica Laus	Western Elite	3L	Filipina	2nd	West
Jillian Wong	Private Metropolitan	3L	Chinese	1.5	South
Joaquin Moran	Western Elite	1L	Argentinian	1st	International
Jocelyn Brady	Western Elite	2L	Korean-white	2nd (mom)	West
Jonathan Song	Western Elite	3L	Korean	2nd	South
Joshua Vera Cruz	Western Elite	2L	Filipino	2nd	South
Julia Mirren	Private Metropolitan	3L	White	3rd+	West
June Taveras	Western Elite	3L	Dominican	2nd	Northeast
Justin Geller	Western Elite	3L	White	3rd+	Midwest
Jyoti Kaur	Western Elite	3L	Indian	2nd	Midwest
Kevin Gu	Private Metropolitan	3L	Chinese	2nd	West
Kurt Waters	Western Elite	3L	Taiwanese-white	2nd (mom)	West

(continued)

Name	Law school	Year in law school	Race or ethnicity	Immigrant generation	Region
KyungHwa Joo	Private Metropolitan	3L	Korean	1st	International
Leah Xie	Private Metropolitan	3L	Chinese	2nd	International
Logan Camacho	Private Metropolitan	1L	Mexican–Native American	3rd+	West
Lori Rasmussen	Private Metropolitan	3L	White	3rd+	Midwest
Luara Castillo	Private Metropolitan	1L	Chicana	3rd+	West
Lucia Gutierrez	Western Elite	2L	Mexican	2nd	West
Luis Pérez	Western Elite	2L	Mexican-Salvadoran	2nd	West
Lydia Kang	Western Elite	2L	Chinese	2nd	Bicoastal
Maisy Sandoval	Western Elite	2L	Chicana	3rd+	West
Manuel Casas	Western Elite	2L	Mexican	2nd	West
Marcia Scott	Western Elite	1L	White	3rd+	West
Marco Saldaña	Western Elite	1L	Mexican	2nd	West
Margaret Cha	Private Metropolitan	3L	Korean	2nd	West
Marie Chiang	Western Elite	1L	Taiwanese	1.5	West
Marta Ortiz	Western Elite	2L	Mexican	1.5	West
Marvin Tambio	Western Elite	2L	Filipino	3rd+	Midwest
Matt Yoon	Western Elite	2L	Korean	2nd	South
Michael Cheng	Private Metropolitan	2L	Chinese	2nd	West
Mila Ahmadi	Western Elite	3L	Iranian	2nd	West
Mina Baek	Private Metropolitan	2L	Korean	2nd	West
Nancy Liang	Western Elite	1L	Chinese	2nd	West

Name	Law school	Year in law school	Race or ethnicity	Immigrant generation	Region
Natalia Melendez	Western Elite	2L	Mexican	2nd	South
Nick Morgan	Private Metropolitan	3L	White	3rd+	West
Noemi Castillo	Private Metropolitan	3L	Salvadoran	2nd	West
Norman Yuan	Western Elite	2L	Chinese	1.5	West
Ofelia Mohammed	Western Elite	1L	Eritrean	2nd	West
Olinda Cruz	Western Elite	1L	Mexican	2nd	West
Phillip Mattson	Western Elite	1L	White	3rd+	Midwest
Raquel Cortez	Western Elite	1L	Salvadoran-white	2nd (dad)	West
Ricardo Colon	Private Metropolitan	2L	Ecuadoran	1st	International
Rose Fong	Private Metropolitan	3L	Chinese	2nd	International
Samuel Zahn	Private Metropolitan	1L	White	3rd+	West
Sara Espinol	Western Elite	1L	Colombian	2nd	South
Scott Fahy	Private Metropolitan	3L	White	3rd+	West
Selena Vallejo	Western Elite	2L	Mexican	2nd	West
Serafina Novak	Private Metropolitan	2L	White	1.5	West
Smriti Kapur	Western Elite	1L	Indian	2nd	South
Spencer Fagan	Private Metropolitan	1L	White	3rd+	West
Stacy Jeong	Western Elite	1L	Argentinian-Korean	1.5	International
Supriya Shah	Western Elite	1L	Indian	2nd	South
Susan de Castro	Western Elite	3L	Filipina	2nd	Northeast
Thomas Cain	Western Elite	1L	White	3rd+	West

(*continued*)

Name	Law school	Year in law school	Race or ethnicity	Immigrant generation	Region
Trent Jackson	Private Metropolitan	3L	Black	3rd+	South
Whitney Hong	Private Metropolitan	2L	Chinese	1.5	West
Will Decker	Private Metropolitan	2L	White	3rd+	Northeast
Yuan Zhang	Western Elite	3L	Chinese	1st	International
Zahra Saatchi	Private Metropolitan	3L	Iranian	1.5	West

Note: For region designations, I use U.S. Census descriptors (Northeast, Midwest, South, and West).

NOTES

INTRODUCTION

1. All quotations come from interviews by the author conducted from 2009 to 2011 with students of two law schools. Unless otherwise noted, all respondent names are pseudonyms to maintain confidentiality.

2. As of 2015, there are 1,300,705 lawyers in the United States, which amounts to roughly 0.4 percent of the population (American Bar Association 2015).

3. This is a common adage among law students when describing their three-year tenure. In year one, law school scares students to death; in year two, it works them to death; but by year three, when they have learned all they need and are eagerly anticipating joining the workforce, law school bores them to death.

4. Richard Abel (1989) describes American law as a profession that restricted access for those who were not white Anglo-Saxon Protestants. While it seemed that law was a profession by which immigrants could acquire prestige, the bar was highly stratified. Americans of Western European heritage entered firms on Wall Street, but countless Eastern European immigrants did not have this opportunity. Instead, members of Eastern European ethnic groups served legal apprenticeships within their respective enclaves, thus permitting them to practice within and for their communities. Nonwhite individuals encountered obstacles to entering mainstream law similar to those of Eastern Europeans. With law's movement from an apprenticeship model to a more academic one, there were still few nonwhite attorneys until the 1980s. As reference, black attorneys made up only 2 percent of the bar in 1960.

5. I intentionally use the following descriptions interchangeably to demonstrate the fluidity among identifiers: nonwhite, minority, and people or person of color. I also use (pan)ethnicity to denote the conflating of ethnicity and race and the racialization processes of ethnic individuals. For example, while *Mexican* is an ethnic identity, *Latino* is panethnic and does not denote race. Whereas *Japanese* is an ethnicity, *Asian American* denotes race or panethnicity.

6. Social scientific research demonstrates time and again that individuals of color undergo discrimination, even for those who are middle class or above. Focusing on professionals in particular, Maria Chávez (2011) finds that Latino lawyers are often questioned about their linguistic proficiency and endure skepticism from colleagues that they, too, are attorneys, among other discriminatory actions. Joe Feagin (1991) argues that black professionals endure discrimination in public spaces, such as restaurants or retail stores. And Mia Tuan's (1998) Asian American respondents negotiate their identities between being seen as a "forever foreigner" and "honorary white."

7. Current available research that does examine the experiences of Asian American and Latino professionals looks at how actual and assumed immigrant backgrounds affect individuals' daily encounters. Some examples include Dhingra 2007, Gándara 1995, and Tuan 1998. Other works focus on issues of race and racism but not racialization; these works include M. Chávez 2011, Costello 2006, and Moore 2008.

8. Some early scholarship on professional socialization focuses on medicine; see Becker et al. 1976 and Bosk 1979. More recent research explores and compares professions, such as work by Carrie Yang Costello (2006), Robert Granfield (1992), Elizabeth Mertz (2007), and Debra Schleef (2005).

9. Joining law journals, especially in leadership roles such as editorships, demonstrates leadership and intellectual prowess. Club membership signals collegiality. Organizations look for and consider seriously these extracurricular markers of success before hiring attorneys.

10. Second-generation immigrants are the children of foreign-born parents, otherwise known as first-generation immigrants. Most current literature on immigrant integration focuses on the second generation and how they become a part of mainstream America. For more discussion on second-generation immigrants, refer to Portes and Rumbaut 2001, 2006.

11. Examples of other works that position panethnicity as the frame of analysis while discussing social phenomena include M. Chávez 2011, Dhingra 2007, Ochoa 2013, and Tuan 1998.

12. The terms *integration, assimilation*, and *adaptation* describe the ways immigrants adjust to life in the United States. I interchange these terms but mostly use *integration* and *adaptation*; *assimilation* connotes the Anglo conformity of European immigrants.

13. European ethnics may assert symbolic or optional ethnicities as Irish on Saint Patrick's Day or as German during Oktoberfest. This form of ethnic allegiance does not affect how they organize their lives or think about their daily interactions. For more discussion, see Waters 1990.

14. Some scholarship is emerging about the Latino middle class; see, for example, Flores 2011, Valdez 2011, and Vallejo 2012.

15. Western Elite and Private Metropolitan are pseudonyms for the two law schools discussed in this book.

16. Law schools are ranked by *U.S. News and World Report*, and prospective students consult these rankings when they apply to law schools. Based on some set criteria, these rankings influence how employers evaluate applicants. For detailed criteria and methodology, see Morse 2016.

17. Interviews lasted anywhere from forty-five minutes to two hours and took place in law school classrooms, university libraries, coffee shops, respondents' homes, public parks, and other spaces conducive to the respondents' schedules and comfort.

18. According to the 2015 U.S. Census, 59.7 percent of the Corvallis population consists of college graduates, in comparison to roughly 30 percent for the state of Oregon (U.S. Census Bureau 2016a, 2016b) and 31 percent for the United States (Ryan and Bauman 2016).

CHAPTER 1

1. The numbers bear this out. Enrollment in graduate programs saw an uptick during the beginning of the economic recession. Starting in 2008, graduate and professional programs experienced a steady increase in applications and enrollments until 2011, when enrollment began to taper. According to a report by the Council of Graduate Schools, degrees awarded increased across the board for certificate programs and for graduate degrees between 2009 and 2011 (Allum, Bell, and Sowell 2012).

2. The Law School Admission Test (LSAT) is required for application to law schools.

3. Biological determinists may attribute these findings to genetics—those who acquire more education are predisposed to scholastic achievement and pass on their genes to their offspring. This explanation, however, overlooks the importance of socialization and cultural capital.

4. For research on the academic successes of immigrant youth, see Fulgini 1997 and Hirschman 2001. Patricia Gándara's *Over the Ivy Walls* (1995) examines the achievements of Chicanos, while Vivian Louie's *Compelled to Excel* (2004) and *Keeping the Immigrant Bargain* (2012) evaluate the educational successes of second-generation Chinese and Latino youth, respectively.

5. Immigrants who migrated before they were teenagers are referred to as the 1.5 generation. See Portes and Rumbaut 2006.

6. All names of student organizations are pseudonyms to maintain confidentiality.

7. Many factors entice law students to consider joining a law firm, student loans notwithstanding.

CHAPTER 2

1. While black Americans continue to experience institutional racism, their American identity is not questioned in the same way that their Asian American and Latino counterparts' is. Further, there is widespread recognition and celebration of African Americans as *Americans*, as evidenced, for example, by Black History Month, whereas Asian Americans and Latinos are not represented (or celebrated) in the same way. Continued foreignizing can be found in daily occurrences, such as animal rights activists in New York City's Chinatown protesting the Lychee and Dog Meat Festival, which is held in Yulin, China, annually and not celebrated in the United States. See Sommerfeldt and Otis 2016.

2. It is also not surprising that Asian ethnics sought to identify as white rather than black given the latter's social position. James W. Loewen (1981) writes about this phenomenon in the case of Chinese in Mississippi, who chose to align with white Americans in an effort to avoid being seen as social pariahs (although there was evidence of considerable racial mixing between blacks and Chinese in the Mississippi Delta).

3. This legacy has had negative repercussions, seen in Asian Americans having to contend with microaggressions that assume lack of fluency or proficiency with American culture and language. Asian Americans are often believed to be foreigners and not bona fide Americans. For more discussion of the intermediary racial space occupied by Asian Americans, see Tuan 1998.

4. The Chinese Exclusion Act was spurred by nativism and fears of laboring Chinese taking jobs from white Americans. Chinese laborers were then barred from immigration to the United States for eighty years—the only ethnicity or race-based immigration policy in U.S. history.

5. Asian ethnics, especially Chinese, were often referred to as Celestials in the 1800s, when China was known as the Celestial Empire. For more discussion, see Takaki 1998.

6. This practice is not atypical, as other books on panethnic Latinos also examine Mexican American history as a proxy to understand the Latino experience. This is not to say that it is acceptable to conflate individual cultural, social, and linguistic traditions; the Latino panethnic group is quite heterogeneous. For the sake of understanding Latino sociohistory, however, the Mexican experience provides telling insight. For examples, see Chávez 2011, Gándara 1995, and Ochoa 2013.

7. I use *Plessy v. Ferguson* as a base for comparison, since most Americans are familiar with this case.

8. The creation of the Oriental School was held unconstitutional after *Brown v. Board of Education* (1956) but was constitutional before that under *Plessy*, as the school provided "equal" opportunity for the Asian students' education even as it institutionally segregated them from white pupils. For more discussion of this case and Asian American school segregation in general, see Kuo 1998.

9. This lesser-known segregation of Asian American children has received increasing attention, however, through educational outlets (both academic and journalistic). For a descriptive account, see Chang 2004; for a sociohistorical analysis, see Payne 1984.

CHAPTER 3

1. The 2012 Law School Admission Council reports the following average LSAT scores for test takers by race and ethnicity: Asian American, 152; black American, 142; Latino, 146; Native American, 145; white, 153 (Dalessandro, Anthony, and Reese 2012). Note that these averages are reported in the aggregate and do not reflect the variation in scores among applicants at differently ranked law schools. The websites of Western Elite and Private Metropolitan report the following median, 75th percentile, and 25th percentile, respectively, LSAT scores for 2014: Western Elite 167, 169, and 164 and Private Metropolitan 150, 153, and 146. To maintain the anonymity of the specific institutions in this study, I do not disclose the URL from which I acquired these data.

2. David B. Wilkins (1998) argues against the notion of value-neutral professional socialization, otherwise known as "bleached out" lawyering. Instead, he argues that racial salience creates different ways for black and white attorneys to think about their careers.

3. Phillip's grandfather, father, and sisters are all lawyers.

4. Interestingly, Nick notes that he has yet to have a Latino professor and surmises, "Maybe they'll do better." This comment could reflect one of two things: he expects that Latino professors may be better at teaching or that he does not yet have a basis for comparing Latino faculty with professors of the other two panethnic groups he mentioned (white and Asian). I suspect the latter, as he seemed pretty apathetic about legal pedagogy in general.

5. Two of the respondents from Private Metropolitan scored above the median LSAT score at Western Elite. Although they were accepted by higher-ranked institutions, these respondents chose Private Metropolitan for personal reasons.

6. Per self-reported law school data on their respective websites, the median undergraduate GPA for the 2009 entering class was 2.98 for Private Metropolitan and 3.79 for Western Elite.

CHAPTER 4

1. Total numbers of first-year law students increased nationally between 2009 and 2011 and began to taper in 2012. According to statistics from the American Bar Association, first-year enrollment increased by more than 2,000 students between 2008–2009 (49,414) and 2009–2010 (51,646) among two hundred surveyed law schools. The increase remained steady from 2009–2010 to 2010–2011 (52,488) but dipped considerably for the 2011–2012 first-year enrollees (48,697).

2. The shift in law school enrollees could be due to a decrease in job prospects for lawyers as the demand for legal services slowed.

3. Only students at Western Elite mentioned a decrease in Asian American representation at law school. Other than the Asian American students themselves, none of the students from Private Metropolitan conveyed this concern. One possible explanation worth exploring is that Private Metropolitan respondents might not have been enrolled in advanced placement classes in high school and college and thus were not accustomed to an overrepresentation of Asian Americans in their classes.

4. The dearth of Asian American law students could reflect cultural expectations or immigrant optimism. Asian American parents could direct their children toward more practical fields of study, such as natural sciences or engineering, versus the less practical fields of philosophy, English literature, or law. Immigrant selectivity could also play a role in the number of Asian American lawyers, more generally. Immigrant selectivity, or the brain-drain phenomenon, characterizes Asian American parents' migration, which could influence their children to major in the fields their parents studied. For more discussion, see Chou and Feagin 2008, S. Lee 1996, and Louie 2004.

5. Jessica noted that the facts of each case did not sufficiently address background factors that might have led to the eventual crime. For example, a domestic violence survivor who never reported her abuse could have decided to retaliate by assaulting her abuser and was then charged with a felony.

6. Kim Scheppele (1992) writes that women's testimonies in courtrooms are often interpreted to be overly emotional, which results in questions about the legitimacy of their stories. Judges often ask women witnesses to just state the facts, disallowing the retelling of stories that are part of their testimonies. For many women, testifying is an emotional exercise that commingles facts and visceral feelings. In the same vein, many

law students inject their feelings into their legal analyses, but they are expected to remain emotionally neutral, to just interpret the facts.

7. According to data compiled by the American Bar Association (2011), international students comprise less than 2 percent of Western Elite's student population.

8. The commonly designated racial groups in the United States are, in fact, multiethnic. Portes and Rumbaut (2006) extensively document the transition of multiethnic into panethnic or racialized groups. For example, the panethnic group "Asian" consists of ethnically Chinese, Filipino, Indian, Korean, Japanese, and Laotian individuals, among others. Similarly, the panethnic group "Latino" or "Hispanic" comprises ethnically Cuban, Mexican, Salvadoran, Peruvian, and Venezuelan individuals, among others. For more discussion on ascription of racialized categories and the assertion of ethnic identities, refer to Cornell and Hartmann 1998.

9. In follow-up interviews in 2013 and 2014, some respondents again recounted these same events, reflecting a strong impression.

10. While the LSAT score is a primary consideration for law school acceptance, studies have shown that standardized test scores are not reliable indicators of law school success, and they do not predict an aspiring attorney's ability to practice law. For more on SAT (Scholastic Aptitude Test) scores and success in college, see Bowen and Bok 1998 and Massey et al. 2003. For a discussion of LSAT scores and success in law school and beyond, see Wilkins 2000.

11. The state of Michigan passed the Michigan Civil Rights Initiative, also known as Proposal 2, in 2006, denying the use of race in law school admissions. This law was challenged in 2013, and in April 2014, the U.S. Supreme Court voted 6–2 to uphold Michigan's law.

12. When asked whether they were familiar with law-school-related blogs, virtually all respondents mentioned *Above the Law*.

CHAPTER 5

1. All law journal names are pseudonyms.

2. Although expressed in different ways, the unequivocal sentiment among most law students without regard to race, gender, socioeconomic background, or law school was that law school was the most difficult task they ever attempted.

3. According to historian Ronald Takaki, these localized affinity organizations provided assistance to new arrivals as they adapted to life in the United States. Specifically, some of the services included providing social centers, establishing temples, transmitting letters and remittances to China, and finding employment. For more discussion on these associations, see Takaki 1998.

4. Nearly 100 percent of the mixed-race Asian American and Latino law students sampled from both schools are involved in the panethnic organization that reflects their nonwhite ancestry, with which they also identify.

5. In contrast, many more white students reported that their parents were attorneys. Lacking this form of built-in familial knowledge and understanding of the law school process, many Asian American and Latino respondents found the panethnic organizations beneficial for learning the ropes of law school.

6. Law students speak of their years in law school through abbreviation—1L, 2L, 3L, or first-year, second-year, third-year, respectively. In this case, Luis is reminiscing about the second- and third-year law students who were a help to him.

7. By comparison, there were no academic advisors in Western Elite's SAALS or SLLS.

8. Maisy is involved in an organization that focuses on women-of-color issues at Western Elite; the members of this organization made phone calls congratulating the accepted women of color (Asian American, black American, Latino, Native American). The organization began informally years ago when a few women of color law students from the law school got together weekly to share their frustrations as minority women in law school. The interest in the group swelled, and within two years, the organization became a full-fledged student group at Western Elite.

9. To practice as an attorney, graduates must take and pass an intensive bar exam that tests legal knowledge and professional responsibility.

10. Many large firms offer mentorship programs that match associates of color with senior associates or partners. These firms also host diversity events, providing practitioners of color with the opportunity to mingle and network. Additionally, diversity task forces strategize to recruit and retain attorneys of color.

11. Affiliation with professional panethnic legal organizations provides resources, offers opportunities to network, and strengthens the recruitment initiative for increasing the numerical presence of Asian American and Latino attorneys.

CHAPTER 6

A version of this chapter was originally published as Yung-Yi Diana Pan, "Becoming a (Pan)Ethnic Attorney: How Asian American and Latino Law Students Manage Dual Identities," *Sociological Forum*, March 2, 2015, pp. 148–169. Used with permission of John Wiley and Sons.

1. Debra J. Schleef finds that elite business and law students manage altruism through redefinition so that "being socially responsible now has little to do with their work lives. Students learn to define pro bono work as similar to the volunteer work that any well-off individual should do to 'give back,' to feel some value in one's personal life, not out of some professional obligation" (1997, 635). For more discussion of how law students rationalize law firm jobs in lieu of altruism, see also Granfield 1992, Schleef 2005, and Stover 1988.

2. Students of color who excel academically are often seen to be acting white on the basis of the stereotype that only white students perform well in school. The non-white students (especially black and Latino) who achieve good grades or participate in extracurricular activities such as orchestra or tennis are seen as acting white. For more discussion, see Fordham and Ogbu 1986, and Ainsworth-Darnell and Downey 1998. Respondents who aspired to law firm positions or were a part of the law review were seen as acting white. Karolyn Tyson, William Darity Jr., and Domini Castellino (2005) contend that explaining underachievement among students of color by their fear of acting white is too simple. They argue that school structure, rather than peer pressure, is important to understanding black students' underachievement.

3. Lower-ranked law schools tend to be more socioeconomically and racially diverse. Judith Fischer (1996) finds more classroom participation at these types of institutions. She also notes that professors at lower-ranked institutions are more student-oriented compared with their counterparts at tier-one institutions, as they are not expected to frequently publish their research. For ethnographic comparisons among women and nonwhite students' classroom participation, see Mertz 2007.

4. Gita Wilder's 2008 *Race and Ethnicity in the Legal Profession: Findings from the First Wave of the After the JD Study* is one of the reports on a longitudinal study, concluded in 2010 and sponsored by the American Bar Foundation, that documented the careers of a cross-national sample of law graduates.

5. Nancy Lopez's (2003) book on Dominican students at an urban secondary school assesses the high dropout rates within this panethnic community, especially among boys. She argues that racial stigma combined with a lack of support and guidance creates inhospitable environments that discourage these boys from remaining in high school.

6. Citation of the specific ABA source would make obvious the law schools in this study; therefore the citation is intentionally omitted.

7. It should be noted that this is a change from the 2009 data collected by the ABA. Over 50 percent of the 2009 Private Metropolitan cohort went on to work for law firms, and fewer were in public interest. The change in employment preference over the past three years reveals how the recession affected the career prospects of graduates at lower-ranked institutions. This data also fails to reflect that because of the recession, many graduates took on temporary or unpaid positions—thus possibly explaining the spike in public interest work.

8. I collected data from four offices of two large, prominent firms on the West Coast and found that 80 percent of the attorneys earned their JDs from top-twenty law schools, and the rest came from schools with regional advantage.

9. Nonwhite attorneys make up approximately 9.7 percent of the American bar—3.9 percent blacks, 2.3 percent Asian Americans, and 3.3 percent Latinos. For more discussion on data and methods, see the 2012 report from the American Bar Association Commission on Racial and Ethnic Diversity in the Profession.

10. David B. Wilkins argues that not all "good" work goes without rewards. The visibility of public interest work could attract the attention of senior attorneys for career mobility. As Wilkins notes, "There are good reasons to suspect that black lawyers have an even greater need for the experience, visibility, and connections that public service potentially brings than their equally pressed but less disadvantaged white peers. It is not surprising, therefore, that these more vulnerable lawyers appear to seek out public service opportunities at a greater rate than other lawyers" (2004, 29).

11. Economists define *liquidable occupations* as those commonly engaged in by immigrant groups and exemplified by jobs that are easily transferable and are not tied up in capital. Examples of such occupations include barber, shoemaker, goldsmith, and tailor.

CHAPTER 7

1. Rosabeth Moss Kanter (1977) pioneered the investigation of gendered inequalities in the professions, revealing that women face gender discrimination despite the

numerical increase toward gender parity. For other discussions of gendered experiences in the professions, see Blair-Loy 2003, Epstein 1993, and Pierce 1995.

2. Professional women experience gendered expectations with regard to caregiving in addition to their professional duties. This phenomenon is particularly striking in law and especially in law firms. For more discussion on professional gendered expectations and stratification, see Blair-Loy 2003. For analysis of the legal profession in particular, see Pierce 1995, and Wallace and Kay 2012.

3. There are only three women of color faculty at Private Metropolitan—two Asian American, and one black; the rest of the faculty consists of men and white women.

4. Coined by Arlie Hochschild (2003), "second shift" refers to the domestic labor that working women are expected to perform in the home in addition to their paid labor.

5. For more discussion on the demure and subservient stereotype, see Pyke and Johnson 2003.

6. For a discussion of such dynamics in Vietnamese families, see Kibria 1993; in Latino families, see Hondagneau-Sotelo 1994.

7. Judith Fischer's field site, Chapman University Law School, is a lower-tiered law school that bills itself as providing a unique law school experience distinct from that offered at larger, highly ranked institutions that teach the philosophy of law as opposed to the logistics of law practice.

8. Rather than a permanent, full-time position, a contract attorney works on limited-time contracts that vary from project to project. They could be hired by firms as needed and given limited tasks, or they could freelance.

9. It should be noted that Helen's retired parents take on the majority of child care so that she and her physician husband can pursue their careers. Having retired parents nearby may also lessen the work-life balance burden for older women law students at Private Metropolitan and local students at Western Elite. This arrangement does not appear to be the anticipated norm among the students in this book.

CONCLUSION

1. The After the JD project is managed by the prominent legal scholars Bryant G. Garth, Robert L. Nelson, Ronit Dinovitzer, Gabriele Plickert, and Joyce Sterling. This longitudinal study tracked the 2002 JD graduating class (a sample of approximately five thousand JD graduates), with follow-up surveys in 2007 and 2010. These data have yielded numerous reports and papers, which can be accessed through the American Bar Foundation, at http://www.americanbarfoundation.org/publications/AftertheJD/AJD_Publications.html.

REFERENCES

The works in this list that are not explicitly cited in the chapters were consulted for general information and have informed the author's analysis.

Abel, Richard. 1989. *American Lawyers*. New York: Oxford University Press.

Ainsworth-Darnell, James W., and Douglas B. Downey. 1998. "Assessing the Oppositional Culture Explanation for Racial/Ethnic Differences in School Performance." *American Sociological Review* 63:436–453.

Alba, Richard D. 1985. *Italian Americans: Into the Twilight of Ethnicity*. Upper Saddle River, NJ: Prentice Hall.

———. 1992. *Ethnic Identity: The Transformation of White America*. New Haven, CT: Yale University Press.

———. 1999. "Immigration and the American Realities of Assimilation and Multiculturalism." *Sociological Forum* 14:3–25.

———. 2005. "Bright vs. Blurred Boundaries: Second Generation Assimilation and Exclusion in France, Germany and the United States." *Ethnic and Racial Studies* 28:20–49.

Alba, Richard, and Victor Nee. 2003. *Remaking the American Mainstream: Assimilation and Contemporary Immigration*. Cambridge, MA: Harvard University Press.

Allum, Jeffrey R., Nathan E. Bell, and Robert Sowell. 2012. *Graduate Enrollment and Degrees: 2001 to 2011*. Washington, DC: Council of Graduate Studies. Available at http://cgsnet.org/graduate-enrollment-and-degrees-2001-2011.

American Bar Association. n.d. "Pre-law." Available at http://www.americanbar.org/groups/legal_education/resources/pre_law.html (accessed December 13, 2016).

———. 2011. "Diversity JD Enrollment Data, 1971–2010." Available at http://www.americanbar.org/content/dam/aba/administrative/legal_education_and_admissions_to_the_bar/statistics/diversity_jd_enrollment_data_1971_2010.authcheckdam.pdf.

————. 2013. "Enrollment and Degrees Awarded, 1963–2012 Academic Years." Available
at http://www.americanbar.org/content/dam/aba/administrative/legal_education
_and_admissions_to_the_bar/statistics/enrollment_degrees_awarded.authcheck
dam.pdf.

————. 2015. "ABA National Lawyer Population Survey: 10-Year Trend in Lawyer
Population by State." Available at https://www.americanbar.org/content/dam/aba/
administrative/market_research/national-lawyer-population-by-state-2005-2015
.authcheckdam.pdf.

American Bar Association Commission on Racial and Ethnic Diversity in the Profession. 2012. "Goal III Report: The State of Racial and Ethnic Diversity in the American Bar Association." Available at http://www.americanbar.org/content/dam/aba/
administrative/racial_ethnic_diversity/REG3Rpt12_finalweb_updated3_13_12
.authcheckdam.pdf.

American Bar Association Commission on Women in the Profession. 2011. "A Current
Glance at Women in the Law, 2011." Available at http://www.americanbar.org/
content/dam/aba/marketing/women/current_glance_statistics_2011.authcheck
dam.pdf.

Ancheta, Angelo N. 1998. *Race, Rights, and the Asian American Experience.* New Brunswick, NJ: Rutgers University Press.

Banks, Taunya Lovell. 1988. "Gender Bias in the Classroom." *Journal of Legal Education*
38:137–146.

Bean, Frank D., and Gillian Stevens. 2003. *America's Newcomers and the Dynamics of
Diversity.* New York: Russell Sage Foundation.

Becker, Howard S., Blanche Geer, Everett C. Hughes, and Anselm L. Strauss. 1976. *Boys
in White: Student Culture in Medical School.* Chicago: University of Chicago Press.

Blackwell, James E. 1987. *Mainstreaming Outsiders: The Production of Black Professionals.* Bayside, NY: General Hall.

Blair-Loy, Mary. 2003. *Competing Devotions: Career and Family among Women Execu-
tives.* Cambridge, MA: Harvard University Press.

Blair-Loy, Mary, and Gretchen DeHart. 2003. "Family and Career Trajectories among
African American Female Attorneys." *Journal of Family Issues* 24:908–933.

Blau, Peter M., John B. Cullen, Rebecca Z. Margulies, and Hilary Silver. 1979. "Dissect-
ing Types of Professional Schools." *Sociology of Education* 52:7–19.

Blumer, Herbert. 1958. "Race Prejudice as a Sense of Group Position." *Pacific Sociological Review* 1:3–7.

Bobo, Lawrence. 1999. "Prejudice as Group Position: Micro-Foundations of a Sociological Approach to Race and Race Relations." *Journal of Social Issues* 55:445–472.

Bobo, Lawrence, and Vincent L. Hutchings. 1996. "Perceptions of Racial Group Competition: Extending Blumer's Theory of Group Position to a Multiracial Social
Context." *American Sociological Review* 61:951–972.

Bolton, Sharon C., and Daniel Muzio. 2007. "Can't Live with 'Em; Can't Live without
'Em: Gendered Segmentation in the Legal Profession." *Sociology* 41:47–64.

Bonacich, Edna. 1973. "A Theory of Middleman Minorities." *American Sociological
Review* 38:583–594.

Bonilla-Silva, Eduardo. 2014. *Racism without Racists: Color-Blind Racism and Racial
Inequality in Contemporary America.* Lanham, MD: Rowman and Littlefield.

Bonilla-Silva, Eduardo, and David R. Dietrich. 2009. "The Latin Americanization of U.S. Race Relations: A New Pigmentocracy." In *Shades of Difference: Why Skin Color Matters*, edited by Evelyn Nakano Glenn, 40–60. Stanford, CA: Stanford University Press.

Bosk, Charles L. 1979. *Forgive and Remember: Managing Medical Failure*. Chicago: University of Chicago Press.

Bowen, William G., and Derek Bok. 1998. *The Shape of the River: Long-Term Consequences of Considering Race in College and University Admissions*. Princeton, NJ: Princeton University Press.

Brems, Christine, Michael R. Baldwin, Lisa Davis, and Lorraine Namyniuk. 1994. "The Imposter Syndrome as Related to Teaching Evaluations and Advising Relationships of University Faculty Members." *Journal of Higher Education* 65 (2): 183–193.

Breton, Raymond. 1964. "Institutional Completeness of Ethnic Communities and the Personal Relations of Immigrants." *American Journal of Sociology* 70:193–205.

Brown, Susan K., and Frank D. Bean. 2006. "Assimilation Models, Old and New: Explaining a Long-Term Process." *Migration Information Source*, October 1. Available at http://www.migrationpolicy.org/article/assimilation-models-old-and-new-explaining-long-term-process.

Carbado, Devon W., and Mitu Gulati. 2004. "Race to the Top of the Corporate Ladder: What Minorities Do When They Get There." *Washington and Lee Law Review* 61:1645–1693.

———. 2013. *Acting White? Rethinking Race in "Post-racial" America*. New York: Oxford University Press.

Carter, Prudence L. 2005. *Keepin' It Real: School Success beyond Black and White*. New York: Oxford University Press.

Castañeda, Alejandra. 2006. "Roads to Citizenship: Mexican Migrants in the United States." In *Latinos and Citizenship: The Dilemma of Belonging*, edited by Suzanne Oboler, 143–165. New York: Palgrave Macmillan.

Cech, Erin, Brian Rubineau, Susan Silbey, and Carroll Seron. 2011. "Professional Role Confidence and Gendered Persistence in Engineering." *American Sociological Review* 76:641–666.

Chang, Iris. 2004. *The Chinese in America: A Narrative History*. New York: Penguin Books.

Chavez, Linda. 1991. *Out of the Barrio: Toward a New Politics of Hispanic Assimilation*. New York: Basic Books.

Chávez, Maria. 2011. *Everyday Injustice: Latino Professionals and Racism*. Boulder, CO: Rowman and Littlefield.

Chou, Rosalind S., and Joe R. Feagin. 2008. *Myth of the Model Minority: Asian Americans Facing Racism*. New York: Routledge.

Clance, Pauline Rose, and Suzanne Imes. 1978. "The Imposter Phenomenon in High Achieving Women: Dynamics and Therapeutic Intervention." *Psychotherapy Theory, Research and Practice* 15 (3): 1–8.

Clydesdale, Timothy T. 2004. "A Forked River Runs through Law School: Toward Understanding Race, Gender, Age and Related Gaps in Law School Performance and Bar Passage." *Law and Social Inquiry* 29:711–769.

Collins, Patricia Hill. 1990. *Black Feminist Thought: Knowledge, Consciousness, and the Politics of Empowerment.* New York: Routledge.

Cornell, Stephen, and Douglas Hartmann. 1998. *Ethnicity and Race: Making Identities in a Changing World.* Thousand Oaks, CA: Pine Forge Press.

Costello, Carrie Yang. 2006. *Professional Identity Crisis: Race, Class, Gender, and Success at Professional Schools.* Nashville, TN: Vanderbilt University Press.

Crenshaw, Kimberle. 1991. "Mapping the Margins: Intersectionality, Identity Politics, and Violence against Women of Color." *Stanford Law Review* 43:1241–1299.

Dalessandro, Susan P., Lisa C. Anthony, and Lynda M. Reese. 2012. "LSAT Performance with Regional, Gender, and Racial/Ethnic Breakdowns: 2005–2006 through 2011–2012 Testing Years." Law School Admission Council LSAT Technical Report 12-03. Available at http://www.lsac.org/docs/default-source/research-(lsac-resources)/tr-12-03.pdf.

Davis-Kean, Pamela E. 2005. "The Influence of Parent Education and Family Income on Child Achievement: The Indirect Role of Parental Expectations and the Home Environment." *Journal of Family Psychology* 19 (2): 294–304.

de Anda, James. 2006. "*Hernandez* at Fifty: A Personal History." In *"Colored Men" and "Hombres Aquí": Hernandez v. Texas and the Emergence of Mexican-American Lawyering,* edited by Michael A. Olivas, 199–208. Houston, TX: Arte Público Press.

Delgado, Richard, and Jean Stefancic. 2001. *Critical Race Theory: An Introduction.* New York: New York University Press.

Deo, Meera E., Walter R. Allen, A. T. Panter, Charles Daye, and Linda Wightman. 2010. "Struggles and Support: Diversity in U.S. Law Schools." *National Black Law Journal* 23 (1): 71–97.

Dhingra, Pawan P. 2007. *Managing Multicultural Lives: Asian American Professionals and the Challenge of Multiple Identities.* Stanford, CA: Stanford University Press.

Dinovitzer, Ronit, and Bryant G. Garth. 2007. "Lawyer Satisfaction in the Process of Structuring Legal Careers." *Law and Society Review* 41:1–50.

———. 2009. "Pro Bono as an Elite Strategy in Early Lawyer Careers." In *Private Lawyers and the Public Interest: The Evolving Role of Pro Bono in the Legal Profession,* edited by Robert Granfield and Lynn Mather, 115–134. New York: Oxford University Press.

Du Bois, W.E.B. 1903. *The Souls of Black Folk.* New York: Penguin Books.

Eccles, Jacquelynne S., and Pamela E. Davis-Kean. 2005. "Influence of Parents' Education on Their Children's Educational Attainments: The Role of Parent and Child Perceptions." *London Review of Education* 3 (3): 191–204.

Epstein, Cynthia Fuchs. 1973. "Positive Effects of the Multiple Negative: Explaining the Success of Black Professional Women." *American Journal of Sociology* 78 (4): 912–935.

———. 1992. "Tinkerbells and Pinups: The Construction and Reconstruction of Gender Boundaries at Work." In *Cultivating Differences: Symbolic Boundaries and the Making of Inequality,* edited by Michèle Lamont and Marcel Fournier, 232–256. Chicago: University of Chicago Press.

———. 1993. *Women in Law.* New York: Basic Books.

Feagin, Joe R. 1991. "The Continuing Significance of Race: Antiblack Discrimination in Public Places." *American Sociological Review* 56:101–116.

———. 2013. *The White Racial Frame: Centuries of Racial Framing and Counter-framing.* New York: Routledge.

Feagin, Joe R., and José A. Cobas. 2014. *Latinos Facing Racism: Discrimination, Resistance, and Endurance.* Boulder, CO: Paradigm.

Fischer, Judith D. 1996. "Portia Unbound: The Effects of a Supportive Law School Environment on Women and Minority Students." *UCLA Women's Law Journal* 7:1–56.

Flores, Glenda Marisol. 2011. "Racialized Tokens: Latina Teachers Negotiating, Surviving and Thriving in a White Woman's Profession." *Qualitative Sociology* 34: 313–335.

Fordham, Signithia, and John Obgu. 1986. "Black Students' Success: Coping with the 'Burden of Acting White.'" *Urban Review* 18:176–206.

Fulgini, A. J. 1997. "The Academic Achievement of Adolescents from Immigrant Families: The Roles of Family Background, Attitude, and Behavior." *Child Development* 68:351–363.

Galindo, René, and Jami Vigil. 2006. "Are Anti-immigrant Statements Racist or Nativist? What Differences Does It Make?" *Latino Studies* 4:419–447.

Gándara, Patricia. 1995. *Over the Ivy Walls: The Educational Mobility of Low-Income Chicanos.* New York: State University of New York Press.

Gans, Herbert J. 1979. "Symbolic Ethnicity: The Future of Ethnic Groups and Cultures in America." *Ethnic and Racial Studies* 2 (1): 1–20.

Garth, Bryant, and Joyce Sterling. 2009. "Exploring Inequality in the Corporate Law Firm Apprenticeship: Doing the Time, Finding the Love." *Georgetown Journal of Legal Ethics* 22:1361–1394.

Gilkes, Cheryl Townsend. 1982. "Successful Rebellious Professionals: The Black Women's Professional Identity and Community Commitment." *Psychology of Women Quarterly* 6:289–311.

Goffman, Erving. 1959. *The Presentation of Self in Everyday Life.* New York: Anchor Books.

Gómez, Laura E. 2004. "A Tale of Two Genres: On the Real and Ideal Links between Law and Society and Critical Race Theory." In *The Blackwell Companion to Law and Society*, edited by Austin Sarat, 453–470. Malden, MA: Blackwell.

Gordon, Milton. 1964. *Assimilation in American Life: The Role of Race, Religion, and National Origins.* New York: Oxford University Press.

Granfield, Robert. 1992. *Making Elite Lawyers: Visions of Law at Harvard and Beyond.* New York: Routledge, Chapman, and Hall.

Guinier, Lani, Michelle Fine, and Jane Balin. 1997. *Becoming Gentlemen: Women, Law School, and Institutional Change.* Boston: Beacon Press.

Hall, Stuart. 1996. "Gramsci's Relevance for the Study of Race and Ethnicity." In *Critical Dialogues in Cultural Studies*, edited by David Morley and Kuan-Hsing Chen, 411–440. New York: Routledge.

Hamilton, Nora, and Norma Stoltz Chinchilla. 2001. *Seeking Community in a Global City: Guatemalans and Salvadorans in Los Angeles.* Philadelphia: Temple University Press.

Haney López, Ian. 1997. *White by Law: The Legal Construction of Race.* New York: New York University Press.

———. 2006. "Race and Colorblindness after *Hernandez* and *Brown*." In *"Colored Men" and "Hombres Aquí": Hernandez v. Texas and the Emergence of Mexican-American Lawyering*, edited by Michael A. Olivas, 41–52. Houston, TX: Arte Público Press.

———. 2011a. "Chance, Context, and Choice in the Social Construction of Race." In *The Latino/a Condition: A Critical Reader*, edited by Richard Delgado and Jean Stefancic, 11–18. New York: New York University Press.

———. 2011b. "Race and Erasure: The Salience of Race to Latinos/as." In *The Latino/a Condition: A Critical Reader*, edited by Richard Delgado and Jean Stefancic, 373–384. New York: New York University Press.

Heinz, John P., Robert L. Nelson, Rebecca L. Sandefur, and Edward O. Laumann. 2005. *Urban Lawyers: The New Social Structure of the Bar*. Chicago: University of Chicago Press.

Hing, Bill Ong. 1997. *To Be an American: Cultural Pluralism and the Rhetoric of Assimilation*. New York: New York University Press.

Hirschman, Charles. 2001. "The Educational Enrollment of Immigrant Youth: A Test of the Segmented Assimilation Hypothesis." *Demography* 38 (3): 317–336.

Hirschman, Charles, and Morrison G. Wong. 1986. "The Extraordinary Educational Attainment of Asian-Americans: A Search of Historical Evidence and Explanations." *Social Forces* 65:1–27.

Hochschild, Arlie Russell. 2003. *The Second Shift*. New York: Penguin Books.

Hondagneu-Sotelo, Pierette. 1994. *Gendered Transitions: Mexican Experiences of Immigration*. Berkeley: University of California Press.

Hughes, Sandra. 2009. "Latinos Celebrate Sotomayor Confirmation." *CBS News*, August 6. Available at http://www.cbsnews.com/news/latinos-celebrate-sotomayor-confirmation.

Kanter, Rosabeth Moss. 1977. *Men and Women of the Corporation*. New York: Basic Books.

Kao, Grace, and Marta Tienda. 1995. "Optimism and Achievement: The Educational Performance of Immigrant Youth." *Social Science Quarterly* 76:1–19.

Kibria, Nazli. 1993. *Family Tightrope: The Changing Lives of Vietnamese Americans*. Princeton, NJ: Princeton University Press

———. 2000. "Race, Ethnic Options, and Ethnic Binds: Identity Negotiations of Second-Generation Chinese and Korean Americans." *Sociological Perspectives* 43:77–95.

Kim, ChangHwan, and Arthur Sakamoto. 2010. "Have Asian American Men Achieved Labor Market Parity with White Men?" *American Sociological Review* 75:934–957.

Kimes, Martha. 2007. *Ivy Briefs: True Tales of a Neurotic Law Student*. New York: Atria Books.

Kleinman, Sherryl. 1996. *Opposing Ambitions: Gender and Identity in an Alternative Organization*. Chicago: University of Chicago Press.

Kuo, Joyce. 1998. "Excluded, Segregated and Forgotten: A Historical View of the Discrimination of Chinese Americans in Public Schools." *Asian American Law Journal* 5:181–212.

Lamphere, Louise. 1992. *Structuring Diversity: Ethnographic Perspectives on the New Immigration*. Chicago: University of Chicago Press.

Lee, Jennifer. 2002. *Civility in the City: Blacks, Jews, and Koreans in Urban America*. Cambridge, MA: Harvard University Press.

———. 2014. "Don't Tell Amy Chua: Mexicans Are the Most Successful Immigrants." *Time*, February 25. Available at http://ideas.time.com/2014/02/25/dont-tell-amy-chua-mexicans-are-the-most-successful-immigrants/.

Lee, Jennifer, and Frank D. Bean. 2004. "America's Changing Color Lines: Race/Ethnicity, Immigration, and Multiracial Identification." *Annual Review of Sociology* 30:221–242.

———. 2007. "Reinventing the Color Line: Immigration and America's New Racial/Ethnic Divide." *Social Forces* 86:561–586.

———. 2010. *The Diversity Paradox: Immigration and the Color Line in Twenty-First Century America.* New York: Russell Sage Foundation.

———. 2012. "A Postracial Society or a Diversity Paradox? Race, Immigration, and Multiraciality in the Twenty-First Century." *Du Bois Review* 9:419–437.

Lee, Stacey J. 1996. *Unraveling the "Model Minority" Stereotype: Listening to Asian American Youth.* New York: Teachers College Press.

Levin, Leslie C. 2009. "Guardians at the Gate: The Backgrounds, Career Paths, and Professional Development of Private US Immigration Lawyers." *Law and Social Inquiry* 34:399–436.

Lobo, Arun Peter, and Joseph J. Salvo. 1998. "Changing U.S. Immigration Law and the Occupational Selectivity of Asian Immigrants." *International Migration Review* 32:737–760.

Loewen, James W. 1981. *The Mississippi Chinese.* Long Grove, IL: Waveland Press.

Lopez, Nancy. 2003. *Hopeful Girls, Troubled Boys: Race and Gender Disparity in Urban Education.* New York: Routledge.

Louie, Vivian S. 2004. *Compelled to Excel: Immigration, Education, and Opportunity among Chinese Americans.* Stanford, CA: Stanford University Press.

———. 2012. *Keeping the Immigrant Bargain: The Costs and Rewards of Success in America.* New York: Russell Sage Foundation.

Massey, Douglas S., Camille Z. Charles, Garvey F. Lundy, and Mary J. Fischer. 2003. *The Source of the River: The Social Origins of Freshmen at America's Selective Colleges and Universities.* Princeton, NJ: Princeton University Press.

McDowell, William C., Nancy G. Boyd, and Wm. Matthew Bowler. 2007. "Overreward and the Impostor Phenomenon." *Journal of Managerial Issues* 19 (1): 95–110.

McGee, Ebony O., and Danny B. Martin. 2011. "'You Would Not Believe What I Have to Go through to Prove My Intellectual Value!' Stereotype Management among Mathematically Successful Black Mathematics and Engineering Students." *American Educational Research Journal* 48:1347–1389.

McPherson, Miller, Lynn Smith-Lovin, and James M. Cook. 2001. "Birds of a Feather: Homophily in Social Networks." *Annual Review of Sociology* 27:415–444.

Mertz, Elizabeth. 2007. *The Language of Law School: Learning to "Think like a Lawyer."* New York: Oxford University Press.

Meyerson, Debra E., and Maureen A. Scully. 1995. "Tempered Radicalism and the Politics of Ambivalence and Change." *Organization Science* 6:585–600.

Moore, Wendy Leo. 2008. *Reproducing Racism: White Space, Elite Law Schools, and Racial Inequality.* Boulder, CO: Rowman and Littlefield.

Morse, Robert. 2016. "Methodology: 2017 Best Law Schools Rankings." *U.S. News and World Report*, March 15. Available at http://www.usnews.com/education/best-graduate-schools/articles/law-schools-methodology.

Motomura, Hiroshi. 2006. *Americans in Waiting: The Lost Story of Immigration and Citizenship in the United States.* New York: Oxford University Press.

National Center for Education Statistics. 2016. "Educational Attainment of Young Adults." Available at https://nces.ed.gov/programs/coe/indicator_caa.asp.

Oboler, Suzanne. 1995. *Latino Lives: Identity and the Politics of (Re)Presentation in the United States*. Minneapolis: University of Minnesota Press.

O'Brien, Eileen. 2008. *The Racial Middle: Latinos and Asian Americans Living beyond the Racial Divide*. New York: New York University Press.

Ochoa, Gilda L. 2013. *Academic Profiling: Latinos, Asian Americans, and the Achievement Gap*. Minneapolis: University of Minnesota Press.

Olivas, Michael A. 2006. "*Hernandez v. Texas*: A Litigation History." In *"Colored Men" and "Hombres Aquí": Hernandez v. Texas and the Emergence of Mexican-American Lawyering*, edited by Michael A. Olivas, 209–222. Houston, TX: Arte Público Press.

Park, Robert E. 1996. "Human Migration and the Marginal Man." In *Theories of Ethnicity: A Classical Reader*, edited by Werners Sollors, 156–167. New York: New York University Press.

Passel, Jeffrey S., and D'Vera Cohn. 2008. "U.S. Population Projections: 2005–2050." Available at http://www.pewhispanic.org/files/reports/85.pdf.

Payne, Charles. 1984. "Multicultural Education and Racism in American Schools." *Theory into Practice* 23 (2): 124–131.

Peller, Gary. 1995. "Race-Consciousness." In *Critical Race Theory: The Key Writings That Formed the Movement*, edited by Kimberlé Crenshaw, Neil Gotanda, Gary Peller, and Kendall Thomas, 127–158. New York: New Press.

Perea, Juan F. 2011. "Buscando América: Why Integration and Equal Protection Fail to Protect Latinos." In *The Latino/a Condition: A Critical Reader*, edited by Richard Delgado and Jean Stefancic, 597–604. New York: New York University Press.

Pierce, Jennifer L. 1995. *Gender Trials: Emotional Lives in Contemporary Law Firms*. Berkeley: University of California Press.

Portes, Alejandro, and Rubén G. Rumbaut. 2001. *Legacies: The Story of the Immigrant Second Generation*. Berkeley: University of California Press.

———. 2006. *Immigrant America: A Portrait*. Berkeley: University of California Press.

Pyke, Karen, and Denise Johnson. 2003. "Asian American Women and Racialized Femininities: 'Doing' Gender across Cultural Worlds." *Gender and Society* 17:33–53.

Rhode, Deborah L. 2015. "Law Is the Least Diverse Profession in the Nation, and Lawyers Aren't Doing Enough to Change That." *Washington Post*, May 27. Available at https://www.washingtonpost.com/posteverything/wp/2015/05/27/law-is-the-least -diverse-profession-in-the-nation-and-lawyers-arent-doing-enough-to-change -that.

Rumbaut, Rubén G. 1994. "The Crucible Within: Ethnic Identity, Self-Esteem, and Segmented Assimilation among Children of Immigrants." *International Migration Review* 28:748–794.

Ryan, Camille L., and Kurt Bauman. 2016. "Educational Attainment in the United States: 2015." Available at http://www.census.gov/content/dam/Census/library/publi cations/2016/demo/p20-578.pdf.

Scheppele, Kim Lane. 1992. "Just the Facts, Ma'am: Sexualized Violence, Evidentiary Habits, and the Revision of Truth." *New York Law School Law Review* 37:123–172.

Schleef, Debra. 1997. "Empty Ethics and Reasonable Responsibility: Vocabularies of Motive among Law and Business Students." *Law and Social Inquiry* 22:619–650.

———. 2005. *Managing Elites: Professional Socialization in Law and Business Schools.* Boulder, CO: Rowman and Littlefield.

Segura, Denise A. 1992. "Chicanas in White-Collar Jobs: You Have to Prove Yourself More." *Sociological Perspectives* 35:163–182.

Small, Mario Luis. 2009. *Unanticipated Gains: Origins of Network Inequality in Everyday Life.* New York: Oxford University Press.

Smith, Robert C. 2006. *Mexican New York: Transnational Lives of New Immigrants.* Berkeley: University of California Press.

Sommerfeldt, Chris, and Ginger Adams Otis. 2016. "Canines and Their Human Supporters Protest Yulin's Annual Chinese Dog Eating Festival in Chinatown." *New York Daily News*, June 17. Available at http://www.nydailynews.com/new-york/canines-human-supporters-protest-yulin-festival-article-1.2678108.

Sommerlad, Hilary. 2007. "Researching and Theorizing the Process of Professional Identity Formation." *Journal of Law and Society* 34:190–217.

Sommerlad, Hilary, and Peter Sanderson. 1998. *Gender, Choice and Commitment: Women Solicitors in England and Wales and the Struggle for Equal Status.* Dartmouth, MA: Ashgate.

Sommerlad, Hilary, Lisa Webley, Liz Duff, Daniel Muzio, and Jennifer Tomlinson. 2010. "Diversity in the Legal Profession in England and Wales: A Qualitative Study of Barriers and Individual Choices." London: Legal Services Board, University of Westminster.

Stover, Robert V. 1988. *Making It and Breaking It: The Fate of Public Interest Commitment during Law School.* Chicago: University of Illinois Press.

Takaki, Ronald. 1998. *Strangers from a Different Shore: A History of Asian Americans.* New York: Little, Brown.

Tang, Joyce. 1993. "The Career Attainment of Caucasian and Asian Engineers." *Sociological Quarterly* 34:467–496.

Tatum, Beverly Daniel. 2003. *Why Are All the Black Kids Sitting Together in the Cafeteria? And Other Conversations about Race.* New York: Basic Books.

Tuan, Mia. 1998. *Forever Foreigners or Honorary Whites? The Asian Ethnic Experience Today.* New Brunswick, NJ: Rutgers University Press.

Turow, Scott S. 1977. *One L.* New York: Penguin Books.

Tyson, Karolyn, William Darity Jr., and Domini Castellino. 2005. "It's Not 'a Black Thing': Understanding the Burden of Acting White and Other Dilemmas of High Achievement." *American Sociological Review* 70:582–605.

Urciuoli, Bonnie. 2006. "Boundaries, Language, and the Self: Issues Faced by Puerto Ricans and Other Latino/a College Students." In *Latinos and Citizenship: The Dilemma of Belonging*, edited by Suzanne Oboler, 169–190. New York: Palgrave Macmillan.

U.S. Bureau of Labor Statistics. 2014. "Labor Force Characteristics by Race and Ethnicity, 2013." *BLS Reports* 1050. Available at http://www.bls.gov/opub/reports/race-and-ethnicity/archive/race_ethnicity_2013.pdf.

U.S. Census Bureau. 2016a. "Welcome to QuickFacts: Corvallis City, Oregon." Available at https://www.census.gov/quickfacts/table/PST045215/4115800/accessible.

———. 2016b. "Welcome to QuickFacts: Oregon." Available at https://www.census.gov/quickfacts/table/PST045215/41/accessible.

Valdez, Zulema. 2011. *The New Entrepreneurs: How Race, Class and Gender Shape American Enterprise.* Palo Alto, CA: Stanford University Press.

Vallejo, Jody Agius. 2012. *Barrios to Burbs: The Making of the Mexican-American Middle Class.* Palo Alto, CA: Stanford University Press.

Vallejo, Jody Agius, and Jennifer Lee. 2009. "Brown Picket Fences: The Immigrant Narrative and Patterns of 'Giving Back' among the Mexican-Origin Middle Class." *Ethnicities* 9:5–31.

Vidal-Ortiz, Salvador. 2008. "People of Color." In *Encyclopedia of Race, Ethnicity, and Society,* edited by Richard T. Schaefer, Shu-Ju Ada Chang, and Kiljoon Kim, 1037–1039. Vol. 3. Thousand Oaks, CA: Sage.

Wallace, Jean E., and Fiona M. Kay. 2012. "Tokenism, Organizational Segregation, and Coworker Relations in Law Firms." *Social Problems* 59:389–410.

Waters, Mary C., 1990. *Ethnic Options: Choosing Identities in America.* Berkeley: University of California Press.

———. 1999. *Black Identities: West Indian Immigrant Dreams and American Realities.* Cambridge, MA: Harvard University Press.

Weiss, Melford S. 1994. "Marginality, Cultural Brokerage, and School Aides: A Success Story in Education." *Anthropology and Education Quarterly* 25:336–346.

Wilder, Gita Z. 2008. *Race and Ethnicity in the Legal Profession: Findings from the First Wave of the After the JD Study.* Overland Park, KS: National Association for Law Placement and American Bar Association.

Wilkins, David B. 1997. "Two Paths to the Mountain Top? The Role of Legal Education in Shaping the Values of Black Corporate Lawyers." *Stanford Law Review* 45:1981–2026.

———. 1998. "Fragmenting Professionalism: Racial Identity and the Ideology of Bleached Out Lawyering." *International Journal of the Legal Profession* 5:141–173.

———. 2000. "Rollin' on the River: Race, Elite Schools, and the Equality Paradox." *Law and Social Inquiry* 25:527–556.

———. 2004. "Doing Well by Doing Good? The Role of Public Service in the Careers of Black Corporate Lawyers." *Houston Law Review* 41:1–91.

Wilkins, David B., and G. Mitu Gulati. 1996. "Why Are There So Few Black Lawyers in Corporate Law Firms? An Institutional Analysis." *California Law Review* 84:493–625.

Wingfield, Adia Harvey. 2010. "Are Some Emotions Marked 'Whites Only'? Racialized Feeling Rules in Professional Workplaces." *Social Problems* 57:251–268.

Wong, Marie Rose. 2004. *Sweet Cakes, Long Journey: The Chinatowns of Portland, Oregon.* Seattle: University of Washington Press.

Wong, Paul, Chienping Faith Lai, Richard Nagasawa, and Tieming Lin. 1998. "Asian Americans as a Model Minority: Self-Perceptions and Perceptions by Other Racial Groups." *Sociological Perspectives* 41:95–118.

Zhou, Min. 2009. *Contemporary Chinese America: Immigration, Ethnicity, and Community Transformation.* Philadelphia: Temple University Press.

Zhou, Min, and Carl L. Bankston III. 1998. *Growing Up American: How Vietnamese Children Adapt to Life in the United States.* New York: Russell Sage Foundation.

INDEX

Yung-Yi Diana Pan is an Assistant Professor of Sociology at Brooklyn College, City University of New York.

www.ingramcontent.com/pod-product-compliance
Lightning Source LLC
Chambersburg PA
CBHW051435270326
41935CB00019B/1831